Enhancing
Learning and Thinking

Enhancing Learning and Thinking

Edited by ROBERT F. MULCAHY,
ROBERT H. SHORT,
and JAC ANDREWS

PRAEGER

New York
Westport, Connecticut
London

Library of Congress Cataloging-in-Publication Data

Enhancing learning and thinking / edited by Robert F. Mulcahy, Robert
H. Short, and Jac Andrews.
    p. cm.
    ''The idea for this book emerged from a major international
conference on thinking that took place at the University of Alberta,
Edmonton, Canada''—Pref.
  Includes bibliographical references and index.
  ISBN 0-275-93666-X (alk. paper)
    1. Learning—Congresses. 2. Thought and thinking—Study and
teaching—Congresses. 3. Cognition—Congresses. 4. Cognition in
children—Congresses. I. Mulcahy, R. F. (Robert F.), 1941–
II. Short, Robert H. III. Andrews, Jac.
LB1060.E544 1991   91-15556
370.15'23—dc20

British Library Cataloguing in Publication Data is available.

Library of Congress Catalog Card Number: 91-15556
ISBN: 0-275-93666-X

First published in 1991

Praeger Publishers, One Madison Avenue, New York, NY 10010
An imprint of Greenwood Publishing Group, Inc.

Printed in the United States of America

The paper used in this book complies with the
Permanent Paper Standard issued by the National
Information Standards Organization (Z39.48-1984).

10 9 8 7 6 5 4 3 2 1

Contents

Part 2   Specific Applications to School Content

Part 3   Assessment and Evaluation

Figures and Tables

FIGURES

TABLES

Preface

The past ten years have been witness to a burgeoning interest in the possibility of enhancing cognitive capabilities in children and adults. This growth is evident in schools, colleges, universities, and businesses, where attempts are being made to develop and apply approaches to improve learning, thinking, and problem-solving abilities in students and personnel. The evidence is more than clear that learning and thinking can be facilitated by intervention.

In addition, society has entered a postindustrial information age, where growth and change are so rapid that in many fields as much as half of the information can become outdated in as few as five years. Dynamic change of this magnitude demands that society look toward its educational and business communities to teach the types of skills that are considered essential in acquiring and using information. It has been suggested that the main goal of education should be to produce learners who have the skills and motivation to learn on their own rather than merely produce learned individuals.

Rapid technological development with its attendant information explosion is resulting in the business sector beginning to place a greater emphasis on the enhancement of cognitive capabilities in its personnel. Thinking is coming to be regarded as a major resource that can be tapped and used. It is because of this that a much closer relationship is now being forged between educational and business communities. This is especially true in the research and development of cognitive intervention programs.

The idea for this book emerged from a major international conference on thinking that took place at the University of Alberta, Edmonton, Canada. The organization of the conference involved close cooperation among university, business, government, and school personnel. It was held so that people involved in education and business might become more aware of the growing resources available to them in their quest to more fully develop human potential. The focal point of the conference was a wide selection of programs and approaches that have been developed around the world to enhance learning and thinking skills. In addition, numerous papers reflecting basic and applied research in cognitive skills training were presented throughout the five-day conference.

This book is divided into three parts. The first part includes seven chapters. The first four chapters discuss the general procedures and principles involved in implementing learning and thinking enhancement programs, while the last three present particular programs and approaches that have been developed to teach general learning and thinking skills. Part 2 has five chapters that look at research and application in specific content areas such as arithmetic, reading, and socially based skills. Finally, part 3 contains three chapters that address educational assessment and program evaluation. The book concludes with a chapter that poses a series of questions and supplies some tentative answers in the area of cognitive skills enhancement.

The conference proved to be a stimulating one for all who participated, and we hope that this book will be just as stimulating for those who read it. Many provocative questions are raised in it and we would like to see these questions lead to further research and development in the field. We challenge readers to pursue them.

We have also attempted to address a wide audience in the business, school, university, and community health professions in the hope that we might encourage greater interest in combined and integrated research in the cognitive skills area.

To produce a book such as this there are many who need to be acknowledged. We would like to express our sincere gratitude to all those who worked so hard to make the conference the success it was and to those involved in the production of this volume. In particular, we would like to thank Arnold Ostfield, Gary Campbell, Joan Cowling, and Ron Spence, members of the conference executive committee, as well as sponsors of the conference—the University of Alberta, the Edmonton Public School Board, Alberta Education, the Northern Alberta Institute of Technology, the Bank of Nova Scotia, Touche Ross, Quality Press Inc., and VENCAP. There are numerous others who made significant contributions, and to them we offer our sincere gratitude.

PART 1

ISSUES AND APPLICATIONS

Interest in cognitive training procedures is not a new phenomenon in education. In fact, as early as the 1880s, programs or approaches that promised to enhance both learning and mental abilities had been established. It should be recognized, however, that contemporary efforts to enhance learning and thinking abilities are distinguishable from early attempts in at least two important ways. First, current approaches tend to emphasize the *process* of cognition rather than the *product* of cognition along with the respect for the fact that cognitive performance is capable of, and indeed often sensitive to, modification. Second, while the enhancement of higher-order thinking ability has been a goal of education for many years, it was generally directed toward a rather elite segment of society and not to the population as a whole. In contrast, most current cognitive training programs are designed for the benefit of the whole range of school-aged and college students with many programs designed specifically for particular groups of individuals. Part 1 provides examples of some of the current approaches that are being used to enhance the learning and thinking of individuals in society.

The first four chapters present some general influences on the development of learning and thinking in students. In chapter 1, Raymond S. Nickerson presents a number of conclusions drawn from his considerable experience with the teaching of thinking. He maintains that although our knowledge of thinking is somewhat limited and fragmented, we actually do know enough about it to justify the hope that it can be improved. He believes that the attitudinal variable is a critical one in the teaching of thinking and also argues that because thinking is so complex and our knowledge of it so limited we should never assume that there is only one way to become an effective thinker.

In chapter 2, Arthur L. Costa delineates what he considers to be twelve critical "climate" factors that can help facilitate intellectual growth. He suggests that if schools would strive to emphasize and promote these factors in their daily routines they would provide the type of intellectual environment conducive to the development of competent and creative thinkers and problem solvers.

In chapter 3, Sandra Falconer Pace provides an insider's view into the process that a government department or agency engages in when it is developing a position statement on the teaching of learning and thinking skills. She also shows how this type of decision making can direct the development of curriculum for school systems. In chapter 4, John B. Biggs takes an interactive approach to the process and discusses the factors that can impede or enhance the development of learning and thinking in schools. He looks at the system, the teacher, and the student factors that interact to either facilitate or hinder the attainment of higher-level cognitive abilities in students. He emphasizes a process approach for the enhancement of such abilities. His integrated model includes a presage component (factors existing prior to learning), a process component (how one goes about the task), and a product component (outcomes of learning and thinking). He concludes by discussing how this model can help in deriving further ways to improve cognitive skills.

The final three chapters in part 1 present more specific approaches and programs for learning and thinking skills enhancement. In chapter 5, M. A. Price provides details of a research project that evaluates a cognitive approach to teaching preschoolers at risk and suggests future directions for evaluating preschool cognitive programs. In chapter 6, Kofi Marfo, Robert F. Mulcahy, David Peat, Jac Andrews, and Seokee Cho present a general rationale for the teaching of learning strategies and review some of the theory and research underlying their own cognitive strategy teaching program. They emphasize the importance of embedding metacognitive training within such programs and provide a description of an instructional model designed to do this task. Evaluation data from a longitudinal study of their learning strategy program is also discussed.

In the final chapter, Selby H. Evans and Donald F. Dansereau provide details of an approach designed to improve the thinking processes involved in generating and receiving communication. The "knowledge-mapping" approach is discussed and research from their laboratory is presented that indicates that mapping can facilitate aspects of instruction and communication. They provide details on how to read maps, how to produce them, and how to use them effectively.

1

Some Observations on the Teaching of Thinking

Raymond S. Nickerson

Over the past several years, I have had occasion to review a considerable amount of material on the teaching of thinking, observe several programs designed to teach thinking in the classroom, and participate in the development of one such program. In this chapter I will state a number of conclusions drawn from these experiences. My apologies to the reader if some of them seem too intuitively obvious to warrant mentioning. My excuse for including them is that, no matter how obvious they are, we see evidence that they are easily forgotten or ignored on occasion.

Thinking is multifaceted. Philosophers have reflected on the nature of thought for many centuries and psychologists have been attempting to study it scientif- ically for at least a hundred years. The resulting literature is far-ranging. Con- sequently, if we wish to talk about thinking, we do well to give some indication about what we mean by that term; otherwise the listener or reader is free to assign to it any of a broad variety of connotations.

In this chapter thinking connotes the kind of cognitive activity in which we engage when we attempt to evaluate conflicting evidence on a controversial issue in order to arrive at a reasonable conclusion, to derive from a collection of disparate symptoms a plausible diagnosis of an automative problem, to de- sign a test of a scientific hypothesis, to construct a counter-argument against which to judge the merits of an argument that we are being asked to accept, to understand the assumptions on which some position is based, or to reflect upon the values that a particular course of action seems to imply. This is the kind of thinking that is often referred to as critical thinking. Unfortunately, this term is sometimes given the negative connotation of fault finding. Finding fault with faulty reasoning is, of course, an important aspect of critical thinking, as philosophers and psychologists typically conceive it, but it is not the only one. The kind of thinking I have in mind in this chapter encompasses criticism in the fault-finding sense, but not to the exclusion of more positive instances of inference making, figuring out, and reflection.

Our understanding of thinking in this sense is fragmentary and very limited. In spite of the considerable attention the topic has received from philosophers and psychologists, the workings of the mind remain enigmatic for the most part. We do not know, for example, why some people are curious and inquisitive while others appear to be uninterested in learning. We do not know why experts in the same area sometimes can examine the same evidence and draw from it diametrically opposed conclusions. We do not know why an argument that is compelling to one knowledgeable person is easily rejected by another, or why beliefs that appear bizarre and irrational to some people are entirely acceptable to others. Beyond simply documenting the fact that we often do not think as logically, consistently, or effectively as we might, which it has done quite convincingly, *research has revealed specific ways in which our thinking commonly goes astray* (Nisbett & Ross, 1980; Tversky & Kahneman, 1974; Wason, 1966). Such documentation may turn out to be very useful because, insofar as it proves to be possible to identify specific reasoning difficulties that many of us share, such knowledge could help guide efforts to improve thinking through education.

There is also evidence that traditional schooling is not having the positive impact on the thinking ability of students that we would hope and might expect it would have. We know beyond doubt that people do not necessarily become good thinkers as a consequence of completing conventional subject matter courses or of doing all that is necessary to graduate from secondary school or even postsecondary institutions (National Assessment of Educations Progress, 1981, 1983; National Commission on Excellence in Education, 1983). This is not to suggest that education never has any effect on the thinking ability of individual students. Training in formal disciplines such as logic and statistics can have a significant positive impact on the quality of thinking (Nisbett et al., 1987). Also, one would have to be cynical indeed not to recognize the likelihood that there are many individuals whose thinking ability has been enhanced by their good fortune of having been exposed to the tutelage of one or more extraordinary teachers who knew how to stimulate them to think and provided tools to help them do so. By and large, however, the educational system as a whole—perhaps it would be more reasonable to say society, of which the educational system is but a reflection—has failed dramatically to develop the thinking abilities of the country's youth to anything near their full potential.

While our understanding of thinking is limited and we have many more questions than answers, we know enough about it to justify the hope of being able to improve some aspect of it through teaching focused on that objective. We know, for example, that domain-specific knowledge is essential to deep thinking about a domain (Glaser, 1984). We know too, however, that such knowledge does not guarantee that deep thinking will be done. We know something of how the ways in which experts typically approach problems differ from the ways in which novices do (Chi et al., 1981; Larkin et al., 1980). We are becoming increasingly aware of the importance of attitudes and dispositions as determinants of intellectual performance (Baron, 1985; Ennis, 1987). We know the effect that specific beliefs can have on the willingness of students to put effort into cognitively demanding tasks (Dweck, in press). And we have some evidence of at least modest amounts of success from systematic efforts to teach thinking, even given the admittedly tentative validity of these techniques (Nickerson et al., 1985).

Finding effective ways of improving the quality of thinking is important for a variety of reasons. Not least among these reasons are potentially disastrous consequences for humanity of widespread inability to think well. There are many examples in history of folly dictating the behavior of large groups of people or even entire nations (Mackay, 1932; Tuchman, 1984). As we become increasingly technologically sophisticated and ever more capable of producing unimaginably large amounts of destructive power, our potential for corporate folly becomes an increasingly serious concern. There is also the point of view, which I share, that the potential to think well has a lot to do with what it means to be human, and that to fail to develop that potential—to settle for less than our genes permit—is a denial of a birthright of a fundamental sort. For these and other reasons, the teaching of thinking should be a high-priority objective of education. It is not clear that education has a more important task.

Teaching thinking is not easy. It requires preparation, deep commitment, and dogged perseverance. Judging from promotional literature, there appear to be people who believe that an intensive workshop of a few days' duration, supplemented with some specially designed material for use in the classroom, is all that is needed to produce an effective teacher of thinking. I do not mean to disparage workshops on the teaching of thinking, or to put down in wholesale fashion material that has been designed to facilitate such thinking in the classroom. Both can be very useful. But I do wish to speak strongly against what I view as "quick fix" approaches to the teaching of thinking that trivialize a complex problem. As a subject of study, thinking is at least as complex as any other in the existing curriculum. We would hardly expect to prepare teachers to teach mathematics or physical science or language by giving them a three-day workshop and some curriculum material and turning them loose in class. If one is going to teach geometry or biology or English literature one should know the subject well. The same applies to the teaching of thinking. It is asking a lot of a teacher and showing considerable naivete regarding what thinking is all about, to expect one to be able to teach thinking well who has never had a course in developmental psychology, cognition, logic, rhetoric, problem solving, decision making, probability, and statistical reasoning, or other pertinent subjects, as well as a modicum of on-the-job experience teaching thinking while in training.

A prerequisite to teaching thinking is being able to think well. Thinking is unlikely to be taught effectively by someone who cannot think well and has no interest in learning to do so. Again, the analogy of teaching traditional subjects is appropriate. We would not expect one who cannot solve mathematical problems to be able to teach students how to do so. We would not expect a nonwriter to be able to teach students how to write, nor would we expect one who has had no experience performing scientific experiments to be a really good teacher of experimental procedure. It is unrealistic in the extreme to expect anyone who is not a skilled "practitioner" of thinking to be good at developing the thinking potential of students to a high degree.

The importance of the principle that a teacher of thinking should be a thinker is underscored by the critical role that attitudes, motivation, and beliefs play in thinking. *Attitudinal variables are at least as critical as anything else we can point to in determining the quality of thinking.* Inquisitiveness, fairmindedness in the treatment of evidence, openness to opinions that differ from one's own, dissatisfaction with quick and superficial explanations, willingness to put effort into gathering facts and understanding opposing views on controversial issues—such attitudes are not easily learned from a book or by being told of their importance. My suspicion is that teachers who teach them best do so by example, and further that they project these attitudes not simply in order to teach by example, but because they *have* these attitudes and would find it difficult *not* to project them. I suggest also that such attitudes are difficult to feign with much consistency and that the teacher who does not display them automatically without thinking about it will find it impossible to teach them effectively by example and consequently will be unable to teach them at all.

Existing approaches to the teaching of thinking have some promise, but they should be viewed as beginnings. We do not yet know how to teach thinking very well. This is not a legitimate excuse for not trying, but it is a good reason for maintaining an attitude of tentativeness and experimentation with respect to approaches we might try and for constantly viewing the results of our efforts with an evaluative eye. As a corollary to the observations above regarding the importance of a teacher of thinking being a thinker, it is also my belief that *level of teacher competence is the single most important determinant of the success or failure of any attempt to implement a program to teach thinking in the classroom.* This is not to suggest that the program itself is unimportant— an excellent program can be an invaluable asset in the hands of a highly skilled teacher—but whereas an outstanding teacher may compensate for a poor program, in my view it does not work the other way around.

Both the view that thinking is multifaceted and recognition that our understanding of it is limited should caution us against assuming that there is only one way to be a good thinker and a single effective method for enhancing thinking ability. If we look at historical figures who have had a significant impact on the world by virtue of the products of their thinking, whether in science, the arts, philosophy, religion, politics, or some other field, we do not find a collection of people who were strikingly alike even with respect to their habits of thought. Invariably too, we find weakness as well as strengths even in the giants. The lesson from history is that one need not be a good thinker in all aspects to be a good thinker in some respects, and that being a good thinker in some respects has often resulted in products of thought of inestimable value to the world. History also encourages the view that while improving all aspects of thinking may be an appropriate goal of education, accomplishments that fall short of attaining that ambitious goal can be very beneficial and worth considerable effort. Perfection is not a reasonable target and never will be, but significant improvement is, even given our current limited understanding of how best to proceed.

It is not reasonable to expect that we shall discover any time soon how to turn our students—or ourselves—into perfectly logical, consistent, thorough, sensitive thinkers who manage to avoid the many reasoning foibles that have plagued humankind in the past. *What is reasonable to expect and to work toward is a gradually better understanding of what it means to think well and how to promote good thinking in the classroom.* Progress can be made through both theoretical research aimed at producing a more complete account of how our minds work and applied research aimed at developing and evaluating instructional methods for helping them to work better than they often do. Given the multifaceted nature of thinking, the question of how best to teach it is probably too general and imprecise to guide research. There are some more specific methodological questions lurking within this very general one, however, that are sufficiently precise to be answerable, at least in principle. Examples include the following:

How can the habit of listening carefully to what other people have to say be fostered?

How can people's willingness and ability to understand points of view differing from their own be increased?

How can the tendency to act impulsively ("without thinking") be restrained?

How can the ability to use analogies appropriately and effectively be enhanced?

How can the skill with which one evaluates arguments be improved?

How can the objectivity with which people deal with evidence be increased?

How can people's ability to find information that is likely to be useful in specific problem-solving or decision-making situations be enhanced?

How can the probability be increased that specific problem-solving heuristics will be used appropriately in contexts other than those in which they were taught?

How can people be helped to be more aware of their own cognitive strengths and limitations so as better to exploit the strengths and compensate effectively for the limitations?

How can people's willingness to revise opinions and beliefs in the light of evidence that indicates the need for revision be increased?

How can people's ability to monitor their own intellectual performance and manage their intellectual resources be improved?

These questions vary in specificity and some of them may have to be unpacked further before getting to forms that will admit of unambiguous answers. But all of them are considerably more specific than the question of how to teach thinking. And each has the virtue that the act of formulating it requires explication of what one believes some aspect of thinking to involve. I believe we must be willing to be at least this specific in our statement of "how" questions if we are to hope to get answers.

We are unlikely to be satisfied with the results of our current efforts to find better ways to teach thinking, but that is as it should be. *The goal of improving thinking should be an unending one.* If we at some point convince ourselves that we now know how to do this well enough and no further efforts for improvement are necessary, we will then be in real trouble.

The maturity of any field of scientific investigation is revealed by the nature of the questions it evokes, perhaps more than in any other way. For an immature field, the questions are couched in general and imprecise terms, and are open to various interpretations. And there can be wide differences of opinion as to the acceptability of answers that are proposed. Progress in a field is marked by a growing understanding of what questions should be asked. Paradoxically, the ability to be specific about our ignorance of a domain depends on our knowledge of that domain; the more limited that knowledge is, the less will we be able to be precise about what we do know. We may presume that we collectively know more about human cognition today than was known one hundred years ago, but current knowledge is surely still a fraction of what is knowable. Maybe we do not yet know enough to appreciate how wide and deep our ignorance really is.

With respect to the teaching of thinking, the metaquestion is, Do we yet know enough to ask any reasonable questions? I believe the answer is yes, that we are able to articulate some questions that are both important and amenable to research. Those mentioned above are examples. Thanks to the research that has been done, especially on problem solving, reasoning, and metacognition, over the past few years, there are at least tentative answers for some of those questions. *What remains unknown about how best to enhance thinking in specific ways surely far outweighs what is currently known, but we do know enough to make a start.*

REFERENCES

Baron, J. (1985). *Rationality and intelligence.* New York: Cambridge University Press.

Chi, M., Feltovich, P., & Glaser, R. (1981). Categorization and representation of physics problems by experts and novices. *Cognitive Science,* 5, 121–152.

Dweck, C. S. (in press). In R. Glaser & A. Lesgold (eds.), *The handbook of psychology and education*. Vol. 1. Hillsdale, N.J.: Erlbaum.

Ennis, R. (1987). A taxonomy of critical thinking dispositions and abilities. In J. B. Baron & R. J. Sternberg (eds.), *Teaching thinking skills*. New York: Freeman.

Glaser, R. (1984). The role of knowledge. *American Psychologist, 39*, 93–104.

Larkin, J. H., McDermott, J., Simon, D. P., & Simon, H. A. (1980). Expert and novice performance in solving physics problems. *Science, 208*, 1335–1342.

Mackay, C. (1932). Extraordinary popular delusions and the madness of crowds. Boston: L. C. Page. (Original work published 1852)

National Assessment of Educational Progress (NAEP). (1981). *Reading, thinking, and writing: Results from the 1979–1980 national assessment of reading and literature*. Report No. 11-L-01. Denver: Education Commission of the States.

————. (1983). *The third national mathematics assessment: Results, trends, and issues*. Report No. 13-MA-01. Denver: Education Commission of the States.

National Commission on Excellence in Education. (1983). *A nation at risk: The imperative for educational reform*. Washington, D.C.: U. S. Government Printing Office.

Nickerson, R. S., Perkins, D., & Smith, E. E. (1985). *The teaching of thinking*. Hillsdale, N.J.: Erlbaum.

Nisbett, R. E., Fong, G. T., Lehman, D. R., & Cheng, P. W. (1987). Teaching reasoning. *Science, 238*, 625–631.

Nisbett, R. F., & Ross, I. (1980). *Human inference: Strategies and shortcomings of social judgment*. Englewood Cliffs, N.J.: Prentice-Hall.

Tuchman, B. (1984). *The march of folly*. New York: Ballantine.

Tversky, A., & Kahneman, D. (1974). Judgment under uncertainty: Heuristic and biases. *Science, 185*, 1124–1131.

Wason, P. C. (1966). Reasoning. In B. M. Foss (ed.), *New horizons in psychology*. Vol. 1. Harmondsworth: Penguin.

2

The School as a Home for the Mind: A Climate for Thinking

Arthur L. Costa

The Greeks had a word for it: *paideia*. The term, popularized by Adler's *Proposal* (1982), is an ideal concept we share—a school in which learning, fulfillment, and becoming more human are the primary goals for all its inhabitants—students, faculty, and support staff. It is the Athenian concept of a learning society in which self-development, intellectual empowerment, and lifelong learning are the most valued core elements.

The development of thinking as a goal of education is not just kid-stuff. If education is to achieve an intellectual focus, then the total school environment must mediate all its inhabitants' intelligent behavior. The school must become a home for the mind for all who dwell there. I offer a hypothesis: Teachers will more likely teach for thinking if they are in an intellectually stimulating environment themselves.

A quiet revolution is taking place across America in corporate offices, industrial factories, government bureaucracies, and schools—a mind/brain revolution. Increasingly, those attributes of a climate conducive to intellectual growth and self-fulfillment are becoming universally recognized and accepted. The conditions that maximize creativity are being described, understood, and installed (Perkins, 1983; Kohn, 1987). The new paradigm of industrial management emphasizes an environment in which growth and empowerment of the individual are the keys to corporate success. Pascarella writes:

Management is heading toward a new state of mind—a new perception of its own role and that of the organization. It is slowly moving from seeking power to empowering others, from controlling people to enabling them to be creative. . . . As managers make a fundamental shift in values . . . the corporation undergoes a radical reorientation to a greater worldview. (1984, p. 6)

Many educators have advocated these conditions for years, believing that a climate that maximizes human potential can be developed, monitored, and sustained. The conditions are equally applicable to any level of the educational organization: classrooms, schools, school districts. What follows are some climate factors that facilitate human intellectual growth; educators at the school, classroom, and district levels for each factor are described.

COLLEGIALITY

Humans mature intellectually in reciprocal relationships with other humans. Vygotsky (1987) points out that the higher functions actually originate in interaction with others:

Every function in . . . cultural development appears twice: first, on the social level, and later on the individual level; first between people (interpsychological), and then inside (intrapsychological). This applies equally to voluntary attention, to logical memory, and to the formation of concepts. All the higher functions originate as actual relationships between individuals. (p. 57)

Together, individuals surface ideas, then bounce and batter them about, thereby eliciting thinking that surpasses individual effort. As individuals engage in problem solving, conversation, and consensus seeking, multiple perspectives are expressed, dissonance created and reduced, discrepancies perceived and resolved, alternatives weighed.

The essence of collegiality is that people in the school community are working together to better understand the nature of intelligent behavior, how it develops, how it is taught and assessed, and how the total school experience can be organized to better promote growth in their own and learners' intellectual abilities.

Professional collegiality at the district level is evident when teachers and administrators from different schools, subject areas, and grade levels form networks to coordinate district efforts toward enhancing intelligent behavior across all content areas as well as in district policies and practices. Committees and advisory groups assess staff needs, identify and locate talent, and participate in district-level decisions and prioritizing. They support and provide liaison with school site efforts, plan districtwide in-service and articulation to enhance teachers' skills, and develop an aligned, coordinated, and developmentally appropriate curriculum for students.

Instructional materials selection committees review and recommend adoption of materials and programs intended to enhance students' thinking. Through districtwide networks teachers share information and materials and teach each other about skills, techniques, and strategies they have learned are effective.

At the school site teachers plan, prepare, and evaluate teaching materials. They visit each other's classrooms frequently to coach and give feedback about the relationship between their instructional decision making and resultant student behaviors. They prepare, develop, remodel, and rehearse lessons and units of study together.

Teachers and administrators continue to discuss and refine their vision of a school as a home for the mind. Definitions of thinking and the teaching and evaluation of students' intellectual progress is continually clarified and refined. Child-study teams keep portfolios of students' work and discuss the development of an individual student's thought processes and learning styles. Instructional problems are explored, and experimental solutions are cogenerated. Faculty meetings are held in classrooms where the host teacher shares instructional practices, materials, and videotaped lessons with the rest of the faculty. Teachers sequence, articulate, and plan for continuity and reinforcement of thinking skills across grade levels and subject areas.

Collegiality and collaboration are in evidence in the classroom as well. Students may be observed working together with their "study-buddies" in cooperative learning groups and in peer problems solving. Students participate in class meetings to establish plans, set priorities, and assess how well they are growing in their own intelligent behaviors.

EXPERIMENTATION AND ACTION RESEARCH

MacLean's (1978) concept of the triune brain helps us understand the need for operating in an environment of trust. For the neocortex to become fully engaged in its functions of problem solving, hypothesis formation, experimentation, and creativity, the "reptilian brain" (R-complex) and the "paleomammalian brain" (limbic system) need to be in harmony. Excessive stress or trauma detracts from neocortical functioning. Basic survival needs demanded by the reptilian brain and for emotional security and personal identity required by the paleomammalian brain can override complex neocortical functioning.

Experimentation implies that an atmosphere of risk taking exists. Data can be generated without fear that it will be used as a basis for evaluation of teachers' or students' successes or failures. Creativity will more likely grow in a low-risk atmosphere (Kohn, 1987).

An experimental, risk-taking climate will be in evidence as various published programs and curricula are pilot tested. Evidence is gathered over time and the resulting effects on students are shared. Teachers become researchers as alternate classroom arrangements and instructional strategies are tested while colleagues observe the resulting student interactions. Experiments are conducted with various lesson designs, instructional sequences, and teaching materials to determine their effects on small groups of students or with colleagues prior to large group instruction.

The classroom climate, too, will foster risk taking as students experiment with ideas, share their thinking strategies with each other, and venture forth with creative thoughts without fear of being judged. Value judgments and criticism are replaced with acceptance of, listening to, empathizing with, and clarifying each other's thinking (Costa, 1984b).

APPRECIATION AND RECOGNITION

Whether it be art, athletic prowess, acts of heroism, or precious jewels, what is valued is given public recognition. Core values are communicated by that which is appreciated. If thinking is valued, it, too, will be recognized by some expression of appreciation. This is true for students in the classroom, and for teachers and administrators as well.

Some observable school indicators might include teachers being invited to describe their successes and unique ways of organizing for teaching thinking; teachers sharing videotaped lessons in faculty meetings; or showcasing the positive results of teachers' lesson planning, strategic teaching, and experimentation.

Some observable classroom indicators might include students being recognized for persevering, striving for precision and accuracy, and expressing empathy. Students should applaud each other for acts of ingenuity, compassion, and persistence. Positive results and consequences of students' restraint of impulsivity are elaborated.

HIGH EXPECTATIONS

"Thinking *is* important. You *can* think, you *will* think, and I'll help you *learn* to think." There is an inherent faith that all human beings can continue to grow and improve their intellectual capacities throughout life—that all of us have the potential for even greater giftedness, creativity, and intellectual power.

Students may perceive thinking as hard work and recoil from situations that demand "too much" of them. Students, teachers, and administrators realize that learning to use and continually refine their intelligent behavior is the purpose of their education. They continue to define and clarify that goal and seek ways to gain assistance in achieving it.

Mottoes, slogans, and mission statements are observable throughout the classroom, the school, and the district. "Lincoln schools are thoughtful schools" is the motto painted on one district's delivery trucks for all the community to see. Bookmarks reminding the community that thinking is the school's goal are distributed to service organizations and the public by the superintendent of Plymouth-Canton Public Schools in Michigan. "Thought is taught at Huntington Beach High" is emblazoned upon the school's note pads. "Make thinking

happen" is printed on Calvin Coolidge Elementary School's letterhead statio-
nery in Shrewsbury, Massachusetts. "Thinking spoken here" is a constant
classroom reminder of Stockton, California history teacher Dan Theile's goals
for students.

Expectations are communicated when staff members periodically report
breakthroughs in their progress toward installing thinking in their schools and
classrooms. Superintendents review with administrators their long-range goals
and visions and their progress toward including the development of intelligent
behaviors in their school's mission. Teachers are invited to share progress in
enhancing students' thinking. In classrooms, journals are kept and students periodically report new insights they are gaining about their own problem-solving
strategies.

PROTECTING WHAT IS IMPORTANT—SAYING "NO" TO DISTRACTIONS

Knowing that thinking is an important goal, all inhabitants of the school
believe that their right to think will be honored and protected. This overarching
and primary goal is kept in focus as district leaders make day-to-day decisions.
This may prove to be difficult as pressures from public and vocal special interest groups distract us from our mission. Our vision may be temporarily ob-
scured by politically expedient and financially parsimonious decisions.

Thinking is valued not only for students and certificated staff, but for the
classified staff as well. A principal of a "thinking school" reported that a
newly hired custodian constantly asked her to check on how well he was clean-
ing the classrooms and to tell him whether he was doing an adequate job. She
decided to help him develop a clear mental image of what a clean classroom
looked like and then worked to enhance his ability to evaluate for himself how
well the room he cleaned fit that image.

Teachers' rights to be involved in the decisions affecting them are protected
and those who do not choose to be involved in decision making are also honored in their choice.

Fads, bandwagons, and other educational innovations that may detract from
our intellectual focus are ignored as irrelevant to our central issue. Philosophical discussions, however, are encouraged because they give voice to alternative
views. Considering other points of view as expressed in such books as Bloom's
Closing of the American Mind (1987), Finn and Ravitch's *What Do Our 17
Year Olds Know?* (1987), and Hirsch's *Cultural Literacy* (1987) creates ten-
sions, honors divergent thinking, and expands and refines our vision. Such
discussion further verifies the staff's definition of literacy to include modes of
thinking and inquiring. It strengthens the staff's commitment to the principle
that to learn anything—cultural literacy or basics—requires an engagement of
the mind.

Since change and growth are viewed as intellectual processes, not events, we are interested in and value the time invested in ownership, commitment, and long-range learning.

TANGIBLE SUPPORT

Like radio transmitters, how school personnel expend their valuable resources—time, energy, and money—sets up a signal system to the staff, community, and students about what is important.

Financial resources are allocated to hire substitutes so that teachers can be released to visit and coach each other. Staff members and parents are sent to workshops, courses, conferences, and other in-service opportunities to learn more about effective thinking and the teaching of thinking.

Instructional materials and programs related to thinking are purchases. Time is allocated to plan for and train teachers in their use and to gather evidence of their effectiveness. Consultants are hired for long-range planning and in-service. Faculty meeting time is used to discuss and report new learnings about intellectual development and implications are generated for program improvement.

Administrators use their time and energy to visit classrooms to learn more about and coach instruction in thinking. Teachers expend their valuable time in planning lessons and observing each other teach for thinking. Time in the classroom is allocated to thinking and talking about thinking. The processes of thinking are explicitly stated so that students know that learning to think is the goal of the lesson. Problem solving and metacognition *are* the "tasks that students are on."

CARING, CELEBRATIONS, AND HUMOR

The value of thinking is exemplified in the traditions, celebrations, and humorous events that indicate thoughtful behavior is being achieved.

Staff members may be heard sharing humorous anecdotes of students' thought processes. ("I observed two seventh-grade boys on the athletic field yesterday. From their behavior, I could tell a scuffle was about to break out. Before I got to them, another boy intervened and I overheard him say, 'Hey, you guys, restrain your impulsivity.' ")

Teachers and administrators share personal, humorous, and sometimes embarrassing anecdotes of their own lack of thinking.

At school assemblies students and teachers are honored for acts of creativity, cooperation, thoughtfulness, innovation, and scholarly accomplishments. Academic decathalons, thinking fairs, problem-solving tournaments, dialogical debates, invention conventions, science fairs, art exhibitions, and musical programs celebrate the benefits of strategic planning, careful research, practice, creativity, and cooperation.

Career days are held in which local business and industry leaders describe what reasoning, creative, problem-solving, and cooperative skills are needed in various jobs and occupations.

COMMUNICATIONS

Thinking skills pervade all forms of communication from and within the school. Report cards, parent conferences, and other forms of progress reports include indicators of students' growth of intelligent behaviors. (Costa, 1984a).

Portfolios of students' work are collected over time as sources of data about growth in organizational abilities, conceptual development, and increased creativity. Test scores are reported that include reasoning, vocabulary growth, critical thinking, analogies, problem solving, and fluency. Parent education meetings are held to help parents know how to enhance their child's intelligent behavior (Feldman, 1986).

Newspaper articles are written and calendars and newsletters are sent home informing parents and the community of the school's intent and progress in teaching thinking. In meetings with parents, suggestions are given for ways to enhance their child's intellectual capacities.

Students maintain journals to record their own thinking and metacognition and to share and compare their growth of insight, creativity, and problem-solving strategies over time. Parents, too, are invited to collect evidence of transference of their child's intellectual growth from the classroom to family and home situations.

CONTINUING TO EXPAND THE KNOWLEDGE BASE

The mark of a school that is becoming a home for the mind is that it is continually expanding the knowledge base instead of striving for conformity to certain specified instructional competencies. Knowledge about thinking and the teaching of thinking is vast, complex, uncertain, and incomplete (Marzano et al., 1987). No one will ever know it all nor do we wish to reduce it to a simplistic step-by-step lesson plan (Brandt, 1987). Teachers and administrators can continually learn more and add to their repertoire of instructional skills and strategies.

Knowing that the school's mission is to develop the intellect and that process is valued as much as content, each teacher at each grade level and within each subject area will strive to invest thoughtful learning, reflection, and metacognition into all instruction. Teachers constantly expand their repertoire of instructional skills and strategies intended to develop in students a wide range of reasoning, creative, and cooperative abilities. They strive to match their instructional behaviors, tactics, and strategies from this vast repertoire with content goals, students' characteristics, and context with which they are working. They vary their lesson designs according to students' developmental levels, cognitive styles, and modality preferences (Jones, 1987).

Teachers and administrators take course work in philosophy, logic, and critical thinking and strive to improve their own thinking skills and strategies while their students expand their range of intelligent behaviors. These include not only knowing how to perform specific thought processes (Beyer, 1985), but also knowing what to do when solutions to problems are *not* immediately known—developing study skills, learning-to-learn, reasoning, problem-solving, and decision-making strategies (Marzano & Arrendondo, 1986). They learn about their own cognitive styles and how to cooperate with those who have differing styles. They learn how to cause their own "creative juices" to flow by brainstorming, inventing metaphor, synectics, and concept mapping.

TRUST, HONESTY, AND OPEN COMMUNICATION

All the school's inhabitants are committed to the improvement of school climate, interpersonal relationships, and the quality of human interaction. Students and classified and certificated personnel strive for precision of language, understanding, and empathy. They practice and improve their listening skills of paraphrasing, empathizing, and clarifying.

At school board, administrative, faculty, and class meetings decision-making processes are discussed, explicated, and adopted. Process observers are invited to give feedback about the group's effectiveness and growth in their decision-making, consensus-seeking, and communication skills.

Furthermore, each group member's opinions are respected. Disagreements can be stated without fear of damaging the relationship. Debates and alternate points of view are encouraged. Responsibility for "errors, omissions, and inadequacies" is owned without blaming others. Responses are given and justified and new ideas are advanced without fear of being criticized or judged. Differing priorities, values, logic, and philosophical beliefs of group members are discussed and become the topics of analysis, dialogue, and understanding.

PHILOSOPHY, POLICIES, AND PRACTICE

Enhancing intelligent behavior is explicitly stated in the school district's adopted philosophy and mission statement. District policies and practices are constantly scrutinized for their consistency with and contribution to that philosophy. Evidence of their use as criteria for decision making is examined. Furthermore, procedures for continuing to study, refine, and improve districtwide practices are aligned so that schools keep growing toward more thoughtful practice.

Personnel practices reflect the desire to infuse thinking. Job specifications for hiring new personnel include skills in teaching thinking. Teachers are empowered to make decisions that affect them—they have a sense of efficacy. Supervision of and staff development for all certificated staff are focused on enhancing perceptions and intellectual growth and honors their role as professional decision makers (Costa & Garmston, 1985).

Selection criteria for texts, tests, instructional materials, and other media include their contribution to thinking. Counseling and discipline, library and psychological services are constantly evaluated for their enhancement of and consistency with thoughtful practice.

In schools and classrooms discipline practices appeal to students' thoughtful behavior. Students participate in generating rational and compassionate classroom and school rules and are involved in evaluating their own behavior in relation to those criteria.

MODELING

Learning to think is probably best learned through imitation and emulation of significant others. All adults in the school, therefore, strive to model in their own behaviors those same qualities and behaviors that are desired in students.

Modeling will be evident as teachers and administrators share their metacognitive strategies in the presence of students and others while they are teaching, planning, and solving problems (Jones, 1987).

Staff members restrain their impulsivity during emotional crises. They listen to students, parents, and each other with empathy, precision, and understanding. Teachers and administrators constantly reflect on, and evaluate their own behaviors and strive to make them more consistent with the core value and belief that thoughtful behavior is a valid goal of education.

The school will become a home for the mind only when the total school is an intellectually stimulating environment for all the participants; when all the school's inhabitants realize that freeing human intellectual potential is the goal of education; when they strive to get better at it themselves; and when they use their energies to enhance the intelligent behaviors of others.

REFERENCES

Adler, M. (1982). *The paideia proposal*. New York: Macmillan.

Beyer, B. (1985). Teaching critical thinking: A direct approach. *Social Education, 49*, 297–303.

Bloom, A. (1987). *The closing of the American mind*. New York: Simon & Schuster.

Brandt, R. (1987). On teaching thinking skills: A conversation with B. Othanel Smith. *Educational Leadership, 45*, 2.

Costa, A. (1984a). Teacher behaviors that enhance thinking. In A. Costa (ed.), *Developing minds: A resource book for teaching thinking*. Alexandria, Va.: Association for Supervision and Curriculum Development.

———. (1984b). How can we recognize improved student thinking? In A. Costa (ed)., *Developing minds: A resource book for teaching thinking*. Alexandria, Va: Association for Supervision and Curriculum Development.

Costa, A., & Garmston, R. (1985). Supervision for intelligent teaching. *Educational Leadership, 43*, 70–80.

Feldman, R. D. (1986, November). How to improve your child's intelligent behavior. *Woman's Day,* pp. 10–12.

Hirsch, E. D. (1987). *Cultural literacy.* Boston: Houghton Mifflin.

Jones, B. F. (1987). Strategic teaching: A cognitive focus. In B. F. Jones, A. S. Palincsar, D. Ogle, & E. Carr (eds.), *Strategic teaching and learning: Cognitive instruction in the content areas.* Alexandria, Va.: Association For Supervision and Curriculum Development.

Kohn, A. (1987). Art for art's sake. *Psychology Today,* 21, (9), 52–57.

MacLean, P. (1978). A mind of three minds: Educating the triune brain. In J. Chall & A. Mirsky (eds.), *Education and the brain.* Seventy-seventh Yearbook of the National Society for the Study of Education. Chicago: University of Chicago Press.

Marzano, R., & Arrendondo, D. (1986). *Tactics for thinking.* Alexandria, Va.: Association for Supervision and Curriculum Development.

Marzano, R., Brandt, R., Hughes, C., Jones, B. F., Presseissen, B., Rankin, S., & Suhor, C. (1987). *Dimensions of thinking.* Alexandria, Va.: Association for Supervision and Curriculum Development.

Pascarella, P. (1984). *The new achievers.* New York: Free Press.

Perkins, D. (1983). *The mind's best work: A new psychology of creative thinking.* Cambridge, Mass.: Harvard University Press.

Ravich, D., & Finn, C. (1987). *What do our 17 year olds know?* New York: Harper & Row.

Vygotosky, L. S. (1978). *Mind in society.* Cambridge, Mass.: Harvard University Press.

3

Government Processes for Including Thinking Skills in the Curriculum

Sandra Falconer Pace

The explosion of information about and published programs for thinking skills has fueled an interest in the topic throughout the whole educational community. Universities are involved in research and dissemination, and school divisions are concerned to develop students' higher-order thinking skills. In both the United States and Canada, agencies responsible for curriculum development are also seeking to incorporate directions on higher-order thinking skills in position statements, curricula, and education policies. Some of the Canadian provinces and seven American states have been active in establishing official positions with regard to the teaching of thinking skills and have included these specifically in curriculum development.

The evolution of a position statement in a published document within a government department is an interesting, albeit lengthy, process. While it is not generally recognized by those outside the government, the primary reason for the length of the process is the necessity for consensus within the educational community. This community is composed of many interests: government officials, the university or research community, parents, taxpayers, and school division personnel. School division personnel are often represented by teachers, school-based administrators, central office consultants, administrators, and school trustees. Members of the public, such as home and school associations or chambers of commerce, may also be consulted in curriculum development, depending upon the particular initiative. Political factors, of course, always affect this process, but the needs for consensus and input from many "stakeholders" or "educational partners" are the intrinsically time-consuming factors in the process. Educators typically decry the length of time required to produce a curriculum or publish a position statement, but jealously guard their right to influence the process.

In Canada, education is the responsibility of each provincial government. It is administered by a department or ministry of education, analogous in structure if not in scope to some American state education agencies. Canada, unlike most other countries, has virtually no federal presence in education (except in the two territories, where the federal government exercises the provincial role). Even where federal funding is provided for programs, such as with French education currently, these funds are administered individually (and to some extent differently) by each province.

The department or ministries are empowered by legislation to set the curriculum for provincial schools and to certify teachers. Jurisdictions and teachers are legally required to follow the provincial programs of study in the various subjects. Locally developed courses may be offered upon approval by the departments of education. Many courses also have components that are open to adaptation according to local needs. Programs of study set the objectives and the content of courses. Frequently, the departments also publish optional curriculum guides and teacher resource manuals, which flesh out content and instructional methods for further assistance to teachers. Position statements on educational issues may be published for two purposes: to guide curriculum developers and to inform educators in the field. Finally, the departments may also publish informational documents as a service to the field. While not having the force of a position statement, informational documents nonetheless assist teachers in understanding the basis of official curricula and in implementing these curricula.

This chapter will attempt to examine the processes by which a government department or agency develops a position statement, and follow how such a statement informs curriculum development. Examples are drawn primarily from two western Canadian provinces, Alberta and Saskatchewan, and one American state, California, which have been particularly forward-looking in the area of thinking skills.

THE DEVELOPMENT OF POLICY STATEMENTS AND INITIATIVES

Frequently, government officials will themselves identify the need to establish a position or direction with respect to a given issue. This will result in staff time being allocated to write an internal position statement or discussion paper on a topic. Internal papers promote discussion and clarify intent within a government agency. They are rarely "secret" agendas—instead they are attempts to identify and promote coherence and direction in government publications and actions. For example, in Alberta, Sharon Mott drafted an internal discussion paper on the integration of communication and critical thinking skills

(Alberta Education, 1982) for use in curriculum development. British Columbia has also drafted an internal discussion paper on thinking skills for use in their curriculum development process.

When an issue reaches political consciousness, government agencies or departments are constrained to act. A minister of education in a province or similar official in a state can direct the department or agency to establish a position on a topic. In many provinces, states, and countries recently, there have been massive reviews of the education system in whole or part. This has led to an interest in establishing the core curriculum for schools. The "core curriculum" includes those subjects that all students must take in order to graduate from basic education. In western Canada, Alberta undertook to evaluate its secondary system (grades 7 to 12). In British Columbia and Saskatchewan, the entire K-12 system was examined. An emphasis on thinking skills has typically been one outcome of these reviews.

The development of policy statements such as those following the reviews of education is generally a combined effort on the part of bureaucratic and political officials. The educators seek to inform the politicians of sound educational practice, and the politicians seek to ensure that their particular issues are addressed. At its most harmonious, this is a mutually informative process, where the will of the electorate, through its elected representatives, is integrated with the educational expertise of the government officials. Policy statements go through numerous drafts as all constituencies are satisfied. Ten drafts are not unusual; in one instance there were twenty-seven changes in the course of the process. Policies rank in importance from being legislated documents, to official policy statements of the government, to official policy statements of the department, to the official policy statement of a unit within the department. Regulations generally interpret legislated policies. Guidelines and procedures generally follow policy statements. Officials then have varying degrees of latitude to interpret these documents, depending on their specificity.

The next level of development, when the initiatives flow from the established policy, is generally under the guidance of the government officials. Approval for initiatives (as opposed to policy) is usually granted by the deputy minister in Canada, rather than the politician. The policy statement, for example, may state that "higher-order" or "critical and creative" thinking skills will be included in the curriculum, taught, and tested. The exact definition of those skills will come from the initiative level. It will be developed by a writer or team of writers under the direction of the government official or advisory committee. More often nowadays, writers are contracted to produce these background papers. It is felt that a career bureaucrat cannot be expected to have expertise in all areas that may be required over the course of a career. Hence, if a person is contracted to each task, expertise can be assured by each *de nouveau* hiring. The more collaborative the model, the more committees will be used to manage the process. The committee structures ensure input, involvement, and ownership for all the interest groups invited to participate. Working committees may actually act as writing teams, while advisory committees provide recommendations that may or may not be accepted.

Alberta's review of its system of secondary education in 1984 resulted in the government policy statement, *Secondary Education in Alberta, June 1985*. This policy statement has subsequently informed curriculum development on a large scale in the province. Two parallel initiatives came directly from this review, the *Developmental Framework* (Alberta Education, 1987a, 1988a, 1988b) and the *Catalogue of Essential Concepts, Skills, and Attitudes* (Alberta Education, 1987c). Both of these initiatives are position statements designed as a basis for curriculum development and both deal in a major way with the development of thinking skills. *The Developmental Framework* is a set of four documents describing students' normal development in the cognitive, affective, and physical domains. The fourth document, which integrates these domains, appeared in 1990 (Alberta Education, 1990). The *Catalogue of Essential Concepts, Skills, and Attitudes* is a statement of the understandings or learnings to which all graduates from grade 12 should be exposed. These essential concepts, skills, and attitudes are then integrated into programs of study to ensure all students have the opportunity to learn them. One section of the *Catalogue* lists critical and creative thinking concepts, skills, and attitudes.

In Saskatchewan, the review of K-12 education culminated in *Directions, The Final Report* (1984). From there, several initiatives were developed, the *Common Essential Learnings* (Saskatchewan Education, 1988) being the primary supporting initiative. All Saskatchewan teachers received a handbook on these Common Essential Learnings (CELs) (Saskatchewan Education, 1988) and two days of in-service on the CELs. It is intended that the CELs will inform the redevelopment of the curriculum, which includes both the seven required areas of study and options, over the 1990s. One of the six common essential learnings is critical and creative thinking.

In California, as in many other American states, the education process seems to be inherently more political at many stages than is usually the case in Canada. The passage of the Hughes–Hart Education Reform Act (Senate Bill 813, State of California, 1983) required the development of model curriculum frameworks to inform school divisions' work (California is a local control state). These curriculum frameworks include goals and objectives for the teaching of higher-order thinking from elementary through high school (Freeman, 1989). In California, the position statement is essentially incorporated in narrative terms into the curriculum frameworks.

THE DEVELOPMENT OF CURRICULA

In California, several of the curriculum frameworks have already been developed and are in use. Science, mathematics, and English language arts are available at the elementary and middle levels. Saskatchewan had several curricula under development while the CELs were being prepared, but the first curricula to come out completely under their guidance are middle social studies and elementary science. The K-6 science program is especially interesting, since it is based on an innovative and well-conceived foundation paper called the *Dimensions of Scientific Literacy*. To ensure consistent development of thinking skills in the Alberta curriculum, and following on work previously done in the department, an Alberta Education committee prepared an internal report on the integration of thinking skills across subject boundaries (Alberta Education, 1987b). Curriculum developers then followed this model in writing recent curricula. These recent curricula include career and life management, junior and senior high mathematics, social studies at all levels, junior and senior high science, and agriculture, among others.

In the Alberta document on cognitive development, *Students' Thinking: Developmental Framework, Cognitive Domain* (1987a), it is noted that many students do not develop formal operational thinking skills until they reach senior high school (if then). Students who are academically gifted or advanced in creative or productive thinking may develop these skills as early as age eleven or twelve, but many more students do so at about age fourteen or fifteen, and some students do not do so even into adulthood. Curricula for upper elementary and junior high students, therefore, should seek to develop abstract thinking skills for students, but recognize that all but some gifted students do not already exhibit such skills.

To assist in developing abstract thinking in all students, and to accommodate the advanced development of gifted students, all curricula at the junior high and the senior high levels have some objectives at the formal operational level. Of course, there are more formal operational objectives in the grade 12 than the grade 7 curricula. The classroom teacher will still need to differentiate instruction and product expectations for gifted, average, and other students; the adaptive portion of the curriculum in each subject will allow time for this purpose.

Objectives for all curricula include thinking skills implicitly. An examination of goals and objectives statements in any curriculum will reveal which thinking skills are to be developed. For those familiar with Bloom's taxonomy, the verbs used in the statements allow quick analysis of thinking skill levels. "List" is not on the same level as "understand" or "analyze." Most state or provincial curricula will have statements at a number of levels of abstraction. This is in fact one difficulty: there may be no consistent terminology or orientation used in the different courses of study. That is, when a science curriculum asks students "to observe," it is asking for a thinking skill, but the relationship between the skill of observing and the processes of scientific thinking is not explicitly drawn for the student. In the language arts curriculum, if the objective "observe" is used again, it will rarely be coordinated with the use of the same term in science.

This lack of coordination among the use of terms in different subject and often different age-level curricula occurs because state, provincial, and local agencies usually develop curricula over time and through committee processes. That is to say, curricula are not all developed, K-12 and in all subjects, by one person or group of people at one time. Curriculum development is staged across developmental levels (typically, four divisions or three levels), and across different subject areas (such as mathematics, science, language arts, etc.). Redeveloping a state or province's entire curriculum is seldom staged across less than a decade, and more often occurs over a twenty-year time scale. (Only British Columbia is attempting a more rapid change, with consequent stresses.) Since curriculum development is such a complex process, it is difficult to coordinate aspects that thread through all curricula, such as thinking skills.

While the curricula are developed by different people over an extended time, they are all taught (in elementary school) by one teacher to one group of students. Each student experiences the whole of the curriculum. This may seem obvious, but it is not a trivial point. As an exercise once, Alberta Education staff added up all the extra minutes each curriculum committee wished for their subject. They determined that a student would have to be in school for twenty-two hours each day in order to accommodate all the committees' requests! Besides difficulties with sufficient time for all subjects, students must also try to integrate across subject boundaries the skills, strategies, and processes that they are taught. In elementary schools, it can be a real challenge to produce integrated units of study when curriculum orientations do not mesh.

Position statements and informational documents are attempts to bridge these differences among curricula. They serve as updates to older curricula and directions to new curriculum development. They inform people who are new to the curriculum development process. In western Canada, departments of education used to be staffed with long-term personnel who directed curriculum development through their own writing efforts or through working committees. In recent times of budget constraints, the departments have attempted to reduce permanent staff. The curriculum redevelopment is then managed through the hiring of contract or seconded staff on a project-by-project basis, or by contracting the projects directly to school divisions. Few departments, however, have the intensive orientation procedures that would allow these short-term personnel to be aware of the departments' position in areas such as thinking skills, so that curricula are consistent in their use of terminology. Saskatchewan is attempting to do this through the establishment of a common format for all the curriculum documents, as well as a reliance on the CELs initiative.

Besides the differences in the use of terms in objective statements, curricula often differ in their use of strategies and processes. For example, Alberta used an overarching process called the inquiry process in science to tie thinking skills together. The Alberta social studies curriculum also used an inquiry process, but it differed from the one in science. Certainly, reading is a process, but (as an example) comprehension was not listed as a process for language arts in the way that inquiry was for science or social studies. In other words, there was no organizing relationship drawn among the levels of thinking in the various curricula. This is not surprising, since most of the earlier curricula were developed before the more recent research on thinking skills began to suggest a synthesis. Following the development of Alberta's internal report on the integration of thinking skills across subject boundaries (Alberta Education, 1987b), new curricula began to be more consistent in their use of terms and processes for thinking.

The approach taken in Alberta was to understand that strategies are developed and used for a purpose. In each subject, the purpose of the strategy is described. This makes differences in the strategies understandable. For example, social studies uses a decision-making strategy for issue resolution, but a research strategy for information gathering. In attempting to develop a framework of thinking skills, Alberta Education sought to accommodate all subject areas while still allowing for subject specificity. The question was, How can there be a consistent and coherent development of thinking skills in all curricula, such that students will have skills learned in one area reinforced in others, while still recognizing that different subjects naturally use different modes of inquiry? The framework sought by the committee attempted to be simple, comprehensive, and inclusive of the various dimensions of thinking.

FRAMEWORKS FOR THINKING SKILLS

Alberta Education began with a structural analysis of the kinds of thinking skills that exist and can be taught. It was not an operational analysis, or examination of how thinking occurs. While Alberta Education supports the stand that thinking can, and in fact must be taught, it does not prescribe one way for this to be done. It supports the idea that thinking must be taught in a variety of ways, because it is a variety of skills and processes. The initial model was conceptualized as shown in figure 3.1.

This framework has four dimensions set against context as a background. A simplified version of the model is outlined in figure 3.2.

In this model, thinking is conceptualized as consisting of three levels: individual skills (such as observing or hypothesizing), organized sequences of skills called strategies (such as the inquiry process or problem solving), and metacognition, or the ability to think about and modify one's own thinking. The attitudes one holds about thinking are conceived of as critical to one's ability to think effectively. The purpose one has for thinking determines (or rather should determine) the skills, strategies, and attitudes one calls into play to accomplish the task. The essential difference, in this schema, between critical and creative thinking is seen as a difference of purpose, and hence of skills, strategies, and attitudes used, as well as of products produced.

This internal document was used by curriculum developers and reviewed by selected educators for about two years while the department sought to further refine the model, simplify it, and gather input for a published discussion on

Figure 3.1
Dimensions of Thinking

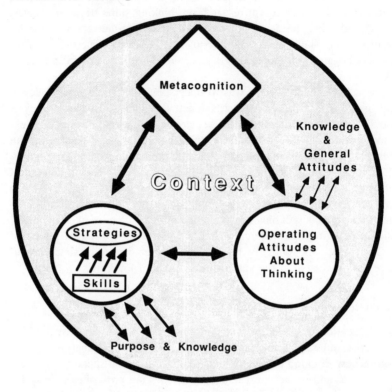

thinking skills. Alberta Education published two informational documents in 1990 detailing directions for thinking skills and practical hints for teachers to encourage the development of students' thinking.

Saskatchewan's model for critical and creative thinking comes from a critical thinking tradition. While it acknowledges the role of creative thinking, twelve of the sixteen suggestions for teachers to create a climate conducive to critical and creative reflection center on critical thinking, two promote both types, and only two foster creative thinking. The model that Saskatchewan uses includes aspects not referred to in the text of the handbook. For example, the bottom lines clearly allude to Gardner's theory of multiple intelligences, but the text makes no reference to these types of intelligences. Nor is Gardner included in the reference list. The primary source quoted is Richard Paul.

Saskatchewan's chapter on critical and creative thinking explicitly mentions that their curricula will take the position that thinking skills must be developed within the subject areas. California has also taken care to explicitly incorporate thinking skills objectives into each subject area through its curriculum frameworks. The other American states that have goals statements on thinking skills

Figure 3.2
Dimensions of Thinking: Simplified Model

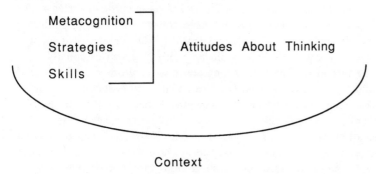

Context

for their curricula are Hawaii, Missouri, New York, North Carolina, and Utah. Indiana has guidelines for thinking skills instead. The inclusion of thinking skills within curricula rather than as a separate subject is a common position among government agencies. The inclusion of thinking skills within subjects has several points to recommend it:

• There is research support for this view.
• Experts in the area support this view.
• Textbook adoption processes keyed to curricula will include thinking skills objectives as a matter of course.
• Curriculum-referenced testing will include thinking skills testing as part of the curriculum to be tested.
• It avoids the problem of authorizing a new subject, "Thinking."
• Time does not have to be found to incorporate the new subject in an overcrowded school day.
• It circumvents having to choose among commercial thinking programs.

Freeman (1989) makes the point that a comprehensive policy in thinking skills should include higher-order thinking skills in all of the following aspects:

• goals and objectives, or guidelines
• in-service programs
• state testing
• textbook adoptions

Only California, Indiana, North Carolina, and Utah, of the seven states identified by Freeman as being active in the incorporation of thinking skills, include consideration of thinking skills within the textbook adoption process. California has been particularly proactive in developing textual resources that support higher-order thinking objectives in its curricula. In this regard, Canadian textbooks are often in advance of American ones. Because the Canadian market is much smaller than the American market for texts, and because curricula differ in each province, frequently Canadian provinces have entered into custom publishing arrangements with publishers. This means that the province agrees to supply a minimum order for a text, and the publisher writes that text essentially under contract to the province. Curriculum congruence is therefore virtually assured, including thinking skills objectives. One particularly apt example is the development of the grade 11 career and life management course for Alberta students. The course and text were developed directly under the guidance of the internal Alberta Education thinking skills model. Custom publishing is an excellent vehicle for single adoption situations, and can promote a local publishing industry. It requires, however, sufficient support from the government agency in terms of numbers of texts purchased and consultative support to be successful.

All states mentioned by Freeman except Utah include consideration of higher-order thinking in state testing programs. California and New York have gone beyond paper-and-pencil testing to include some performance testing such as group problem solving. Some Canadian provinces are now examining types of performance testing for different subject areas. Alberta's process for preparation of graduation or diploma examinations explicitly includes higher-order thinking questions. In fact, 50 percent of a student's grade 12 English examination consists of one or more short and one long essay question. (The examination forms 50 percent of the student's final grade, and so the written portion of the examination is 25 percent of the student's overall final English grade. Other subject examinations, including the sciences, also have written portions.)

TEACHING THINKING:
ALBERTA EDUCATION'S DESCRIPTION

Use and review of Alberta Education's initial model led to a need for a description of thinking that is simpler in structure and that highlights what needs to be done in curriculum documents and in the classroom. This model, built on Costa's discrimination among teaching for, of, and about thinking (Costa, 1981, 1985), emphasizes the development of metacognitive thinking. Thinking is defined as the mental processes and skills we use to shape our life world. Drawn from the philosophical tradition, this definition recognizes the breadth of influence and fundamental importance of thinking skills for each person.

Since curricula already encompass the development of thinking skills and strategies, a major emphasis in this document is put on the development of metacognitive awareness. Where good teachers have always taught students to think implicitly, now the emphasis is expanding to explicit teaching of thinking for all students, not just those with special needs or giftedness. It is felt that if people are aware of the skills, strategies, and processes they use in thinking, they are more able to modify and improve those thinking skills, strategies, and processes. Thus metacognitive awareness is an important component of independent lifelong learning.

Eleven guiding principles inform curriculum development in Alberta and ensure the best possible teaching of thinking skills.

1. *Students should learn thinking skills in order to live successfully now and in the future.* The complexity and rapid change of today's society require that citizens have high levels of critical thinking in order to evaluate claims and situations, develop diverse creative thinking strategies, solve complex problems, and show a willingness to engage in cooperative and group activities to improve society.

2. *Students of all ages and of varying abilities can improve their thinking skills.* Much research has and is being undertaken on the improvement of thinking skills in students of all ages and at all ability levels. Many study and "learning-to-learn" skills are aspects of thinking skills. Becoming effective learners requires that all students develop their thinking skills to higher levels.

3. *Thinking skills instruction encourages the development of cognitive abilities, and the skills of critical reasoning, information processing, and creative exploration.* Children learn through constructing meaning from their experiences. The study of this process can help teachers to understand how material can be presented to children in optimal ways. Teaching for thinking will encourage students' cognitive development. Teaching for metacognition is teaching for formal operational thinking, since one aspect of formal operational thinking is metacognition. The different representations used to teach different aspects of thinking in many information-processing applications enhance a person's skills at encoding problems in various ways until a fruitful representation or solution is found.

4. *Thinking skills are taught and learned in various ways.* Thinking skills are a wide variety of skills. Since they are not one unitary operation or structure, it follows logically that a variety of methods must be used to teach them. In particular, critical reasoning and creative exploration are likely to be taught and learned through very different means. A complete thinking skills program will include a variety of methods to teach a variety of thinking skills.

5. *Teachers can facilitate the development of thinking skills and metacognitive awareness through specific approaches.* While many programs for teaching thinking skills exist and have their uses, there are also some more general instructional techniques that will assist students' thinking skills development, regardless of the subject matter. Examples of such techniques include cooperative learning, peer teaching/tutoring, and cognitive modeling. These techniques are likely to assist students' learning because they increase the mediated learning experiences to which students are exposed. Mediated learning is defined as the ongoing interactive process through which thinking or experiences are explained and shown to students.

6. *Language is a major symbol system, universally used to represent the content and processes of thinking.* Language is one of many modalities that

reflect thought as a mirror does an image. It is a particularly useful one, and very widely used. While young children require heavily contextualized language, the beginning of decontexualized language is accelerated with learning to read and write. Schooling increasingly uses written language as a proxy for thought. Teachers should be aware that language is a reflection of thought rather than thought itself, and help students to understand its uses and effects.

7. *Thinking skills should be taught within the context of school subjects and the student's life world.* Thinking must be thinking about *some thing,* and so the teaching of thinking should be embedded in all subjects. People readily use only what they have practiced, and so students need to practice thinking skills in all possible contexts. Students are most likely to transfer the use of thinking skills if they have used them in all subjects. Furthermore, each subject matter is a way of knowing, or a way of representing and solving problems. As such, each subject has some unique thinking skills and forms of representation that can and should be taught.

8. *Curriculum documents should make explicit the teaching of thinking skills.* Just as explicit teaching of thinking skills assists students, so explicit description of thinking skills, strategies, and metacognitive strategies will assist teachers to teach these well. A common framework within which all curricula are developed will help teachers to see opportunities to involve students in thinking. Techniques that aid in representing situations or problems or in organizing knowledge should be explicitly described in curriculum documents. Some of these techniques include questioning, webbing, use of metaphors, concept mapping, diagramming, charting, and classifying. Suggestions for critical and creative thinking in the context of the subject should be made. Real-life applications should always be drawn, and should in fact often be starting points for the lessons.

9. *Assessment of thinking skills development requires appropriate evaluation strategies.* Alberta Education's student evaluation and records branch designs its examinations to test students' abilities at all levels of thinking. In fact, provincial achievement tests are innovative in this regard. The reading diagnostic testing program is also exemplary in providing an example of testing that goes beyond the knowledge level to examine thinking skills development in the context of reading. Teacher-made testing must emulate this model, but evaluation at the classroom level cannot begin and end with testing. A variety of evaluation methods should reflect the variety of instructional methods. The role of teacher's professional judgment in observation and conferencing with students is critical to the development of a range of thinking skills and attitudes. If students are to develop metacognitive skills, they must be involved in self-evaluation. In evaluating their writing, problem solving, or productions, students are evaluating the thinking process through which they arrived at that piece of writing, solution, or production.

10. *Supportive administrative practices enhance classroom instruction and the development of positive attitudes toward thinking.* Administrators support

teachers in teaching thinking when they create an environment conducive to risk taking, enthusiasm, and intellectual discussion. Allocation of resources to materials and activities that encourage thinking demonstrates commitment. Teacher supervision and evaluation policies and practices must reward teaching that encourages thinking. The contribution of all staff and students to the discussion of thinking must be valued.

11. *Preservice and in-service opportunities to explore the teaching of thinking should be available to all educators.* Teaching thinking is a subject as complex to study as any other subject. Since it is so significant to students' lives, and should be so pervasive in the curriculum as a whole, it would be a worthy subject of study in preservice and in-service teacher education.

California's process of including higher-order thinking is comprehensive in its approach. The description of the role of thinking for Alberta schools espouses a holistic and explicit perspective to teaching thinking. It emphasizes the role of metacognition, and in doing so goes beyond earlier statements and curricula that used a skill and strategy basis to teaching thinking. Saskatchewan's model and handbook chapter on critical and creative thinking have strong support for teaching thinking skills in all subjects.

The provinces of Alberta and Saskatchewan and the state of California are in fortunate positions in the development of their curricula. In the past, school curricula have not typically been developed under a guiding framework that brings common purpose to the teaching of thinking in all subjects while allowing for subject specificity. Of course, resource documents, such as Alberta's and Saskatchewan's descriptions of thinking, will not, of themselves, ensure the teaching of thinking. By helping establish a climate of acceptance and encouragement for the teaching of thinking, however, the curricula that are and will be developed can be in the forefront of educational practice. They will still need to be followed by effective pre- and in-service opportunities for teachers, and relevant testing practices.

REFERENCES

Alberta Education. (1982, July). *Preliminary report on the integration of communication skills and critical thinking skills with the Alberta curricula.* Edmonton.

———. (1985, June). *Secondary education in Alberta: Policy statement.* Edmonton.

———. (1987a, March) *Students' thinking: Developmental framework, cognitive domain.* Edmonton.

———. (1987b, May) *Report of the committee on thinking skills.* Unpublished internal report. Edmonton.

———. (1987c, May) *Essential concepts, skills and attitudes for grade 12.* (Often referred to as the *Catalogue of essential concepts, skills and attitudes.*) Edmonton.

———. (1988a, March). *Students' interactions: Developmental framework, social sphere.* Edmonton.

————. (1988b, July) *Students' physical growth: Developmental framework, physical dimension*. Edmonton.

————. (1990). *The emerging student: Developmental framework, language and interactions among domains*. Edmonton.

Costa, A. (1981). *Teaching for intelligent behavior: An awareness workshop*. California State University, Sacramento.

Costa, A. (ed.). (1985). *Developing minds: A resource book for teaching thinking*. Alexandria, Va.: Association for Supervision and Curriculum Development.

Freeman, D. J. (1989). State guidelines promoting teaching for understanding and thinking in elementary schools: A 50-state survey. *Educational Evaluation and Policy Analysis,* 11(4), 417–429.

Jones, B. F., Palincsar, A. S., Ogle, D. S., & Carr, E. G. (1987). *Strategic teaching and learning: Cognitive instruction in the content areas*. Alexandria, Va.: Association for Supervision and Curriculum Development.

Marzano, R., Brandt, R., Hughes, C., Jones, B. F., Presseisen, B., Rankin, S., & Suhor, C. (1988). *Dimensions of thinking*. Alexandria Va.: Association for Supervision and Curriculum Development.

Presseisen, B. (1987). *Thinking skills throughout the curriculum*. Bloomington, Ind.: Pi Lambda Theta.

Saskatchewan Education. (1984, August). *Directions: The final report*. Regina.

————. (1988, August). *Understanding the common essential learnings: A handbook for teachers*. Regina.

4

Enhancing Learning in the Context of School

John B. Biggs

GOOD LEARNING: IDEAL AND INSTITUTIONAL

While it is important to enhance motivation and/or higher-order cognitive processing by special interventions, it is even more desirable to maximize the quality of learning in its traditional ecology, the school. In this chapter, we will focus on how far it is possible to improve learning in existing learning institutions. There are two problems. The first is knowing what is holding back the quality of learning and what is likely to enhance it. The second, and more difficult, is changing reality in the school so that the inhibitors of learning quality are removed, and what promotes quality is made more salient.

The first, drearily familiar, point to be made is that one of the most reliable findings in educational research is that innovations, in the end, often achieve no better results than the traditional practices they replace: the more things change, the more they remain the same (Sarason, 1971). Whatever the research and developmental evidence for the worth of a practice, the practice, once officially installed, merges indistinctly with the general institutional profile, and things tend to go on much as before. Are schools then operating at their optimal functional level? If change is so difficult, must we settle for what we currently have? If that is so, exotic intervention would appear to be the best hope for improved learning.

Schools are not operating at their functional best, educationally speaking. There is too much evidence to suggest that people can learn far more effectively than they typically do in most public schools. Further, change does occur; there is little doubt that schools have changed in the last fifty years, and that most children are learning more effectively than they did fifty years ago. These changes often occur, however, as a result of the sociology of institutions rather than of the psychology of student learning.

There are clearly two dynamics at work here. The first is *substantive,* to do with the psychological value of a practice or procedure; as mentioned above, there is much evidence that under ideal conditions people can learn more effectively than they currently do. The second is *institutional,* to do with how a practice actually functions once it is installed in the natural ecology of the classroom. Let me illustrate with an example from the U.S. Navy.

The following describes how continuous aim firing—a method of keeping a ship's guns trained on an enemy ship when both ships are steaming in different directions—was introduced into the U.S. Navy.

The Navy's standard method, in Theodore Roosevelt's time, employed a very heavy set of gears and a highly trained crew with a kind of football coach/naval captain who gave directions. . . . Although there was a gun sight, nobody dared put his eye to it because of the recoil of the gun. Sims, a young naval officer, developed a new method which took advantage of the inertial movement of the ship; he simplified the gearing procedure and isolated the sight from recoil. . . . He tested the system and was able to effect a remarkable increase in accuracy.

Sims then wrote back to naval Headquarters . . . and the Navy wrote back that it was not interested . . . (but Sims) finally persuaded the Navy to test the method. . . . The test, as devised by the Navy, consisted in strapping the device to a solid block in the Navy Yard in Washington, where, deprived of the inertial movement of the ship, it failed. . . . Sims was not deterred. Finally he reached President Roosevelt directly, and the President forced the device down the Navy's throat. Under these conditions the Navy accepted it, and achieved a remarkable increase in accuracy. (Schon quoted in Reid, 1987, p. 11)

As Reid comments, the Navy was trying to protect a social system from an innovation that would have destroyed the existing system—never mind that the innovation greatly enhanced the official purpose of the system.

What, then, is a "system" in this sense? A system is an interconnected set of elements in equilibrium, so that change to any one element will bring about change in others, and thus establish a new equilibrium (Von Bertalanffy, 1968). In institutional systems, the equilibrium has usually evolved as the one that best suits: (1) the aims of the institution, (2) the social structure surrounding the individuals within it, and (3) the technology that makes it function (Reid, 1987). Various levels of schooling, from individual classroom, to school, to school board, form systems in this sense.

THE CLASSROOM AS A SYSTEM

Let us take the classroom. There are various elements here to do with learner, teacher, task, learning processes, and learning outcomes. The point of departure here is the student. "If students are to learn desired outcomes in a reasonably effective manner, then the teacher's fundamental task is to get students to engage in learning activities that are likely to result in their achieving those outcomes" (Shuell, 1986, p. 429). And "It is helpful to remember that what the student does is actually more important in determining what is learned than what the teacher does" (ibid). This quotation contains several important points: that the learner is the focus, that what learners do is determined by why they do it; that outcomes are determined by the learner's activity; and that the teacher's focus is on learning activities, not teaching activities.

Students undertake learning for a variety of reasons; these reasons determine how they go about their learning; and how they go about their learning will determine the quality of the outcome. This chain of events is captured in figure 4.1.

The model represents an integrated system with three main components: presage, process, and product (hence the "3P" model). Presage factors exist prior to learning, and are of two kinds: those pertaining to the student, and those pertaining to the teaching context. Students bring to the classroom relatively stable, learning-related characteristics: abilities, expectations and motivations for learning, conceptions of what learning is, prior knowledge, and the like.

The teaching context contains the superstructure set by the teacher and the institution: the course structure, curriculum content, and methods of teaching and assessment. This context, apart from its cognitive aspects, also generates a "climate" for learning, which, whether "cold" or "warm," has important motivational consequences.

The students are immersed in this teaching context, and interpret it in the light of their own preconceptions, motivations, and expectations. Their interpretation, and what they decide they should do about it, comprise a metacognitive activity called "metalearning" (Biggs, 1985), which focuses on the processes of learning—how one goes about a task—rather than on the content of what is learned. Metalearning is the means by which students derive their approaches to learning, and the approach adopted will in turn determine the outcome of learning.

The outcome may be described and evaluated in various ways. Quantitative evaluation assesses how much was learned, an aspect emphasized by conventional testing procedures, which use the total number of items—any items—correct for evaluation purposes, rather than focus upon which particular items were correct. Essays are not immune from quantitative assessment, which all too frequently operates on the "weight" principle. Qualitative evaluation, on the other hand, focuses precisely on how well a particular topic is learned or a problem is solved; defining "how well" then becomes the problem. One aspect of quality that can be generalized across subject areas is the structural complexity of the learning outcome (Biggs & Collis, 1982), but other aspects are defined specifically by the subject matter in question, and by the individual grader, with the frequent result that quality tends either to be very subjective, or is

Figure 4.1
Presage, Process, and Product in Student Learning

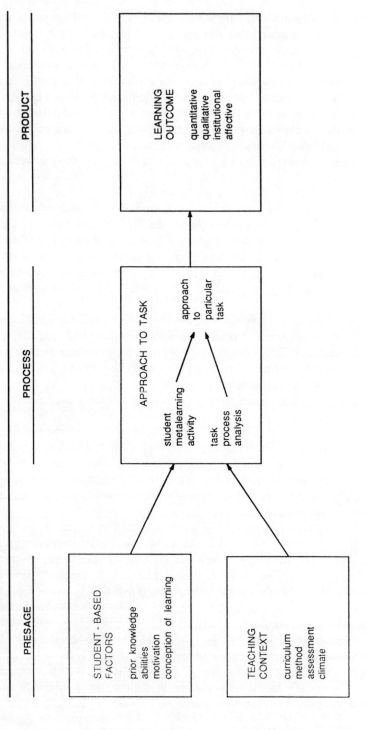

neglected. Institutional evaluation is, of course, expressed in grades and other forms of public recognition. Institutional evaluation may emphasize qualitative or quantitative aspects of performance, but for various reasons the latter have dominated. Another important kind of outcome is affective—whether the student feels that the learning experience was positive and fulfilling, or not. As is elaborated below, the emphasis the teacher places on these aspects of evaluation provides important messages to students about what is valued in learning.

The 3P model thus describes a system comprising student characteristics, the teaching context, student learning processes, and learning outcomes. The improvement of learning involves the interaction of all these components.

APPROACHES TO LEARNING

Students enter school with different motives and intentions. They may learn in order to obtain something they want, such as a credential, or to avert further pressure from a teacher or parent; it may be that they are interested in something and want to find out more about it; perceived excellence in formal learning may be a way to achieve status and recognition, in the form of high grades and prizes. Whatever those reasons might be, they help determine, through the process of metalearning, the way students go about their learning.

This combination of motive and strategy is called an "approach" to learning, three of which—surface, deep, and achieving—have been identified by factor analysis, and replicated several times (Biggs, 1979, 1987a; Entwistle & Ramsden, 1983; Watkins, 1983a). The two basic dimensions of surface and deep have been isolated in closely similar form, but with an entirely different methodology, by Marton and Saljo (1976) (see table 4.1).

The *surface approach* is based on extrinsic motivation: the student sees school learning as a means toward some other end, such as obtaining a job or keeping out of trouble. Students adopting this approach need to balance avoiding failure against working too hard. The strategy appropriate to meeting that intention is to limit the target to essentials, reproducible through rote learning. A student who adopts a surface approach sees the task as a demand to be met, and focuses on the concrete and literal aspects of it, such as the actual words used, rather than on their meaning. The components of the task are thus seen as unrelated to each other or to other tasks, and as being learned through memorization of the components.

The *deep approach* is based on interest in the subject matter of the task. The strategy is to maximize understanding so that curiosity is satisfied. A student adopting a deep approach sees the task as interesting and personally involving, and focuses on underlying meaning rather than on the literal aspects. The task components are integrated with each other and with other tasks. The student reads widely, discusses with others, and may "play" with the task, theorizing about it and forming hypotheses about how it relates to other known or interesting items.

Table 4.1
Prototypical Approaches to Learning

Approaches

	Motive	Strategy
Surface	Extrinsic: avoid failure but don't work too hard	Focus on selected details and reproduce accurately
Deep	Intrinsic: satisfy curiosity about topic	Maximise understanding: read widely, discuss, reflect
Achieving	Achievement: compete for highest grades	Optimise organisation of time and effort ("study skills")

The *achieving approach* is based on a particular form of extrinsic motive: the ego-enhancement that comes out of visibly achieving, and in particular through high grades. The related strategies refer to organizing time, working space, and syllabus coverage in the most efficient way (usually known as "study skills"). A student adopting an achieving approach sees high grades and marks as important, is competitive about obtaining them, sees it as important to be self-disciplined, neat, and systematic, and plans ahead, allocating time to tasks in proportion to their "importance."

While at any given time surface and deep approaches are mutually exclusive, an achieving approach may be linked to either surface or deep. Surface achievers, for instance, systematically rote learn selected detail to obtain high grades; deep achievers, who often are the better students, are organized and make plans in their search for both meaning and high grades.

An approach to learning can be discussed at two levels of generality. First, at its most general, a student's "approach" can refer to the way that individual characteristically goes about most academic tasks. Second, an "approach" can describe how a student handles a particular task at a particular time.

Thus students who characteristically use a surface approach may be given an essay assignment on a topic in which they are passionately interested. For a while, and on that task, their approach may well be deep. Or deep achievers have to take an extraneous subject to make up course units; the result is unimportant as long as they pass, so they may well use a surface approach.

There is usually a negative relationship between surface approach and examination performance (Biggs, 1987a), although a surface approach is effective for recalling unrelated detail (Biggs, 1979). The relationship with grades depends on what the marker values. In one study, a surface-achieving approach to writing a history essay led one grade 11 student to write an extremely long essay, full of biographical detail that strictly speaking did not meet the requirements of the compare-and-contrast question. The teacher nevertheless commended her on her "thoroughness," and gave her the highest mark in the class (Biggs, 1987b).

A deep approach leads to performance of high structural complexity. In secondary school, the deep approach correlated positively with external examination results only in the subjects in which students were interested, which fits the theory that deep approach springs from intrinsic interest. The achieving approach correlates generally with school performance (Biggs, 1987a).

With respect to affective outcomes of learning, students who use a surface approach feel negatively about their learning; they see the task as an imposition and resent the time spent on it, but are afraid of failing.

Students using a deep approach feel challenged and involved, while those using an achieving approach are in it for high grades, and if successful, will feel positive about their achievement.

What a surface or a deep approach to a particular task specifically means will depend on the task in question. In the case of writing expository essays, subtasks include planning, composing, reviewing, and revising; surface writers employ fewer subtasks, which are deployed on low-order textual units (semantically no more than is contained in a sentence), whereas deep writers plan, compose, and review up to the level of the main theme (Biggs, 1987b). Similar task analyses can be carried out for virtually any academic task; existing analyses include text comprehension (Kirby, 1988), map reading (Moore, private communication), and medical problem solving (Ramsden et al., 1989).

A deep approach to a particular task involves several features, including a well-structured knowledge base, comprising the content relevant to the task and also the procedural knowledge needed to handle the task appropriately; the expert knows what to do and is potentially aware of doing it. A writer, for instance, is aware of the need for focusing on main ideas and themes, as well as on specific word searches, and knows when to leave a less than adequate section for subsequent revision. Expert mathematicians classify problems according to solution modes rather than content (Sweller et al., 1983); readers induce unknown word meanings from context (Kirby, 1988). This content specificity in fact makes it difficult to teach a general deep approach; only some aspects are detachable from the given context.

When specific approaches to given tasks are related to outcome, relationships are much stronger than when general approaches are related to overall performance. In one study of twenty-four students, ranging from year 11 to postgraduate, there were no cases of writers using a surface approach who produced essays that had a more complex internal structure than a linear narration of detail, while deep writers without exception produced essays with a coherent and integrated structure that was appropriate to the question (Biggs, 1987b). Van Rossum and Schenck (1984) obtained similarly stark results in the case of a history task, as did Watkins (1983b) with literary and computing science tasks.

Such findings make a convincing case for deriving deep/surface descriptions for important academic tasks, and for arranging the teaching context to maximize the likelihood that deep approaches will be used by students, and that surface approaches will be discouraged. These propositions provide the substantive thrust for improving learning through better teaching. How possible that is institutionally speaking is a separate question we will address later.

ENHANCING LEARNING THROUGH BETTER TEACHING

The 3P model can be used as a focus for deriving ways of improving learning. The learning outcome can be affected in two main ways: (1) by taking presage factors, from either student or teacher domains, and treating them independently of other factors; and (2) by taking the interaction of student and teaching presage factors on students' approaches to learning. The first leads to a deficit, and the second to a process, approach to the improvement of teaching.

The Deficit Approach to Improving Teaching

Here we focus on one presage aspect of the 3P model, and treat it as if it related independently to the outcome, as indeed some factors do. IQ, for example, correlates directly with attainment. Such a focus assumes that something is lacking in either one of the presage variables, student or teacher.

In the blame-the-student version, the student is held deficient in motivation, ability, home background, previous teaching, or in some other characteristic. Thus if learning outcomes are inadequate, we might decide to screen out the dullards more rigorously, or give a crash course in study skills, if these are presumed to be the deficit. If the problem is home background—about which we cannot be expected to do anything—we sit around the staffroom, cursing our fate for being saddled with such poor material. This model, as far as the teacher is concerned, is extrapunitive; the blame lies beyond teaching, so that possible problems to do with curriculum design, teaching, or other institutional factors, are excluded from consideration. The school becomes a selection device, its role being to sort students for employers or for higher education. Such a conception of schooling was dominant fifty years ago, but it is not dead yet, and may even be reasserting itself in the coming decade.

In the blame-the-teacher version, the teacher is held deficient in various teaching skills, so the focus is on improving those skills and widening the teacher's repertoire, but little attention is paid to student outcomes. Much staff development is based on this version, with the emphasis on in-service work, workshops, teachers' centers, and so on. Such work is of course valuable—it *is* important to know to use the right-sized print on an overhead transparency—

but only in so far as the skillful orchestration of technique gets students to relate appropriately to the task at hand.

The Process Approach to Improving Teaching

The process approach to enhancing teaching takes the constructivist model of teaching and learning, recognizing that it is the students who construct knowledge, not the teacher who imparts it (Driver, 1983). The quality of the outcome thus depends on how the students approach the task; what the teacher does is important only in so far as it bears upon the way students go about their work. Good teaching should minimize those factors that lead to surface learning, and maximize those leading to deep and achieving learning.

Minimizing Surface Approaches

The first task involves finding out what factors in the teaching context encourage surface approaches, and then taking steps to minimize their effect. This may be a little more difficult than it seems.

Students read their messages from what teachers actually do in their teaching and assessing, not from what they say. It is important, then, to discover what messages there are in the contexts of teaching and assessment. Many studies have drawn attention to the wide gap between the rhetoric describing the qualities teachers say they want in their students' responses, the tasks they set, and the teaching and classroom arrangements (e.g., Ramsden, 1985; Tobin & Gallagher, 1987). Tobin and Fraser (1988) summarize the position, at least with respect to science and mathematics teaching in Australia and the United States:

Academic work is mainly directed towards earning points for a grade and preparing for tests and examinations which require recall of factual information and application of procedures. Thus examinations and tests have a strong effect on how students engage in classrooms. (p. 76)

Reward and punishment systems provide their own messages. Stipek (1986) cites examples of students preferring to hand in work they know to be incorrect, because the reward system punishes late submission more than it punishes error. At the same time, administrative efficiency prescribes deadlines, and fairness in their enforcement. How the teacher resolves that conflict will tell the students a great deal, both about the teacher's priorities and about how to live least uncomfortably with them.

The very fact of assessment is threatening to many students, however humanely it is administered. Whenever there is a formal evaluation, and a result "published" in some sense, the student has to live with the result and to account for it. The healthiest attributions for success are those that emphasize self-efficacy, and for failure, changeable factors such as luck, or better, insufficient effort. Low achievers, however, attribute success to luck, and failure to low ability (Dweck & Elliott, 1983). To some extent these attributions are derived by virtue of being "that sort of person," but they are also shaped by messages from the teaching context, and from personal interactions between teacher and student. Interactions that say, on success, "You were lucky that time!" or, on failure, "That was stupid of you, wasn't it?" convey attributions that may well become permanently debilitating.

Messages that convey to students that—whatever the teacher's real intentions—the assessment procedures are there just to sort students into categories for grading purposes invite a cynical kind of bargaining; they will jump through the hoops, and in return they will get their qualification. Deep engagement in the task is no part of the bargain and is unlikely therefore to occur.

In short, then, surface approaches may be encouraged in two main ways:

- affectively, by optimizing the conditions for extrinsic motivation, where rewards and punishments become the salient things to acquire or to avoid, respectively. In particular, a "cold" classroom climate, generating anxiety or cynicism, leads to surface learning.
- cognitively, by setting tasks that require low-level rote responses, and evaluating performance in ways that tell the students that rote recall is rewarded.

Encouraging the Achieving Approach

Encouraging the achieving approach to learning is handled by directly teaching learning and study skills to students across subject areas. Teaching study skills is a beguiling concept. The evidence is equivocal. Positive results have been found under certain conditions, particularly with highly motivated students in contexts emphasizing the metacognitive skills of self-management, rather than direct instruction of particular study techniques (Biggs, 1988; McKeachie et al. 1985; Weinstein & Mayer, 1984).

The problem is that teaching study skills is essentially based on the deficit model: the aim is to straighten out the student, independently of changes in teaching. Unless such changes do occur, study skill training can even become counterproductive. For example, Ramsden et al. (1986) gave a course in study skills to first-year undergraduates in a variety of faculties, focusing on such topics as managing study time efficiently, reading and note taking, examination preparation, and writing skills. The only discernable effects of the program, compared to a control group, were that the students increased their use of surface strategies, the opposite of the intended result. Subsequent interviews indicated that the students believed that effective first-year study comprised accurate retention of a great deal of content, so they took from the study skills course what they believed they needed. This study could not illustrate more clearly how important the student's perspective is in determining the learning process, and how that perspective is in turn dependent on the messages received from the teacher. If students are to be expected to drop a surface approach to learning then one should see what it is in the ecology of the teaching context that is maintaining it; in an interactive system, things do not happen in isolation.

Encouraging Deep Approaches

While some of the study skill intervention studies have provided some evidence for an increase in deep learning (Biggs, 1988), deep approaches are more likely to be ecologically sound, and therefore more enduring, when they arise as adaptations to the context of teaching and assessing a particular subject. Deep approaches may be engendered:

- affectively, by creating conditions that are likely to foster intrinsic motivation.
- cognitively, by teaching specifically the procedural knowledge for a deep approach to particular academic tasks, and by setting and evaluating tasks in an integrative context that tells students that higher-level outcomes are expected.

Intrinsic motivation is the direct spring to deep learning by providing a felt need-to-know. Such curiosity—if that is not too weak a word for it—is very difficult to instill, although there are conditions under which it is extremely unlikely to occur, and others under which it is rather more likely. Intrinsic motivation is unlikely to occur under conditions of high external stress (Biggs & Telfer, 1987), whether interpersonal (threats, harassment, surveillance) or situational (work overload, time stress, excess difficulty). It is more likely to occur in a "warm" classroom climate, where student and teacher feel good working together, where teacher enthusiasm for the task may be contagious, and where student "ownership" of the task may be encouraged through individual or joint planning in the selection and delivery of the task.

As regards procedural knowledge of deep approaches to key tasks, teachers need to know themselves what good readers do when they extract meaning from text (Kirby, 1988), or what good writers do when they create text (Biggs, 1987b), or what good problem solvers do when solving math problems (Sweller et al., 1983). They then need to devise teaching devices and prompts that will elicit these procedures for deep processing; it is not enough to assume, as it often is assumed, that these processes occur "naturally," with practice.

Teachers need also to provide opportunities that allow misconceptions to be made explicit. This means that teachers need to be expert in a range of teaching skills, particularly involving teacher-student interaction, so that students' conceptions of key course material can be made explicit and challenged. It is very difficult to obtain the appropriate conditions when the teaching flow is one-way, as in expository teaching, or even in interactive teaching when the "interaction" is responding "yes" or "no" to closed questions (Tobin & Fraser, 1988).

Roth and Anderson (1988) cite extracts from two teachers' lessons in elementary school science. Ms. Lane appeared to be an excellent teacher on the surface; she carefully planned her lessons around the text so that all the relevant material would be covered, and she used praise to reinforce students' answers to the topic question on light (''Why can't we see around walls?''). She sought to find something to praise in every child's response, however, so that responses revealing misconceptions of the travel of light were praised along with correct responses, both reinforcing the misunderstanding in the responder and possibly causing that misconception to spread. Ms. Ramsey, on the other hand, did not accept incorrect responses and invited others in the class to build progressively on unsatisfactory responses, leading the whole class to a correct understanding of the topic in question:

Ms. Ramsey's teaching focused on getting key concepts across rather than on covering all the pages in the text. Unlike Ms. Lane, Ms. Ramsey focused on the key issues that seemed to represent critical barriers to student learning. Her content coverage could be described as narrow and deep compared to Ms. Lane's. This focus conveyed to students that science was about understanding and making sense of a few ideas, rather than a process of collecting and memorizing facts and words. (Roth & Anderson, 1988, pp. 127–128)

Tobin and Fraser (1988) selected a group of ''exemplary'' science and mathematics teachers—their criterion of exemplary being consensus among colleagues, tertiary lecturers, and senior administrative personnel—and studied their personal characteristics, classroom practice, and student work. There were several consistent differences between the exemplary and comparison teachers. Exemplary teachers knew their subject matter exceptionally well; they had high expectations of their students' level of performance, and were sensitive to misunderstandings they might have; they consistently used a wide repertoire of teaching strategies; and they were open to trying different ways of involving their students. They could recognize misconceptions for what they were, and could rephrase questions that would lead the students to a better understanding. They made the connections between questions and items of knowledge explicit, and they intervened to test students' understandings. They all held the constructivist conception of teaching; they insisted that it is the children who must make the connections in the end.

Exemplary teaching follows the 3P model. At the presage stage, it is important to formulate clearly what a reasonable objective might be. It is then a matter, at the process stage, of activating deep learning on the part of the students, which again involves an understanding of teaching technique and how that integrates with student learning processes. Finally, the student product needs to be evaluated qualitatively. Such evaluation should not be confused with the summative aspect only; much more important for student learning is the formative aspect of evaluation. Teaching logically demands that students' current progress be known, and that the gap between that and the desired objective be closed.

As with the attempt to discourage surface learning, encouraging deep learning depends on the messages students receive; and again, assessment becomes a major source of these messages. To date, there seems little doubt that traditional tests have sent the wrong message. "While it may appear obvious that assessment methods should be so designed that they encourage (and test) deep approaches, the reality revealed in the studies of student learning is very different" (Ramsden, 1985, p. 59).

In summary, then, students and teachers will, according to the systems hypothesis, achieve a working equilibrium in the classroom, so that further improvement of learning is not best achieved by concentrating on aspects pertaining either to student or to teacher. Even if the students are deficient in one basic ingredient—knowledge of effective learning/thinking skills, say—a crash course in study skills is not likely to be effective unless teaching is readjusted to suit temporarily induced changes. Rather the point of leverage is on the students' learning processes—to adjust the teaching context so that desirable— that is, deep—learning is the ecologically valid resultant. At the moment, there are too many factors that maintain surface learning in the ecology of the classroom.

THE SCHOOL AS A SYSTEM

Exemplary teachers use the systemic properties of the classroom in order to achieve their effects. Tobin and Fraser's (1988) exemplary teachers taught considerably more effectively than their colleagues, and operated in the classroom in qualitatively different ways. Yet on the basis of the systems model there appears to be something of a paradox here:

These exemplary teachers operated in the same schools as the contrast teachers and their implemented curricula were exposed to the same powerful driving forces as those teachers. . . . Yet the exemplary teachers were able to create a positive learning environment and the comparison teachers generally could not. (Tobin & Fraser, 1988, p. 91)

The point is that there are at least two systems working here: that of the classroom, and that of the context of the whole school in which teaching takes place. This second system is just as surely interactive as the classroom context in which student learning takes place.

The implications for implementation at the level of the classroom are simply that improvements to the teaching context need to be evolved within the system of the classroom, where student-based factors are seen as just as important as implementing this or that teaching method. One can work only so far, however, when the individual teacher is at the point of inflection. The school is the context in which the teacher works, and so we come to the second system, which has its own values, checks, and balances. This version of the 3P model is given in figure 4.2.

Teacher-based factors refer to those determinants of teaching that reside in

Figure 4.2
The School as a System

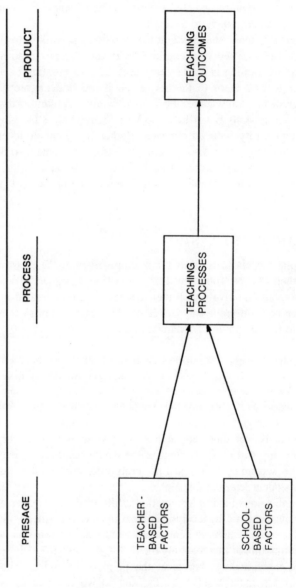

the individual teacher: repertoire of teaching skills, experience, conception of teaching, content knowledge, and the like. *School-based* factors refer to the espoused aims and policies of the school, and to what Reid (1987) calls "the social system" of the school. The "official" aims of the system do not determine what goes on in classrooms so much as traditional role expectations and other aspects of the social system. Such aspects include resource allocation, rules and routines, administrative structures, industrial stipulations, and the expectations and norms of fellow teachers and students, and which teachers are expected to conform to. The teacher has thus to work out a set of teaching processes and procedures within the given institutional constraints; "metateaching" is thus exactly analogous to the teacher as metalearning is to the student. The teaching outcomes include curriculum, teaching method, classroom climate, and rules and procedures, as well as the values that underwrite them. These teaching outcomes in fact define the classroom-based presage factors that set the context for student learning.

Reid (1987) suggests that the social system of an institution frequently affects learning adversely. Some of the values taught are likely to be deleterious, such as emphasis upon an impeccable product, isolation from tools and other resources (including one's peers), the attribution of success to having been taught rather than to having learned. Likewise, many assessment practices are interpreted by students in ways that are unexpected or even irrational from the teacher's perspective (Stipek, 1986).

Several studies confirm Reid's pessimism. A national study of Australian high schools showed that from years 8 through 11, boys' (but not girls') use of deep and achieving approaches declined (Biggs, 1987a). Both male and female undergraduates not intending postgraduate study drop deep and achieving approaches (Biggs, 1982; Newble & Clarke, 1986; Watkins & Hattie, 1985). Institutions often appear to discourage the very things that they officially are committed to foster.

Yet, as there are exemplary teachers within otherwise unexceptional schools, so there are exemplary schools within the broader educational system. Innovations can target the school, rather than lay the responsibility on individual teachers. Thus, White and Baird (in press) emphasize that researchers—or administrators—should not impose teaching methods by prescription from top-down. White and Baird devised a metacognitively based program, originally for science teaching, which had every promise of success; attempts *by individual teachers* to introduce the ideas into their classrooms were, however, only partially successful. These teachers were beaten by the system that prevailed in their particular school. Nonetheless, the Project for the Enhancement of Effective Learning (PEEL) was hugely successful when the social system of an entire school was built around PEEL, from collective teacher initiatives. By the same token, however, the time and effort involved in producing this result were correspondingly greater.

Schools, of course, are part of a larger system still, the community itself. A similar model to those outlined in figures 4.1 and 4.2 could therefore be constructed. School-based, and community-based, factors would comprise the presage variables, deep and surface analogues at the community level the process variables, and the quality of the school system and its quantitative results the product. At this level, we are not dealing with the psychology of learners, but with the sociology of institutions, however.

A STRATEGY FOR ENHANCING LEARNING

Student, teacher, classroom, school, and community are nested in a hierarchy of systems. One level can modify the other from the bottom-up or from the top-down. In the way of things, top-down influence tends to be more powerful than bottom-up, but that depends very much on the system in question. In centralized systems, the action in the classroom is determined by authorities outside the school and well beyond the classroom; in systems involving school-based curriculum development and assessment, the school, and again in the nature of things, the individual classroom teacher, are much more free to determine what goes on in the classroom.

Change can be directed at any of these levels:

- the student (e.g., poor study skills)
- the teachers (e.g., poor content knowledge; poor teaching skills)
- the classroom, where student and teacher factors are in equilibrium (figure 4.1)
- the school, where teaching and schoolwide factors are in equilibrium (figure 4.2)

Each of these targets is both a system within itself, and a component in a larger system; each level is both a result and a further cause. Thus, the system as far as the individual student is concerned comprises the students' motives and intentions; training students to use learning strategies that are not congruent with those motives and intentions is predicted to be ineffective (Biggs, 1987a). On the other hand, if the teaching context does not then require those same strategies in which students have been trained to be used, they will atrophy, not because they are inappropriate as far as the student is concerned, but because of an inappropriate interface with the teaching context. Encouraging a deep approach when the student perceives that teaching demands a surface approach will be futile until that perception—and probably the teaching as well—can be changed (Ramsden et al., 1986).

It is thus inappropriate to say that there is only one target for intervention. There is sufficient "slip" for an intervention to work at one level, before it begins to interact with the next higher level. Thus, "exemplary" teachers work within the same *school* system, but can achieve a different and more effective *classroom* system than do other teachers. Nevertheless, if we want the whole school to teach in exemplary fashion, then the focus is not the individual teacher, but as White and Baird (in press) point out, the whole school. Clearly, the "higher" the system one targets, the more scope there is for effective change.

REFERENCES

Biggs, J. B. (1979). Individual differences in study processes and the quality of learning outcomes. *Higher Education*, 8, 381–394.

——. (1982). Student motivation and study strategies in university and CAE populations. *Higher Education Research and Development*, 1, 33–55.

——. (1985). The role of metalearning in study processes. *British Journal of Educational Psychology*, 55, 185–212.

——. (1987a). *Student approaches to learning and studying*. Australian Council for Educational Research, Hawthorn, Victoria.

——. (1987b). Process and outcome in essay writing. *Research and Development in Higher Education*, 9, 114–125.

——. (1988). The role of metacognition in enhancing learning. *Australian Journal of Education*, 32, 127–138.

Biggs, J. B., & Collis, K. F. (1982). *Evaluating the quality of learning: The SOLO taxonomy*. New York: Academic.

Biggs, J. B., & Telfer, R. (1987). *The process of learning*. Sydney: Prentice-Hall of Australia.

Driver, R. (1983). *The pupil as scientist*. Milton Keynes: Open University Press.

Dweck, C., & Elliott, E. (1983). Achievement motivation. In P. Mussen (ed.), *Handbook of child psychology*, vol. 4, *Socialization, personality and social development*. New York: Wiley.

Entwistle, N., & Ramsden, P. (1983). *Understanding student learning*. London: Croom Helm.

Kirby, J. R. (1988). Style, strategy, and skill in reading. In R. R. Schmeck (ed.), *Learning styles and learning strategies*. New York: Plenum.

McKeachie, W. J., Pintrich, P., & Lin, Y. G. (1985). Teaching learning strategies. *Educational Psychologist*, 20, 153–160.

Marton, F., & Saljo, R. (1976). On qualitative differences in learning—I: Outcome and process. *British Journal of Educational Psychology*, 46, 4–11.

Messick, S. (1984). The psychology of educational measurement. *Journal of Educational Measurement*, 21, 215–237.

Moore, P. J. (private communication). Students' approaches to map-reading. University of Newcastle.

Newble, D., & Clarke, R. M. (1986). The approaches to learning of students in a traditional and in an innovative problem-based medical school. *Medical Education*, 20, 267–273.

Ramsden, P. (1985). Student learning research: Retrospect and prospect. *Higher Education Research and Development*, 5(1), 51–70.

Ramsden, P., Beswick, D., & Bowden, J. (1986). Effects of learning skills interventions on first year university students' learning. *Human Learning*, 5, 151–164.

Ramsden, P., Whelan, G., & Cooper, D. (1989). Some phenomena of medical students' diagnostic problem solving. *Medical Education*, 23, 108–117.

Reid, W. A. (1987). Institutions and practices: Professional education reports and the language of reform. *Educational Researcher*, 16(8), 10–15.

Roth, K., & Anderson, C. (1988). Promoting conceptual change learning from science textbooks. In P. Ramsden (ed.), *Improving learning: New perspectives*. London: Kogan Page.

Sarason, S. B. (1971). *The culture of the school and the problem of change*. Boston: Allyn & Bacon.

Shuell, T. J. (1986). Cognitive conceptions of learning. *Review of Educational Research, 56*, 411–436.

Stipek, D. (1986). Children's motivation to learn. In T. Tomlinson & H. Walberg (eds.), *Academic work and educational excellence*. Berkeley, Calif.: Mc-Cutchan.

Sweller, J., Mawer, R., & Ward, M. (1983). Development of expertise in mathematical problem solving. *Journal of Experimental Psychology; General, 112*, 634–565.

Tobin, K., & Fraser, B. J. (1988). Investigations of exemplary practice in high school science and mathematics. *Australian Journal of Education, 32*, 75–94.

Tobin, K., & Gallagher, J. (1987). Target students in the science classroom. *Journal of Research in Science Teaching, 24*, 61–75.

Van Rossum, E. J., & Schenk, S. M. (1984). The relationship between learning conceptions, study strategy and learning outcome. *British Journal of Educational Psychology, 54*, 73–83.

Von Bertalanffy, L. (1986). *General systems theory*. New York: Braziller.

Watkins, D. A. (1983a). Assessing tertiary students' study processes. *Human Learning, 2*, 29–37.

———. (1983b). Depth of processing and the quality of learning outcomes. *Instructional Science, 12*, 49–58.

Watkins, D. A., & Hattie, J. (1985). A longitudinal study of the approach to learning of Australian tertiary students. *Human Learning, 4*(2), 127–142.

Weinstein, C., & Mayer, R. (1984). The teaching of learning strategies. In M. C. Wittrock (ed.), *Handbook of research on teaching*. New York: Macmillan.

White, R. T., & Baird, J. (in press). Learning to think and thinking to learn. In J. B. Biggs (ed.), *Learning processes and teaching contexts*. Hawthorn: Australian Council for Educational Research.

5

Teaching Thinking to Preschoolers

M. A. Price

The influence of the cognitive approach to education has been increasing over the past twenty-five years and there is a wave of interest in the teaching of thinking and problem solving (e.g., Chance, 1986; Costa, 1981, 1984; deBono, 1985; Jones, 1986; Sternberg, 1984). In addition to an emphasis on assisting all children to be more effective in problem-solving situations, there are examples of numerous applications of a cognitive approach to the teaching of children with learning difficulties (e.g., Alley & Deshler, 1979; Feuerstein, 1980; Reid & Hresko, 1981). Although less attention has been given to the cognitive education approach at preschool levels, there is a growing interest in the benefits of this approach for young children who are at risk for difficulty in school. In this chapter, the focus will be on an example of theory into practice in the area of cognitive education for young children with special needs.

In the Learning Centre Early Childhood Services program, the Cognitive Curriculum for Young Children (CCYC) (Haywood et al., in press) is used to teach four- and five-year-old children with special needs to think and learn more effectively. The CCYC is unique in its emphasis on a cognitive and metacognitive approach to teaching young children with special needs. The developers of the curriculum have paid careful attention to the process of translating theory into classroom practice. The CCYC is used in Belgium, France, Israel, and in over fifty sites across North America, one of which is the Learning Centre in Calgary, Alberta. In this chapter, the structure of the Learning Centre Early Childhood Services (ECS) program will be described. The theoretical bases of the CCYC will be presented and the practical applications of the theoretical concepts will be demonstrated in the descriptions of the components of the Learning Centre ECS. The success of cognitive education for young children will be addressed.

THE STRUCTURE OF THE LEARNING CENTRE ECS PROGRAM

The Learning Centre ECS is operated by the Calgary Society for Students with Learning Difficulties, which has operated the Learning Centre since September 1979. The center is concerned with improving services to persons with learning difficulties by means of an integrated program of research, demonstration, client services, and professional development. The major thrust of the work at the center is to contribute to the development of new approaches to assessment and treatment of learning difficulties, to critically evaluate the effectiveness of these approaches, and to disseminate this information to other professionals and the public (Samuels & Brown, 1989). In 1985, the Learning Centre, in conjunction with Alberta's Children's Hospital, implemented a cognitive education program for preschool children (Samuels et al., 1988). The project involved the comparison of the cognitive education approach with more "traditional" content-oriented programs. The experience of that project (described later in this chapter) led to the formation of a permanent cognitive education ECS program for children with special needs. The Learning Centre ECS began in the 1987–1988 school year as a cooperative project of the Learning Centre and Alberta Children's Hospital with the support of Alberta Education grants.

The Learning Centre ECS combines the mandate of the Learning Centre with the goals of CCYC to meet the primary goal of providing a high-quality educational readiness program to young children with special needs who are at risk for learning difficulties. Specific goals are as follows.

1. To incorporate the CCYC, which has the primary goal of "stretching the mind" of young children by broadening their understanding of their own thought processes in order to increase their educability. Specific goals of CCYC are:

   To enhance and accelerate the development of basic cognitive skills.

   To identify and remediate deficient cognitive functions.

   To develop task-intrinsic motivation.

   To develop representational thought.

   To enhance learning effectiveness and readiness for school learning.

   To prevent special education placement (Haywood et al., in press)

2. To meet the complex needs of young children with special needs and their families through the expertise of a transdisciplinary staff providing an integrated educational experience.

3. To involve parents in the design and implementation of programs for their children.

4. To act as a demonstration and professional development center for others in the community.

5. To evaluate the effectiveness of approaches to assessment and intervention.

Twenty to twenty-four children attend the ECS program each school year, with ten to twelve children in each of two half-day programs. The children attend five days per week for the ten-month school year.

The following criteria are used in determining which children and families will benefit most from enrollment in the program;

1. The child is at least four years of age and less than five years, six months of age on September 1 of the school year.

2. The child's developmental profile shows significant scatter in functioning level across and/or within the major domains of development.

3. The child requires a specialized educational placement (i.e., could not function independently in a regular ECS program) and intervention by at least one specialty area (i.e., speech-language pathology, occupational therapy, physiotherapy, psychology).

Generally, the children present with delays in the following areas of development: cognition (thinking/problem solving), speech and language, fine motor, gross motor, social and emotional development. Cognition, speech and language, and attention tend to be the major areas of difficulty. Referring agencies (primarily clinics of Alberta Children's Hospital) provide assessment and observational data to indicate each child's areas of strength and weakness.

A transdisciplinary program staff approaches the areas of development in an interrelated way, recognizing that each influences the other. The therapies are integrated with the cognitive education program through cooperative and complementary efforts of the staff (Price & Reid, 1988).

The full-time staff includes a coordinator, teacher, child care worker, speech and language pathologist, and teaching assistant. The part-time staff includes an occupational therapist, psychologist, social worker, and physiotherapist.

Five components of the CCYC have been adapted to form the basis for the Learning Centre ECS: mediational teaching style, curriculum units, daily activities, cognitive mediational approach to behavior management, and parent participation. A strength of the Learning Centre ECS derives from a sixth component—the integration of therapy services with the education program.

THEORETICAL COMPONENTS
OF THE COGNITIVE CURRICULUM

The developers of the CCYC have been conscientious in attending to the relationship between theory and practice in cognitive education. Theory has stimulated the development of the curriculum. The assumption that children acquire processes of thought set the process of curriculum development in motion. Theories have guided decisions regarding the selection of "content" and the style of teaching. The developers looked to theory to answer important questions: Which processes of logical thought are important at ages three through six? What influence does the social environment have in facilitating the growth of problem solving? Can we identify key qualities of the interaction between the social environment and the child that facilitate the development of problem solving? Assuming that methods in cognitive education should be derived from theories of cognitive development and cognitive modifiability, the CCYC is well grounded in four major domains of theoretical thought.

First, the impetus for developing a "cognitive" curriculum came largely from the theoretical assumption that we can influence the development of intelligent behavior. Haywood and Brooks (1990) describe a transactional view of intelligence in which intelligence is viewed as multifaceted, recognizing a variety of qualities of intelligence, and multidetermined, recognizing the influence of both genetics and environment. "Thinking (cognition) is a product of native ability and learned processes and strategies of thinking, perceiving, learning and problem-solving" (Haywood et al., 1986, p. 130). CCYC is directed toward the development of learned cognitive processes.

Second, decisions regarding the content of the curriculum were influenced strongly by Piaget's observations of processes of logical thought that usually develop between three and six years of age, such as classification, class inclusion, relations (seriation, transitivity, space, time, causality), conservation, and number (Haywood & Brooks, 1990). During development, interactions between children and the environment may be characterized by two processes: assimilation and accommodation. In assimilation, children apply existing cognitive structures to new information, fitting the new information into the existing structures. In accommodation, children themselves are changed so that they become more and more competent in understanding and applying new information. CCYC aims to stimulate the process of accommodation to encourage change in the thought processes of children.

Third, the developers of the CCYC recognized the important role of adults and the social environment in the development of logical thought and drew upon the views of Vygotsky (Haywood & Brooks, 1990). The acquisition of cognitive structures through learning is a social process. Adults assist children in learning to solve problems by modeling problem solving, guiding, correcting, and rewarding as children attempt to understand and control their world. Adults become progressively less directive as children gain independence and regulate their own thought processes. Vygotsky describes the "zone of proximal development": "Distance between the actual developmental level as determined by individual problem solving and the level of potential development as determined through problem solving under adult guidance or in collaboration with more capable peers" (Vygotsky, 1978, p. 86). The CCYC is directed toward reducing the distance between a child's typical performance and potential performance (Haywood et al., in press).

Recognizing that children benefit from a social environment that includes instruction in problem solving, the developers of CCYC drew on the theories of Feuerstein to identify the important qualities of the interaction between the social environment and the child (Haywood & Brooks, 1990; Haywood et al., 1986; Haywood et al., in press). Feuerstein's theory of structural cognitive modifiability emphasizes the necessity of acquiring cognitive functions through learning and identifies qualities of social interactions that promote the development of cognitive processes (Feuerstein et al., 1979; Feuerstein et al., 1980). Central to Feuerstein's theory is the mediated learning experience (MLE), whereby children come to understand the generalized meaning of their experiences with the assistance of older and more competent individuals, such as parents, grandparents, or older sibillngs. MLE is assumed to be essential to adequate cognitive development and forms the basis of the mediational teaching style of the cognitive classroom. Children with special handicapping conditions acquire fewer cognitive functions through direct exposure learning and require more frequent, intense, and repetitious MLE to learn essential cognitive processes. Feuerstein and his colleagues have provided detailed descriptions of criteria that define MLE (Feuerstein et al., 1979; Jensen & Feuerstein, 1987). Haywood (1987) stresses the following criteria as most important in guiding the interactions between teacher and children in a cognitive classroom. Consciousness of these criteria and efforts to provide quality MLE in the classroom are the basis of the mediational teaching style used in CCYC classrooms.

Intention. The adult intends to use the elements of the interaction to produce cognitive change.

Transcendence. The intended change goes beyond the content of the immediate experience, that is, it is a generalizable process useful to the child in novel situations.

Communication of meaning and purpose. There are no secrets. The mediator communicates to children the long-range, structural, or developmental meaning and purpose of a shared activity.

Mediation of a feeling of competence. The mediator acknowledges good performance and specifies the correct (or incorrect) aspects of that performance so children can be sure exactly what is being acknowledged and what should be repeated.

Regulation of behavior. The mediator helps the child to control impulsive responding or encourages the unwilling child to respond.

Shared participation. The mediator and child participate together and share in the learning experience.

ECS PROGRAM COMPONENTS

The five components of the CCYC provide the structure of the ECS program. A sixth component relates to therapies (e.g., speech and language, occupational therapy, physiotherapy) that have been changed from "supplemental services" to services that are woven together with the components of the CCYC (Price & Reid, 1988).

Mediational Teaching Style

This style of teaching is used by teachers and therapy staff and is derived from Feuerstein's theory of structural cognitive modifiability and MLE. The role of staff is to interact with the children as "mediators" to help the children interpret the generalized meaning of experiences. There is emphasis on extracting generalizable principles and strategies that go beyond the immediate content and which the children can apply in other situations. Through in-service training, all ECS staff are aware of the criteria of MLE and attend to developing the cognitive functions that promote effective ways of perceiving the world, of thinking systematically, of learning, and of solving problems.

Observers to the Learning Centre ECS note several features of the adult-child interaction that are characteristic of cognitive education classrooms using CCYC. First, the style of questioning focuses on the process of thought rather than on the outcome. For example, "What is it?" may be replaced or followed by "How do you know it is a ———?" "How many cookies do you need?" may by replaced by "How will you find out how many cookies you need?" The focus on the processes of thinking heightens metacognitive awareness.

Children are encouraged to reflect on how they came to a conclusion. Cognitive education teachers challenge correct responses as another way to help children focus on the thinking that led to a response. For example, "Yes, that is a square, but how do you know it is a square? How is it different from a triangle?" or, "Yes, the cow belongs in this group, but how do you know it belongs with the horse and pig? Why doesn't it belong with the zebra and camel?" As the year progresses, children are observed to spontaneously justify their responses with "because" and an explanation. They appear to understand that evidence is important, that there are reasons for choices.

The children receive further assistance in providing logical evidence and generalizing strategies because there is an emphasis on rules in a cognitive education class. Children are encouraged to talk about how rules help them. They make rules in a variety of contexts, such as behavior, planning tasks, and social problem solving. The children are exposed to a variety of adults in various contexts in the ECS program and the applicability of rules across these different situations is emphasized. ECS staff attempt to be aware of the classroom rules for behavior, for planning a task, and for social problem solving. Consistency is stressed so that children are encouraged to follow the same rules in all contexts.

In a cognitive education classroom there is an emphasis on generalization of processes. The mechanism of "bridging" involves the process whereby children are encouraged to think of different applications beyond their concrete experience in the classroom (Haywood, 1987; Haywood et al., in press). In the ECS classroom, children engage in a dialogue in which the teacher elicits applications of the principles to areas of their experience. They are also given important concrete opportunities to generalize cognitive functions to different content areas, to different activities (e.g., speech/language therapy, occupational therapy, gym, music, etc.), and to experiences with different people. All staff consciously attempt to bridge the cognitive functions to their area of involvement with the children. For example, the occupational therapist may encourage bridging of planning and organizational strategies at the beginning of a copying task by asking, "Do you remember when you did something like this before? What were the rules?"

Cognitive education teachers model thinking. They talk aloud, verbalizing the steps of problem solving, describing rules, and justifying responses. They also emphasize order, predictability, system, sequence, and strategies (Haywood, 1987). All staff in the ECS draw attention to the organization of events and materials. Similarities and differences across people and contexts are discussed with the children. Children are encouraged to apply the same strategies in different situations. For example, having a starting point and going in order are useful for counting activities in the classroom, for games in the gym, for cooking, for drawing a square, for assembling a book, for sequencing events, and so on.

Curriculum Units

Cognitive functions are taught explicitly to small groups of children by the ECS teacher. The functions are organized in seven units that target specific cognitive processes important for academic learning in the primary and elementary grades, and based on the theoretical thrusts described above. In the CCYC manual (Haywood et al., in press) teachers are given a series of suggested lessons. Each lesson includes a specification of particular cognitive functions to be emphasized, a rationale for the selected activities, a description of a main activity and variations, bridging and generalization, and minimal mastery criteria for judging a child's mastery of the cognitive functions. The units are: self-regulation, quantitative relations, comparison, role taking, classification, seriation, and distinctive features. The systematic teaching of cognitive functions provides the children with the language of thinking. They acquire labels for important thinking processes (e.g., systematic search, comparing, classifying) and are better able to manipulate their ideas and approach to solving problems.

Daily Activities

In the Learning Centre ECS, planning, small group (curriculum units), and summary time are the building blocks of the CCYC and emphasize the cognitive function(s) stressed on a particular day. They are integrated with a variety of activities that address the major areas of development and incorporate cognitive functions, a thematic approach, and mediational teaching style. Daily activities include: planning time, small group, rotating activities (gym, share and sing, library, cooking), table time (fine motor activities), snack, play centers, and summary.

Behavior Management

A cognitive mediational approach to behavior management stresses the processes of thought and systematic problem solving (Haywood & Weatherford, in press). Children are encouraged to share the responsibility for managing troublesome behaviors. They learn to define problem behaviors, to generate alternatives, to choose and evaluate action plans. Initially, the problem-solving approach to behavior management requires considerable adult input, modeling, coaching, and guidance. The children become increasingly more independent, however, in regulating their own behavior and in solving problems in social interactions. Social skills are enhanced.

The cognitive mediational approach to behavior management also has positive effects on the children's motivation in learning situations. Intrinsic motivation is recognized as a key factor in effective learning (Haywood et al., in press). Intrinsic motivation (curiosity, exploration, joy in learning) is encouraged in the absence of an external adult-controlled reward system (e.g., stickers for completing a task). In a cognitive education classroom, the emphasis is upon engaging children in the process of learning and problem solving and assisting them to control behaviors that interfere with their learning or the learning of others.

Parent Participation

The theoretical bases of the CCYC approach to cognitive education give parents an important role in the cognitive development of their children. Parents can learn to be better "mediators." They can learn to interact with their children in ways that assist their children to be more effective thinkers. Thus, a major thrust of the parent participation component of the Learning Centre ECS involves teaching parents to be better "mediators" and advocates for their children. Parents are exposed to the notions of mediated learning experience and the mediational style of interacting with children and are encouraged to use the approach at home. Parents participate in the classroom on a monthly basis, attend formal discussions, and meet with the ECS staff to discuss their child's program and home carryover ideas.

Therapy Services

In the Learning Centre ECS, therapy services (speech and language, occupational therapy, physiotherapy) are integrated with the cognitive education program (Price & Reid, 1988). The therapists use a mediational teaching style and cognitive mediational behavior management, are aware of the cognitive functions and attempt to provide opportunities for generalization of the functions, and plan activities related to the classroom themes. The shared theoretical base and consistent approach across ECS staff is a particular strength of the program.

EVALUATION

There is general agreement that preschool intervention programs benefit children with handicapping conditions. There is little consensus, however, about which models of early intervention are most effective, or which program features contribute to long-lasting positive outcomes. The cognitive education approach to early intervention has sound theoretical bases and the potential for long-term benefits. Although evaluative research is limited and there are many unanswered questions, there is evidence that preschool cognitive education has both short- and long-term benefits.

Cognitive education based on the CCYC has been shown to have positive effects on the cognitive development of preschoolers. The effects on cognitive development have been measured indirectly using a standardized measure of cognitive functioning (McCarthy Scales of Children's Abilities) (Haywood et al., 1986). High-risk preschoolers (ages three-and-a-half to five years) in cognitive education classrooms made significantly greater gains in performance on a standardized measure of cognitive functioning (McCarthy Scales of Children's Abilities) compared with high-risk preschoolers in traditional programs. Children in the cognitive education classrooms gained an average of nine points compared with an average of one point gained by the comparison group. Change scores on the McCarthy for twenty-seven handicapped children in the CCYC classrooms also reflected the positive benefits of the program. The average increase on the General Cognitive Index was twelve points for the handicapped preschoolers.

The positive effects of cognitive education on specific cognitive and language measures were demonstrated in a study by Dale and Cole (1988). The effectiveness of two contrasting early education programs for mildly handicapped children (ages three through five, six through eight) was examined. The Mediated Learning program was based on the Cognitive Curriculum for Young Children (Burns et al., 1983) and emphasized the development and generalization of cognitive processes. The Direct Instruction program (Becker, 1977; Becker et al., 1975) emphasized the systematic and explicit teaching of academic skills. Children in both programs made gains. Children in the Mediated Learning program made greater gains on the verbal and memory scales of the McCarthy Scales of Children's Abilities and mean length of utterance. Children in the Direct Instruction program made greater gains on the test of early language development and the basic language concepts test.

Immediate positive outcomes are of interest. Benefits over the longer term are even more important, however, and were considered in an evaluation in Calgary. The Learning Centre ECS was set up as a cooperative project of Alberta Children's Hospital and the Learning Centre following a two-year research/treatment project that compared the effects of intensive therapeutic and educational interventions (Samuels et al., 1988). In the research project, children's responses to two classroom programs were compared. One program followed a skills- or activity-based approach in which acquisition of basic motor, social, language, and preacademic skills was emphasized. The other program was based on a cognitive education model and incorporated the CCYC with an emphasis upon the explicit teaching of rules for perceiving, analyzing, understanding, and solving problems. Children had access to therapy support services in each program, including speech and language therapy, occupational therapy, and physiotherapy. Children in both educational programs made gains on standardized tests of cognition, receptive language, expressive language, and fine motor development. Children in both programs also made gains on a dynamic assessment measure, CATM (Tzuriel, 1989). There was an impressive differential outcome for the programs when actual school placement was examined one year following the intervention program, however. Significantly more children from the cognitive education program were later placed in regular education programs as compared to the children from the skills-based program. Samuels et al. (1988) suggest that the higher success rate for the cognitive education program may be due to long-term cumulative effects of the processes learned. Another factor that may affect long-term benefits of cognitive education involves the effects of the program on parents. Parents of children in the cognitive education program reported being more involved and learning more than parents of children in the skills-based program and reported more types of gains made by their children (Marshman, 1986).

Evaluative data are being gathered each year to assess the effects of cognitive education for children with special needs who attend the Learning Centre ECS. The data include educational outcomes of the "graduates," parental observations and ratings, and pre-/post- comparisons on standardized tests of cognition, language, fine motor development, and gross motor development. Long-term effects are of interest and the school placement of the children will be tracked over several years. To date, two cohorts have been tracked for at least one year following the cognitive education program. Does preschool cognitive education prevent special education? One year following the program, 43 percent of the thirty-seven children were entering regular education programs and 54 percent were entering special education classes. The significance of this outcome, however, is limited by the lack of a control group for comparison purposes. The special class placements reflected the diversity of special needs of the children: classes for students with learning disabilities, classes for slow learners, classes for children with behavior problems, and mental health classes. These children continued to demonstrate significant learning needs and the special class placements appear to be appropriate to meet their needs. As a larger database develops, the profiles of the children who enter regular and special education will be compared in detail to determine characteristics that may predict their response to cognitive education and educational outcomes.

Although approximately half of the children continued to need special education placements, observations by parents supported the view that the children made observable gains in the cognitive education program. Phone interviews of parents were conducted by a core advisory group of parents at the end of each school year to obtain feedback about the program, and particularly about the changes observed in the children. All thirty-three parents interviewed reported that their children had benefited from the program and made gains. While 15 percent reported that their children had made gains in all areas, the descriptive comments of the parents indicated that there were consistent changes in speech and communication skills (63%), fine motor development (24%), social interaction and play (24%), and self-esteem and independence (39%). Parents also described planning, organization, and problem solving as areas of improvement (18%). Parents' comments were supported by pre-/post- comparisons of the Minnesota Child Development Inventory completed by the parents at the beginning and end of the school year. Data for twenty-five children indicated significant pre-/post- gains on all but the personal-social scale.

Given the small number of children served each year, the diversity of their special needs, and some inconsistency in the available pretest data, a database is being developed to facilitate pre-/post- comparisons. Preliminary analyses of pre-/post- changes on standardized measures of language and fine motor development available for twenty-five to thirty children indicate that they benefited from the program. Changes were significant on several measures: Peabody Developmental Scales, Peabody Picture Vocabulary Test-Revised, Test of Comprehension of Language-Revised, and the Preschool Language Assessment Instrument.

Preschool cognitive education appears to have positive short- and long-term effects. Yet, the data to date is limited. Suggestions for future directions for the evaluation of preschool cognitive education programs include:

• the use of dynamic assessment of cognitive potential to more closely evaluate the goal of assisting children to be more effective learners (Tzuriel, 1989)

• longitudinal studies to monitor long-term effects that include a variety of criteria of success, such as educational placement, observation of the child's problem solving, and dynamic assessment of learning potential

• evaluation of the effects of the parent component of cognitive education programs on parent-child interactions

• comparison of the profiles of children who make substantial gains in preschool cognitive education with children who make minimal gains

• greater use of observational criteria to determine how effectively children are acquiring the cognitive functions being taught in a cognitive education classroom

REFERENCES

Alley, G., & Deshler, D. (1979). *Teaching the learning disabled adolescent: Strategies and methods*. Denver: Love.

Becker, W. C. (1977). Teaching reading and language to the disadvantaged—What we have learned from field research. *Harvard Educational Review*, 47, 518–543.

Becker, W. C., Engelmann, S., & Thomas, D. R. (1975). *Teaching 2: Cognitive learning and instruction*. Chicago: Science Research Associates.

Burns, S., Haywood, C., Cox, J., Brooks, P., Green, L., Ransom, O., Goodroe, P., & Willis, E. (1983). *Let's think about it: A cognitive curriculum for young children*. Paper presented at the Handicapped Children's Early Childhood Conference, Washington, D.C.

Chance, P. (1986). *Thinking in the classroom*. New York: Teachers College Press.

Costa, A. (1981). Teaching for intelligent behaviour. *Educational Leadership*, 39, 29–32.

————. (1984) Thinking: How do we know students are getting better at it? *Roeper Review*, 6, 197–199.

Dale, P., & Cole, K. (1988). Comparison of academic and cognitive programs for young handicapped children. *Exceptional Children*, 54, 439–447.

deBono, E. (1985). The CoRT Thinking Program. In J. W. Segal, S. F. Chapman, & R. Glaser (eds.), *Thinking and learning skills*, vol. 1, *Relating instruction to research*. Hillsdale, N.J.: Erlbaum.

Feuerstein, R. (1980). *Instrumental enrichment: An intervention program for cognitive modifiability*. Baltimore: University Park Press.

Feuerstein, R., Rand, Y., & Hoffman, M. (1979). *The dynamic assessment of retarded performers: The Learning Potential Assessment Device; theory, instruments and techniques*. Baltimore: University Park Press.

Feuerstein, R., Rand, Y., Hoffman, M. B., & Miller, M. J. (1980). *Instrumental enrichment*. Baltimore: University Park Press.

Haywood, H. C. (1987). A mediational teaching style. *Thinking Teacher*, 4 (1), 1–6.

Haywood, H. C., & Brooks, P. (1990). Theory and curriculum development in cognitive education. In M. Schwevel, C. A. Maher, & N. S. Fagley (eds.), *Promoting cognitive growth over the life span*. Hillsdale, N.J.: Erlbaum.

Haywood, H. C., & Weatherford, D. L. (in press). Cognitive-mediational behavior management. In H. C. Haywood, P. H. Brooks, & S. Burns (eds.), *Cognitive curriculum for young children*. Watertown, Mass.: Charlesbridge.

Haywood, H. C., Brooks, P. H., & Burns, S. (1986). *Stimulating cognitive development at developmental level: A tested, nonremedial preschool curriculum for preschoolers and older children*. Hillsdale, N.J.: Erlbaum.

Haywood, H. C., Brooks, P. H., & Burns, S. (eds.). (in press). *Cognitive curriculum for young children*. Watertown, Mass.: Charlesbridge.

Jensen, M. R., & Feuerstein, R. (1987). The Learning Potential Assessment Device: From philosophy to practice. In C. Lidz (ed.), *Dynamic assessment*. New York: Guilford.

Jones, B. F. (1986). Quality and equality through cognitive instruction. *Educational Leadership*, 44, 4–11.

Marshman, M. E. (1986). Parental perception of generalization in preschool children with special needs. Master's thesis, University of Calgary.

Price, M. A., & Reid, G. (1988). Integration of therapy services with a cognitive education program. *Thinking Teacher*, 4 (3), 1–3.

Reid, D. K., & Hresko, W. P. (1981). *A cognitive approach to learning disabilities*. New York: McGraw-Hill.

Samuels, M. T., & Brown, R. I. (1989). *Research and practice in learning difficulties: A demonstration model*. Toronto: Lugus.

Samuels, M. T., Fagan, J., MacKenzie, H., & Killip, S. M. (1988). *Cognitive education for preschool children with severe learning difficulties*. Final Report. The Learning Centre, Calgary, Alberta.

Sternberg, R. J. (1984). How can we teach intelligence? *Educational Leadership*, 42 (1), 38–48.

Tzuriel, D. (1989). Dynamic assessment of learning potential in cognitive education programs. *Thinking Teacher*, 5, 1–3.

Vygotsky, L. S. (1978). *Mind in society: The development of higher psychological processes*. Cambridge, Mass.: Harvard University Press.

6

Teaching Cognitive Strategies in the Classroom: A Content-Based Instructional Model

Kofi Marfo, Robert F. Mulcahy, David Peat,
Jac Andrews, and Seokee Cho

Over the past two decades, developments occurring contemporaneously in the fields of education and psychology have culminated in substantial intensification of the cognitive education movement. In the field of education, growing discontent—both within and outside the education community—about the progressive decline in educational outcomes has resulted in a constant search not only for improved instruction techniques but also for alternative approaches to selecting and defining the content of instruction.

The forces shaping the discontent with educational outcomes all over the world often have their origins in broader concerns of a socio-politico-economic nature. For example, the politics of technological advancements in space travel, touched off by the launching of Sputnik by the Soviets, was a critical factor in the emergence of the cognitive movement in education in North America during the early 1960s. American educators began to turn away from behaviorism and toward cognitivism in their search for alternative methods and contents of instruction to produce generations of thinkers and problem solvers capable of launching America competitively into the space age. Similarly, concerns about widespread socioeconomic imbalances and about the need to ensure equality of educational opportunity in American society also gave birth in the 1960s to massive national educational initiatives, like Project Head Start, designed (largely but not solely) to boost intellectual functioning in disadvantaged preschoolers. In more contemporary times, the educational "soul searching" that has been going on in North America has been fueled by the perception that rapidly developing economies like Japan pose a serious threat to North America's traditional economic supremacy. In report after report, cognitively oriented innovations in education have been recommended as the remedy for the problems outlined above.

Of course, today's view of cognitive education as a potential panacea for addressing the social, economic, and political problems of nationhood is not inconsistent with traditional philosophical foundations of education. Throughout time, educational philosophers have perceived the creation of an informed and intellectually able citizenry as a sine qua non to the building of a democratic, economically viable, and morally strong society. Consequently, the ability to think has become synonymous with becoming educated, and preparing students to be able to think has remained one of the central goals of education in all societies. The achievement of this goal, however, has remained relatively elusive, and the cognitive movement in education represents an intensified, systematic effort to bring this age-old goal more closely within reach.

TRADITIONS IN COGNITIVE EDUCATION

There are two distinct traditions within the cognitive education movement. The first tradition, which we will label as the *thinking skills approach* to cognitive education, has its roots in both cognitive psychology and philosophy (largely in the philosophy of science and education) and emphasizes the teaching of traditional critical, analytical, and productive thinking skills. Specific examples of such skills include organizing and using information, discovering and formulating problems, generating ideas, evaluating and improving ideas (Covington, et al. 1974); drawing inferences, making distinctions, uncovering assumptions, evaluating reasons, seeing analogies (Lipman, 1985); and comparing, classifying, and observing (Wasserman, 1986). In the past decade or so there has been an upsurge of theoretical and basic empirical research on critical thinking, for example (see Norris, 1985, for a review of some of this research), leading to the development and validation of instruments for assessing a variety of critical thinking skills (e.g., Ennis & Millman, 1985; Norris, 1985; Norris & King, 1984; Norris & Ennis, 1989; Watson & Glaser, 1980).

Parallel to the increased theoretical and basic empirical research activity, there has been a proliferation of largely "packaged" instructional programs for teaching thinking skills as part of the school curriculum (see Chance, 1986, for a summary of some of the more popular programs). Among the more established programs are Productive Thinking (Covington et al, 1974), Philosophy for Children (Lipman et al., 1980), Problem Solving and Comprehension (Whimbey & Lockhead, 1982), and CoRT (deBono, 1985). By and large, most of these programs are designed to be taught independently of the subject matter areas in the curriculum, and seem to operate under the assumption that thinking ought to be taught as a subject in its own right.

The second tradition within the cognitive education movement has its roots mainly in cognitive psychology, particularly in cognitive information-processing theories. This tradition typically emphasizes the teaching of a broad range of cognitive and metacognitive strategies relevant to the acquisition, storage, retrieval, and application of knowledge. One of its distinguishing characteristics is that it concerns itself not only with the improvement of basic cognitive functioning per se, but also with the application of cognitive functions and strategies to the improvement of academic learning and performance. Consequently, in much of the work in this tradition, the labels "learning and thinking strategies," "cognitive learning strategies," and "learning strategies" are frequently used. We will label this tradition as the *cognitive strategies approach* to cognitive education.

Among the better-known programs and/or approaches in the cognitive strategies approach are the following:

1. Informed Strategies for Learning (Paris, 1986; Paris et al., 1984; Paris et al., 1986a, 1986b)

2. Reciprocal Teaching (Palincsar, 1986; Palincsar & Brown, 1984)

3. Dansereau's Learning Strategies Course (Dansereau, 1978, 1985; Dansereau et al., 1979)

4. Weinstein's Cognitive Learning Strategies program (Weinstein, 1978, 1982; Weinstein & Underwood, 1985)

5. The Learning Strategies Curriculum (Deshler et al., 1980; Deshler et al., 1983; Schumaker & Clark, 1982)

Each of the above programs has had a rather restricted application. Even Paris' Informed Strategies for Learning program, which targets a broader population of students (regular elementary school students), focuses mainly on reading comprehension. Reciprocal Teaching focuses mainly on reading comprehension and has largely been used with junior high school students enrolled in Chapter 1 remedial reading classes (Palincsar, 1986). The Learning Strategies Curriculum of Deshler and associates has been used primarily with learning disabled adolescents. Dansereau's course targets college-level students, while Weinstein's program has been used with armed services technical trainees and with high school and college-level students. One remarkable feature of all five curricula is that they have either emerged out of, or been developed alongside, empirical research programs.

The work to be described in this chapter, like the five programs mentioned above, is located within the cognitive strategies approach. The Strategies Program for Effective Learning and Thinking (SPELT) (Mulcahy & Marfo, 1987; Mulcahy et al., 1986a, 1986b) was developed and tested as part of a major longitudinal evaluation of cognitive education. Unlike the other programs mentioned above, however, our work attempts to develop a more inclusive learning and thinking strategies curriculum that can be implemented across all subject areas within the primary, junior high, and high school curriculum. We will now shift the discussion to an examination of key developments and issues in both cognitive psychology and education that are responsible for the emergence of cognitive strategy instructional programs. Before we do that, however, we will make two passing observations about the relationship between the thinking skills and cognitive strategies approaches.

First, cognitive education programs may not always fit neatly into one of the two traditions we have identified. Feuerstein's Instrumental Enrichment program provides a good illustration of this point. Feuerstein's program is based on a psychological theory of cognitive modifiability, a theory that blends very neatly concepts from both Piagetian developmental theory and information-processing theory. On the basis of the program's underlying theory, its emphasis on repairing cognitive deficits or dysfunctions, and its formal use of bridging techniques to link thinking exercises with academic learning, Instrumental Enrichment belongs legitimately to the cognitive strategies tradition. Yet by virtue of its actual content and packaging and its out-of-content approach to teaching thinking, the program also shares a great deal with traditional thinking skills programs.

Second, at both the theoretical and empirical levels, there is a growing cross-fertilization between the two traditions. It is now not uncommon to see citations of the cognitive strategies literature by researchers working in the thinking skills tradition, and vice versa. For example, in his review of research on critical thinking, Norris (1985) draws on the psychological literature, linking work on critical thinking with Ann Brown's research on metacognitive strategies. Paul Chance's recent book, *Thinking in the Classroom: A Survey of Programs* (1986), reviews Dansereau's learning strategies program for college students along with more traditional thinking skills programs like CoRT, Philosophy for Children, and Productive Thinking. A more dramatic evidence of this cross-fertilization is seen in a recent paper by Norris and Phillips (1987). In this paper, the authors argue that schema theory does not adequately explain difficulties in reading comprehension, and suggest critical thinking theory as an alternative framework for explaining breakdowns in reading comprehension. The degree of concordance between the critical thinking theory explanation offered by Norris and Phillips and a metacognitive explanation as would be offered by someone like Ann Brown is phenomenal. In fact, so striking is the concordance that when the authors presented aspects of this paper at the 1987 AERA conference, Bonnie Ambruster, the discussant, spent most of her discussion time commenting on the parallels between the two perspectives. Essentially, then, while it is conceptually important to distinguish between the two traditions in cognitive education, there are significant commonalities between them.

THE THEORETICAL BASIS FOR COGNITIVE STRATEGY-BASED INSTRUCTION

There is greater optimism now than ever before about the viability of a marriage between cognitive psychology and classroom instruction. Several factors account for this increased optimism. The notion of cognitive modifiability has become increasingly popular in more recent theorizations about human cognitive performance. There is a definite trend toward defining human intelligence as being made up of different components, some of which are amenable to change through systematic intervention. Haywood and Switzky (1986), for example, have proposed that there are two requirements for intelligent human behavior: native ability and cognitive functions. Native ability is genetically determined, as suggested by traditional psychometric theories of intelligence; cognitive functions are largely acquired and therefore can be trained.

Sternberg's work, which blends traditional psychometric and contemporary information-processing approaches to the study of human intelligence, has focused on the analysis of intelligent behavior into specific information-processing components (Sternberg, 1980, 1985). Based on evidence that some components of intelligent performance are trainable (see Sternberg et al., 1982, for a review), Sternberg (1986) has suggested the need for programs that train intelligence.

Feuerstein's theory of cognitive modifiability (Feuerstein et al., 1980), for example, specifies that variables like genetic inheritance, maturation, organicity, and a variety of environmental factors—traditionally considered to be critical influences on cognitive functioning—are only distal etiological determinants. These are factors that when deficient in some respect "can, but do not necessarily, lead to inadequate cognitive development." They are determinants that "neither directly nor inevitably cause" (p. 17) deficient cognitive performance. The more proximal determinant of deficient cognitive functioning is what Feuerstein and his associates refer to as mediated learning experience, the way in which stimuli emitted by the environment are transformed by a "mediating" agent, usually a parent, sibling, or other caregiver who, "guided by his (her) intentions, culture, and emotional investment, selects and organizes the world of stimuli for the child" (p. 16). Theoretical frameworks like this one are highly interventionist in orientation; they make intentional or incidental intervention a critical variable in the shaping of cognition and cognitive performance.

Most contemporary cognitive information-processing perspectives on cognition and learning imply, one way or another, that because we can systematically analyze cognitive performance into its component processes and strategies, it is possible to design interventions to improve the performance of those who manifest deficiencies in their performance. Educators find these ideas appealing because of the hope it provides for the improvement of learning and performance in the classroom.

Also, cognitive psychologists are increasingly applying their work to problems of education, a situation that has raised phenomenal awareness and hope, among educators, about possible revolutionary changes in the way children are instructed. It is no wonder, then, that educators and educational researchers are increasingly turning to cognitive psychology for direction in the design of instructional interventions.

INSIGHTS FROM COGNITIVE DEVELOPMENTAL THEORY

One major criticism of efforts to apply cognitive psychological theories to the design of educational interventions is that often the conceptual bridges between psychological theory and instructional theory are either very weak or altogether nonexistent. Educational and instructional psychologists are often too eager to apply the raw contents of psychological theories without first pausing to consider what necessary theoretical extensions and/or modifications need to be made to enhance the viability of any perceived educational applications.

The use to which educators have put Piaget's theory of genetic epistemology provides a vivid illustration of this criticism. Piaget's preoccupation was to explain the mechanisms by which human thought processes developed, and although some general principles of educational relevance may be derived from the theory (Ginsburg, 1981), it is essentially a developmental theory and not a learning or instructional theory. Indeed Piagetians of the Genevan school held a strictly horticulturalist view on the question of whether Piagetian concepts are teachable—that is, cognitive development can hardly be modified through learning and, indeed, that any "attempts at such modification, though well intentioned, may do more harm than good" (Brainerd, 1983: p. 26). Yet many of the initial efforts to apply Piaget's theory to education were efforts to teach Piagetian concepts directly. Lavatelli's Early Childhood Curriculum (1970, 1971) and Weikart's Open Framework program (Weikart et al., 1971) are representative examples of early Piagetian curricula in North America. Like Kohlberg and Mayer (1972), these program developers viewed the promotion of Piagetian concepts as a major aim of education. Today, on the basis of both critical analysis of the theory itself and empirical evaluations of experimental Piagetian preschool curricula, there is some consensus that the relevance of Piaget's theory for education does not lie in the direct teaching of Piagetian concepts. As Ginsburg (1981) points out, the theory "is limited in its explanatory power with respect to academic knowledge" (p. 328).

What precautions can be taken to ensure more valid and fruitful applications of psychological theories to instruction? Resnick (1984) has provided a sketch of three major elements necessary for an applied theory of development. She defines applied developmental theory as psychological theory designed to guide interventions in development; its purpose is to either correct problems in children's functioning or further enhance the functioning of children who have no difficulty. A theory with these purposes in mind, according to Resnick, should: (1) describe clearly both the overt behaviors and underlying competencies to be acquired (i.e., a theory of *competence*); (2) explain the processes and mechanisms by which those behaviors and competencies are acquired (i.e., a theory of *acquisition*); and (3) describe the kinds of actions that can be taken to aid the acquisition or improvement of the competencies, delineating the circumstances under which intervention may work or fail (i.e., a theory of *intervention*).

Resnick's three elements should serve as useful criteria for determining whether a given theory has all the ingredients necessary to allow direct application to instructional settings or whether extensions will be needed as an intermediate step to application. It is crucial that this or some similar set of criteria be applied to psychological theories before the contents of such theories are translated into classroom activities.

LINKING COGNITIVE-DEVELOPMENTAL THEORY AND INSTRUCTIONAL DESIGN

The work of Case (1980a, 1980b) at the Ontario Institute for Studies in Education is a good illustration of the kind of extension or modification that can be done to an existing psychological theory to make the theory more directly applicable to instruction. Representing a bridge between the cognitive developmental theory of Piaget and present-day information-processing approaches, Case's work includes the analysis of cognitive problems and performance into component processes. While preserving some traditional Piagetian postulates (e.g., that experience is only a partial explanation of the stages and substages of intellectual development, or that learning is under the control of cognitive development), Case reconceptualizes the process of cognitive development around the following three central ideas:

1. The operational structures of each Piagetian stage can be thought of as groups of executive strategies.
2. A working memory of a specifiable size is required for the acquisition and application of any given executive strategy.
3. Greater familiarity with an intellectual operation reduces the amount of attention required to execute the operation.

Thus, according to Case (1980b) the three major processes that underlie cognitive development and cognitive performance are cognitive strategies, working memory, and automaticity. All cognitive tasks require strategies to solve, and the complexity of a task is, in fact, related to the number and complexity of strategies required to execute it. The efficient application of strategies, however, depends in part upon the ability to hold and utilize information in working memory. While working memory capacity is constant (at least after age two), it increases functionally as cognitive operations become increasingly automatized. In practical terms, frequent practice and overlearning lead to a situation whereby knowledge and strategies are applied with very little or no conscious mental effort, a process that frees up working memory space. In a nutshell, Case views cognitive development (and perhaps for that matter cognitive performance) as "the product of acquiring new strategies, an ever increasing capacity for working memory, and increasing automaticity in applying strategies"

(Yussen & Santrock, 1982, p. 280). One significant difference between Case and Piaget lies in Case's concern for intervention.

Unlike Piaget, Case provides a formal bridge between developmental theory and educational intervention. In several of his works, Case (1978, 1980) has succinctly described instructional applications of this developmental framework. Essentially, he hypothesizes that difficulties or failures in performing a cognitive task may be associated with one or more of the three central cognitive processes. For example, the student may be applying a defective or an oversimplified strategy. A second possibility is that the student may be finding it difficult to cope with the informational demands that the task places on short-term memory. Finally, it is also possible that the basic operations required by the student to accomplish the task may be so difficult that their execution is not under automatic control; consequently, additional demands are made on short-term memory.

Case suggests the following sequence of instructional steps to address, respectively, each of the three potential sources of failure or difficulty presented above:

1. Diagnosis and subsequent modification of the defective or oversimplified strategy, after first demonstrating its inadequacy
2. Reduction of the load on working memory, by controlling task demands
3. Maximization of automaticity of basic operations through the provision of massive practice

These ideas have significant implications for designing cognitive strategy-based instruction. Implied in step 1 are the views that strategy interventions must be tailored to the unique needs of individual students, and an important component of strategy intervention is raising the learner's awareness about deficiencies in strategic behavior. Step 2 underscores the importance of the management of memory in cognitive performance. While the teacher can manipulate tasks to control demands on students' memory capacity, strategies that enable students themselves to manage their own memory would appear to be desirable. Finally, strategy instruction may require systematic identification and hierarchical analyses of operations and processes underlying specific cognitive tasks to facilitate both diagnosis and corrective action. Such corrective action would include the provision of opportunities for extensive practice and overlearning to bring basic operations and processes under automatic control.

INSIGHTS FROM LEARNING THEORY

Cognitive Strategies as Learnable Capabilities

In his classic work on the classification of learnable human capabilities, Gagne (1985) identifies cognitive strategies as a distinct learnable human capability with instructional implications. According to him there are five classes of learnable capabilities: intellectual skills, cognitive strategies, verbal information, motor skills, and attitudes. The distinction he makes between intellectual skills and cognitive strategies is an important one. While intellectual skills have to do with the acquisition and use of symbols, concepts, and rules, cognitive strategies have to do with regulating and monitoring the utilization of symbols, concepts, and rules. Thus, as Gagne puts it, cognitive strategies are "more general and also more generalizable than intellectual skills" (Gagne, 1985, p. 138).

As a learnable capability, cognitive strategies—especially lower-level strategies—can be imparted through direct instruction, and their acquisition is under the same principles of learning that guide all other learnable capabilities.

Internal versus External Conditions of Learning

Gagne's dichotomization of the conditions of learning into *external* and *internal* also has significant implications for cognitive strategies curricula. Conditions external to the learner pertain to all the events and activities of the learning environment that have to be arranged (usually by an instructor) in order to promote learning. Conditions internal to the learner, on the other hand, include the learner's prior knowledge or skills and the internal learning processes that activate such prior knowledge or skills.

The distinction between the internal and external conditions of learning reflects what we will refer to as a transactional view of learning and instruction. Briefly stated, a transactional view posits that the teaching-learning process occurs around at least two principal players: the teacher or instructional system and the learner. Actions and processes undertaken by both the teacher and the learner interact in a dynamic fashion to influence not only the quantity but also the quality of learning. Thus, at the least, the outcome of instruction depends as much on the learner's own role as it does on the effectiveness of the teacher/instructional system. Traditional behavioristic theories of learning and instruction tended to emphasize external conditions almost to the exclusion of those conditions that are under the control (conscious or otherwise) of the learner. Consistent with the behavioristic orientation, traditional practices in education promoted a view of the teaching process as the sole determinant of instructional outcomes. Teacher educators and educational researchers invested most of their effort in developing effective teaching practices, most of which concentrated on techniques of delivery and the use of teaching aids. The implicit assumption behind this orientation seemed to be that once the teacher does a good job delivering content, the learner is bound to learn.

Gagne's work suggests, as does our transactional framework, that designing instruction to promote learning is a process of selecting and organizing external conditions of learning in a manner that helps to activate and support the learner's own internal learning processes. Cognitive strategy instructional programs are generally designed to make this process of activating and supporting the learner's own internal processes the cornerstone of the teaching-learning enterprise.

INSIGHTS FROM METACOGNITIVE THEORY
AND RESEARCH

From Flavell's early work (1979), in which he identified and discussed relationships among metacognitive knowledge, metacognitive experience, and cognitive monitoring, has emerged a view of metacognition as involving two separate phenomena: knowledge or awareness about cognition, and regulation of cognitive behavior (Baker & Brown, 1984). From a developmental perspective, it has been suggested that even at a very young age, children possess a considerable amount of metacognitive knowledge (i.e., knowledge about different aspects of cognition, about their own cognitive capabilities in relation to different types of tasks, and about the relative effectiveness of different strategies for different types of tasks), and that this knowledge continues to grow with age. The ability to take advantage of this knowledge for the purpose of spontaneously selecting and applying the appropriate strategies when faced with a cognitive challenge, however, lags behind considerably (see Nisbet & Shucksmith, 1986). Evidence from the research of Brown (1977) indicates that children's strategic difficulties are in the form of production deficiencies—that is, many children can perform a strategy when prompted to do so, although they may not manifest possession of the strategy when presented with a task requiring its use.

This evidence suggests that perhaps instruction in specific strategies alone may not be enough. To ensure spontaneous utilization of strategies, it may be necessary to formally establish linkages between the strategy to be taught and metamemory information (i.e., knowledge about the variety of tasks and task situations that will call for the use of the strategy). Insights from a number of applied studies in the area of mental retardation reviewed by Campione and his associates (Campione, et al., 1982) confirm the utility of such an approach. These researchers compared results yielded by three different types of strategy training: blind training (subjects are taught or induced to use a strategy without understanding the significance of the strategy); informed training (subjects are not only taught or induced to use a strategy but provided information regarding the significance of the strategy); and self-control training (subjects receive training in the use of a strategy as well as explicit instruction in how to use, monitor, and evaluate the strategy). Campione and his associates concluded that self-control training, which included the greatest amount of metacognitive input, resulted in a more durable use and greater generalization of a trained strategy.

The above conclusion is corroborated in a series of experimental studies conducted by Pressley and his associates (see Pressley et al., 1984) to examine the relative effectiveness of three different ways of providing metacognitive information during strategy training. Experiments were set up in such a way that knowledge about a strategy was: (1) derived by the subject only as an incidental by-product of using the strategy; (2) provided explicitly by the experimenter; or (3) extracted by the subject as a result training in and use of special higher-level processes, called metacognitive acquisition procedures (MAPs). Pressley and his associates concluded that all three approaches promote efficient strategy use, an indication that metacognitive training need not be explicit. They noted also, however, that children were not as efficient as adults "at deriving strategy knowledge and translating it into cognitive actions," and consequently, "more explicit metamemory interventions are needed in order to have a pronounced effect with youngsters" (p. 104).

From an applied perspective, some of the questions that have frequently been asked in relation to cognitive and metacognitive training are the following: Does development place limitations on the acquisition of metacognitive strategies? If so, what is the earliest age at which metacognitive strategies can be taught successfully? Is it sufficient to teach specific task strategies (or tactics) alone, or should such instruction include explicit metacognitive information? With regard to the first and second questions, it is significant to note that some of the studies reviewed by Pressley et al. (1984) involved the teaching of metacognitive acquisition procedures to grade 2 students (e.g., Lodico et al., 1983). With regard to the third question, the two sets of reviews (Campione et al., 1982; Pressley et al., 1984) and further evidence from the work of Belmont et al. (1982) suggest that to achieve durable and generalizable effects, specific strategy training should be accompanied by metacognitive training.

TOWARD A COGNITIVE STRATEGY-BASED INSTRUCTIONAL MODEL

The principal defining attribute of a cognitive orientation to learning is the proposition that learning is an active, constructive process (Shuell, 1980, 1986; Wittrock, 1974, 1986) involving the learner's use and management of internal cognitive processes to acquire, store, retrieve, and apply knowledge. Any theory of instruction that is premised on this view of the learning process thus has to deal with the interrelationships that exist among at least three sets of variables: instructional variables; internal learning mechanisms or cognitive processes; and the expected learning outcomes (Gagne, 1985; Shuell, 1980). Instructional variables are essentially variables external to the learner and under the control of the teacher (or instructional system) that are employed for the purpose of accomplishing certain learning outcomes in the learner. The desired learning outcomes are, however, accomplished by designing and employing instructional events in such a way that they stimulate, support, and facilitate learning processes internal to the learner.

Two interrelated conditions must be fulfilled if learners are to be fully and actively involved in the learning process. First, as is implied in the above conceptualization, control over the management of the cognitive mechanisms underlying learning must ultimately be placed in the hands of the learner. The teacher plays the role of a guide and facilitator, gradually socializing children to discover their own role in, and to assume total control over, the learning process. Thus, over the course of instruction and schooling, teacher control should decrease while learner control increases.

The successful transfer of control from teacher to learner, however, depends on a second condition, namely, that the cognitive processes underlying learning and performance be made more explicit to the learner over the course of instruction and schooling. Teachers and school curricula have always had cognitive agendas that have remained hidden from the learner, the supposed beneficiary of the cognitive goals of instruction. For example, based on the notion of knowledge subsumption in Ausubel's theory of meaningful verbal learning, advance organizers are employed routinely as a tool for activating preexisting cognitive structures that are deemed pertinent for the learning of related new knowledge. Such activation of related prior knowledge structures helps the learner to encode new knowledge meaningfully; when advance organizers are used, however, students are rarely told explicitly about their purpose. Similarly, following the work of Rothkopf and his associates (Rothkopf, 1976; Rothkopf & Bisbicos, 1967), the interspersion of questions within text has become a popular comprehension-enhancing technique for getting readers to allocate more cognitive resources to important segments of text. Informing students explicitly about the purposes of such questions would very likely foster spontaneous self-generation of questions by students during reading, but this is a rare instructional practice.

We consider *control* and *explicitness* as key constructs in our conceptualization of learning strategy instruction. Learning strategy instruction should seek to increase the learner's control of the learning process by increasingly making explicit to the learner the relevant cognitive processes, operations, and activities that make it possible to learn and perform effectively under a given task situation.

Rigney (1978, 1980) employs the concepts of control and explicitness to describe four different conditions for using cognitive learning strategies. According to Rigney, strategy use may be viewed along the two dimensions, explicitness of the strategy and source of control of strategy initiation.

Explicitness of strategy use. A strategy may be detached from or embedded in content. A detached strategy is one that can be described independently of the content or subject matter to be processed. In other words, a detached strategy is used consciously (Derry, 1985), and the learner is aware that is exists and can be applied in an appropriate context.[1] An embedded strategy, on the other hand, is so intrinsically tied to the nature of the assigned task that its use is rather subconscious; the nature of the task dictates the deployment of the strategy but in a way that the learner is not necessarily aware of consciously.

To illustrate, consider assigning the following arithmetic task to a class and barring students from using a calculator or performing paper-and-pencil calculations: $240 \times 15 = ?$ The nature of this task forces the student to use mental imagery to keep track of operations, intermediate products, and carries. In fact, mental arithmetic exercises like this one are designed purposely and used routinely to train the use of mental imagery. Thus, embedded in the task is the strategy of mental imagery that must be employed, regardless of the specific method of attack used by individual students.

A conventional method for solving this computational problem calls for the following sequence of actions:

1. Vertically rearrange the task as follows:
   240
   $\times 15$

2. Multiply the multiplicand by the units column of the multiplier, right-justifying the answer from the units column.

3. Multiply the multiplicand by the tens column of the multiplier, this time right-justifying the answer from the tens column.

4. Sum up the two products.

A student may consciously employ any one of several computational strategies to reduce the number of steps, products, or carries that needed to be tracked mentally. One such strategy would be to employ one's knowledge of the ease of multiplying numbers by 10 and further exploit the relationship between the 5 and the 10 in the multiplier 15 (i.e., 5 is one-half of 10) to save processing time and reduce demands on short-term memory. By employing this strategy, the task is reduced to 2,400 (from the rule: to multiply any number by 10, simply append a zero to that number) plus 1,200 (since 5 is one-half of 10, 240×5 is the same as 2,400/2). A heuristic or rule employed in this fashion to simplify processing is an example of a detached strategy—one that is deployed through conscious decision making—and is not necessarily available to all students.

The distinction between embedded and detached strategies is not always as clear-cut as the example given above. Often the same strategies may be both embedded and detached, depending upon the perspective from which they are considered. For example, reading comprehension tasks train readers in a variety of strategies, such as scanning forward for contextual cues, rereading to pick up important cues that may have been missed, and using inference to derive meaning that may not be readily apparent. That is, whenever we assign comprehension tasks, these are some of the strategies that we force students to devise and use in order to answer questions correctly. These strategies can be said, then, to be embedded strategies by nature. They are embedded because their use is necessitated by the nature of the task. We do know, however, that not all readers employ these strategies, and those who do so do not employ them to the same degree. If a teacher sets out to spell out to students what these strategies are, when they can be employed, and why their use will enhance comprehension, the strategies would have been elevated to a detached status. What this teacher has done essentially is to make more explicit for the students underlying cognitive activities that are necessary to perform well on a given task.

Control of strategy initiation. While cognitive strategies are always performed by the learner, initiation of their use may come from one of two sources: the student's own "self-instruction" or the teacher or the instructional system.

The two dimensions (explicitness and control), each with its two levels, give rise to the four modes of strategy use summarized in figure 6.1. Rigney's work provides the conceptual framework for the SPELT instructional model, which employs both direct instruction and incidental learning techniques. Derry and her associates at Florida State University have employed the same framework to develop a purely incidental strategy instructional model that is currently being tested (Derry, 1985; Derry & Murphy, 1986). There is a major difference between Derry's application and ours. Derry and her associates prefer a computer-assisted instruction (CAI) application to a "somewhat less promising paper curriculum" (Derry, 1985, p. 16) application. We, on the other hand, think that implementing strategy instruction within the regular ("paper") curriculum is a bigger, and perhaps more ecologically valid, challenge.

We have utilized Rigney's model as an analogue for describing four different levels of strategy use, and, consequently, as a guide to describing a cognitive/learning strategy instructional sequence. Each quadrant in figure 6.1 represents a particular approach to nurturing strategy use.

Quadrant 1 is perhaps the commonest instructional model in the traditional academic curriculum. Most traditional instruction is designed within subject matter. The "how" of learning or processing information is taught implicitly rather than explicitly. Control over what is learned and how best to learn it is exercised completely by the instructional system. The reading comprehension example we cited above provides a good illustration of this point.

Quadrant 2 depicts an instructional situation under which cognitive strategies are taught explicitly or imposed by the instructional system. This may take the form of a teacher instructing students to employ specific strategies or presenting to-be-learned material in a way that tells students exactly what strategies to employ to process the material.

Under quadrant 3, we have a situation whereby students consciously decide or generate for themselves what strategy to adopt when confronted with a learning or problem-solving task. Finally, quadrant 4 represents the ultimate goal of learning and instruction. It describes a state of instructional accomplishment whereby the generation or use of strategies by the student is spontaneous and occurs with little or no conscious effort.

THE SPELT INSTRUCTIONAL SEQUENCE

The SPELT instructional sequence is premised on the view that the highest level of cognitive performance is characterized by efficient and spontaneous use of strategies, whether such strategies are self-generated or learned. Quadrant 4 in figure 6.1 represents this level. The attainment of this level occurs through two forms of automaticity: automaticity in self-generation of strategies, and automaticity in the use of learned or acquired strategies. Through constant practice and guidance, the processes of spontaneously utilizing acquired strategies or devising appropriate ones, in situ, come under automatic control. In a sense, the student comes to generate or apply strategies not only spontaneously but often also unconsciously. Strategic behavior, from the perspective of our framework, then, need not always be deliberate or effortful (for more detailed discussions of what makes cognitive behavior or processing strategic, see Baron, 1985; Howe & O'Sullivan, 1990; Pressley et al., 1987).

To attain the level of cognitive functioning represented in quadrant 4, however, it is important that students be taken systematically through the two instructional stages depicted by quadrants 2 and 3. Our instructional model (figure 6.2) is designed to accomplish this. The model has the following components.

A A general teaching style or orientation

B The teaching of a set of recommended strategies, including other strategies generated or identified by the teacher

C Teaching toward student control and generation of strategies

Component A reflects a general teaching style that should permeate the entire teaching-learning relationship between the teacher and students. That teaching style/orientation is characterized by efforts on the part of the teacher to actively involve the student in the learning process. Among the principal hallmarks of this orientation are: raising cognitive and metacognitive awareness; leading students to discover rather than revealing facts to them; and constantly challenging students to be critical, systematic, and strategic in their behavior and attitude toward learning. Nurturing metacognitive skills is one of the major cornerstones of the SPELT approach, a feature that distinguishes it from other strategy programs. For every single strategy that is taught the teacher should provide information, either directly or through class discussion, regarding the significance of the strategy, how and when to use it, and what modifications may be made to it in order to apply it to a broader range of problems.

Our decision to embed metacognitive training within the SPELT program has strong support from both theory and research, aspects of which we reviewed in an earlier section. From a theoretical standpoint, it has been suggested that the greater the knowledge and awareness that students have about a strategy and its significance the more likely it is that the strategy will be em-

Figure 6.1
Alternative Instructional Models

Control of Strategies

		Student Generated	Teacher Imposed
Explicitness of Strategy	Detached from Content	A	B
	Embedded in Content	C	D

Adapted from Rigney (1978)

ployed (Pressley et al., 1984). Some of the recent efforts to develop theories of intelligence from a cognitive processes perspective identify metacognitive skills as an important key to generalization (e.g., Belmont et al., 1982; Borkowski, 1985; Butterfield et al., 1980; Campione & Brown, 1978). More important, there is evidence from research suggesting that strategy training programs that result in longer-term and generalized effects are those that include explicit training in metacognitive skills (Baker & Brown, 1984; Campione et al., 1982; Pressley et al., 1984).

Components B and C represent the hierarchy of moving from traditional instruction (quadrant 1) to instruction that includes in its content explicit cognitive processes necessary for learning and performance in any subject matter area. These two components are the basis for the three SPELT instructional phases (figure 6.2), which represent a progression from the lowest level of strategy acquisition and use (acquisition and use through teacher imposition) to the highest level (self-generation and self-initiated deployment).

SPELT Instructional Phases

Phase 1: Direct Teaching of Strategies

Phase 1 instruction, also called the teacher-imposed phase, consists of the direct teaching of program-recommended, teacher-identified, or teacher-generated strategies. Teacher-imposed strategy instruction is designed to expose students to the idea that cognitive strategies exist, and to demonstrate to students that organized, goal-directed, and efficient use of cognitive strategies increases one's ability to acquire, store, think about, retrieve, and apply knowledge.

A key feature of this phase is *metacognitive empowerment,* a process of increasingly making the students aware of the benefits of strategic behavior. As various strategies are taught, the teacher should structure the instructional experience in such a way as to enable students to compare their performance under strategy-use and nonstrategy-use situations. Providing opportunities for students to share their impressions as they apply various strategies not only aids the process of developing strategy awareness but also makes for a smoother transition to phase 2 instruction. As students become aware and convinced that their use of strategies results in improved learning and performance, they are more likely to invest more effort into the activities of phases 2 and 3.

While phase 1 provides the student with the opportunity to begin the process of consciously building a personal repertoire of useful strategies in different subject areas, its primary purpose is to establish a rudimentary strategy knowledge base and to lay the groundwork for phase 2 and phase 3 instruction. Keeping strategy instruction at phase 1 runs counter to the cognitive goals that underpin the program, namely, increasing control, active involvement, and independence on the part of the learner. If overdone, phase 1 instruction can only lead to a passive, outer-directed learner.

Phase 2: Maintenance and Generalization of Strategies

The primary emphasis during phase 2 instruction is facilitating maintenance and systematic transfer of the strategic repertoire established in phase 1 across tasks and content areas. The direct instructional methodology of phase 1 gives way to more interactive and reflective methods like Socratic dialogue, in which the teacher leads the students, through questioning, to discover relationships and applications for themselves. Socratic dialogue, as employed in the SPELT approach, is operationalized along lines suggested by Collins (1977). It employs such guidelines as: (1) starting with what is known; (2) asking for multiple reasons; (3) asking for intermediate steps in the student's reasoning; (4) requesting formulations of general rules from specific cases; (5) picking counterexamples when insufficient reason is given; (6) using extreme cases to illustrate a misapplication of given strategies; (7) probing for differences among alternative strategies; and (8) asking for predictions of the potential outcomes of employing alternative strategies.

The process of metacognitive empowerment, begun in phase 1, continues in phase 2, but this time with more control beginning to shift from the teacher to the student. Students are asked to identify other settings and task situations where strategies taught previously could be applied, and to evaluate the effectiveness of these strategies as they employ them in new situations. To facilitate this process of comparison, analysis, and evaluation, students are also taught— in the style of phase 1 instruction—specific generalization and critical thinking strategies.

Figure 6.2
The SPELT Instructional Model

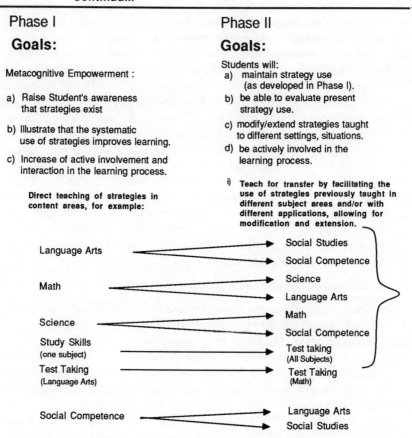

Continuum

Phase I	Phase II
Goals:	**Goals:**

Metacognitive Empowerment :

a) Raise Student's awareness that strategies exist

b) Illustrate that the systematic use of strategies improves learning.

c) Increase of active involvement and interaction in the learning process.

Direct teaching of strategies in content areas, for example:

Students will:
a) maintain strategy use (as developed in Phase I).
b) be able to evaluate present strategy use.
c) modify/extend strategies taught to different settings, situations.
d) be actively involved in the learning process.

i) **Teach for transfer by facilitating the use of strategies previously taught in different subject areas and/or with different applications, allowing for modification and extension.**

Language Arts → Social Studies / Social Competence

Math → Science / Language Arts

Science → Math / Social Competence

Study Skills (one subject) → Test taking (All Subjects)

Test Taking (Language Arts) → Test Taking (Math)

Social Competence → Language Arts / Social Studies

ii) **Strategies presented in Phase II are used as a means to facilitate transfer and to develop critical thinking skills.**

Phase 3: Strategy Generation by Students

Instruction in this phase is designed to nurture in students the ability to generate strategies on their own as well as the ability to apply previously acquired strategies spontaneously. The extensive practice that phase 2 instruction provides in evaluating, modifying, and applying strategies prepares the student to

Figure 6.2—*Continued*

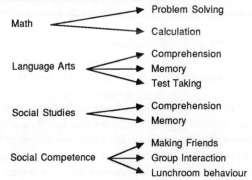

Phase III
Goals:

Students will:

a) monitor, evaluate, and generate effective
   and efficient strategies to improve learning.

b) be actively involved in the learning process.

Following a problem solving model,
the presentation of content based assignments,
from which the students generate strategies
to complete. The use of Socratic dialogue acts
as a catalyst for student evaluation of present
strategic use, leading to their modification,
extention, and/or the generation of new strategies.

**All Subject areas should be involved with strategies
used in skill areas such as those illustrated:**

Math ──── Problem Solving
       ──── Calculation

Language Arts ──── Comprehension
           ──── Memory
           ──── Test Taking

Social Studies ──── Comprehension
            ──── Memory

Social Competence ──── Making Friends
               ──── Group Interaction
               ──── Lunchroom behaviour

begin to look for the most efficient and effective ways of dealing with learning and performance tasks. The teacher employs a problem-solving approach to instruction during this phase. Both basic (content-free) cognitive tasks and content-related problems are assigned to students, with the expectation that students come up with their own strategies for performing the tasks. Individualized as well as total class discussions of such assignments focus on analyses of task requirements, alternative strategies, and avenues for ascertaining the relative effectiveness of potentially useful strategies.

The use of group or paired problem-solving techniques is especially recommended, as such techniques help students to think aloud and make it possible for others and themselves to evaluate the cognitive processes behind their overt problem-solving behaviors. Special teacher- or instructional system-prepared tasks are not the only vehicles for teaching student strategy generation. The teacher also takes advantage of incidentally occurring situations, such as when students manifest specific failures or breakdowns in problem solving, to work with students in locating the source of such failures, identifying reasons why such failures may have occurred, and generating more effective strategies. Continued exposure to phase 3-type of teaching-learning activities is expected to lead ultimately to automization of strategy generation and utilization.

A Spiral Strategy Curriculum

The notion of instructional phases may appear to connote that the goals associated with the three phases are tied to a fixed time continuum. At least in one independent attempt to evaluate our strategy instructional approach, our instructional phases were erroneously interpreted in this fashion. We should emphasize that except in situations where students are being introduced to strategy instruction for the very first time (in which case it is crucial that phase 1 teaching occur extensively around a variety of strategies), the phases may overlap and indeed occur concurrently. Within any given classroom, a teacher and students may be operating in phase 1 in connection with strategies in one subject area and in phase 2 or even phase 3 in another subject area. Similarly, the rate at which a student or a class moves from one phase to another in connection with any given strategy is not predetermined; it is based on the teacher's assessment of student progress in grasping and working with the strategy.

The three phases are indeed designed to operate within a spiral strategy instruction curriculum. The essential cognitive strategies that facilitate academic learning, problem solving, and thinking may be the same for all grade levels. Variations across grade levels tend to be variations in complexity and the degree to which students can begin to employ them in a controlled manner. Thus, similar to Bruner's (1960) notion of a spiral curriculum, the same strategies may be taught at all grade levels but at varying degrees of complexity and sophistication. Conceptualized in this manner, the relative significance of each of the instructional phases will vary as students progress through higher grades. For example, phase 1 instruction for a group of grade 7 students who have been receiving strategy instruction for three years will be diminished significantly, compared to another group of grade 7 students who have been in a strategy instructional program for only one year.

SPELT Strategies

Two strategy classifications are used within SPELT: (1) primary versus support strategies (Dansereau, 1978), and (2) general versus specific strategies (Deshler et al., 1983). Primary strategies are those used to operate directly on material to be learned; they may be specific (such as a summarization strategy for reading) or general (such as a planning strategy). Support strategies, on the other hand, are those used to operate on the learner to create and maintain an internal psychological climate that is conducive to learning (e.g., a concentration or relaxation strategy).

The second classification—general versus specific—are subcategories of the first classification. General strategies are in most cases content-independent mechanisms for inducing purposeful, planful, and reflective behavior. They serve as guides that enable students to develop a systematic routine of assessing problem situations, determining their requirements, selecting appropriate goal-specific strategies for arriving at solutions, and monitoring the problem-solving process.

Specific strategies, on the other hand, have limited relevance or applications to a very small range of tasks. They may be task-limited, content-specific, or domain-independent. A task-limited specific strategy has a limited application to a particular task or operation within a given domain or content area. One of our strategies (MR. DoL1) is designed to aid a quick determination of the direction in which to move the decimal point when doing mental multiplication or division of by 10s, 100s, or 1,000s. While this strategy employs a first-letter mnemonic, its application does not go beyond this kind of task in mathematics. A content-specific strategy is one that could apply to more than one task but is usually limited to one subject domain. Finally, a domain-independent specific strategy is one that involves a specific cognitive process; because this cognitive process is necessary across a variety of content areas, however, the strategy can be applied equally well in many domains. Remembering and comprehension strategies, for example, can be very specific and yet have a broader utility across subject areas.

Beyond the above general description, the strategies taught within SPELT fall into the following areas:

- General problem-solving strategies
- Social problem-solving strategies
- Math problem-solving strategies
- General metacognitive strategies
- Reading strategies
- Memory strategies
- Study and time management strategies

- Test-taking strategies
- Mood-setting (support) strategies

The SPELT model recognizes that not all categories of strategies can be taught through direct instructional methods. Direct instructional techniques are used primarily with task- and content-specific strategies. More generic and metacognitive strategies are *nurtured* through the overall teaching orientation described earlier. A key principle underlying the SPELT approach is that the acquisition of strategic behavior, like all other forms of learning, is not something that can be expected to take place within a brief period of instruction. It takes a systematically designed and consistently implemented program of instruction spread over a reasonably long period to gradually nurture and give expression to strategic learning and performance

SPELT In-service Training for Teachers

In-service training for SPELT instruction is given over five full days, broken into two blocks. Part 1 is a three-day session, and is followed by part 2 about three weeks later. During part 1 training, teachers are introduced to the program's theoretical foundations in cognitive psychology, to the three-phase instructional model, and to the practical application of the model in the classroom. A great deal of the time is spent exposing the teachers to, demonstrating, and having them practice a number of specific and general strategies from the teacher's manual (Mulcahy et al., 1986a). They get ample opportunities to experience each of the three instructional phases through an interactive exposure to a series of activities associated with each phase. The principal goal of part 1 is to provide teachers with the structure necessary to enable them to begin systematic implementation of strategy instruction in the classroom right after the workshop.

Teachers leave the third day of the workshop with the understanding that they will experiment with the principles and practical ideas in their classrooms during the succeeding three weeks, keeping track of their experiences and concerns for discussion during part 2 of the training. Part 2 is a two-day session designed to reinforce the activities and goals accomplished in part 1. It begins with a group sharing and discussion of each member's experiences during the preceding three weeks of implementation. Greater emphasis is placed on practical ways of moving students to self-generation and spontaneous utilization of strategies (phase 3).

Both small and large group discussions and activities are significant features of the workshops; modeling is perhaps the most important teaching technique employed throughout the training sessions. The in-service instructor models the methodology and the instructional sequence in much the same way as they are expected to be implemented in the classroom.

The SPELT program has been extensively evaluated in the context of a longitudinal study (Mulcahy et al., 1989). The major study involved approximately 4,500 students from about twenty school jurisdictions in North-Central Alberta. This cooperative venture involving the faculty of education at the University of Alberta, the department of education of the government of Alberta, and various school districts, has involved the implementation of two experimental programs in both elementary and junior high classrooms over a three-year period. The evaluation involved pupil progress (cognitive ability, academic achievement, self-concept, perceived competence, and cognitive strategies), teacher assessment of program and in-service, as well parental and administrator perceptions.

The results of the study have been reported in detail elsewhere (Mulcahy et al., 1989), so we will only summarize briefly some of the major findings here. The most encouraging effects were observed with respect to the perceptions of both teachers and parents. The participating teachers viewed the in-service training to have been adequate in preparing them to implement the program, and that the program procedures were suitable for group instruction given the number of students in their classes (i.e., 15–55). At the end of one and two years of instruction the vast majority of teachers observed their students using the learning/thinking strategies across different classrooms and subjects. Teachers also indicated that they would continue to use the instructional procedures even after their involvement in the project had ended. Over 95 percent of all the teachers indicated that they would recommend the approach to other teachers and many indicated the approach should be made a mandatory component for all preservice teachers. In a followup of twenty teachers one and one-half to two years after their involvement with the research project had ended, 85 percent indicated that they were continuing to teach aspects of the program to their present classes. All of these teachers indicated they would recommend the program to their colleagues.

The majority of parents indicated that they observed a number of important behavioral changes in their children over the course of the two years of instruction. The most frequently reported behavior changes over grades were in increased attention to homework, recognizing alternate points of view, willingness to tackle more difficult tasks, self-confidence, and questioning. The parental perceptions suggested that program effects were indeed being generalized outside of the school context.

The program did appear to be effective in increasing achievement in reading comprehension for elementary students with learning difficulties and to some extent appeared also to result in increased use of more effective cognitive strategies in reading and math for all participants regardless of grade or ability.

The evaluation data, while indicating some positive effects, should be treated with caution as it is impossible to attribute the changes observed to the program with 100 percent certainty.

We are currently following up with more specific evaluations of program effectiveness utilizing both within-class and within-subject designs to further elucidate the efficacy of components of the approach.

The results have clear implications for the mainstreaming of students with learning difficulties, as well as gifted students. The impact of the teaching of cognitive strategies on the learning disabled students, particularly at grade 4, suggests that if the teaching approaches are used systematically throughout the elementary school, they may prevent some students from developing severe learning problems, and keep them in the mainstream.

The recent research on the teaching of learning/thinking strategies to learning disabled students also demonstrates significant effect with respect to achievement (see, for instance, Palincsar & Brown, 1984; Paris & Oka, 1986).

These approaches should be effective for mildly mentally retarded as well as native children in regular classrooms. Indeed some researchers have suggested this (Mulcahy & Marfo, 1987; Brown, 1974). There is a need for further research on teaching learning/thinking strategies for these populations. Further investigation into the effects of extending cognitive instruction to primary, senior high, and postsecondary levels is also required. Current research at the preschool level with high-risk children appears to hold significant promise.

NOTES

The work reported in this chapter is based on a longitudinal Cognitive Education Project funded by Alberta Education and supported by the University of Alberta and school jurisdictions in North-Central Alberta. We are grateful to the Planning Services Division of Alberta Education, in particular Drs. Nelly McKeown and Clarence Rhodes, for their invaluable support. Dr. Fred French contributed in many significant ways to initial work on the development of the instructional model described in the chapter. We wish also to acknowledge Dr. Charles Norman and Jonas Darko-Yeoboah for their assistance with data management and analysis.

1. This is not meant to restrict the definition of strategic behavior to the conscious use of a cognitive strategy. In fact, as pointed out later in the discussion, the ultimate goal of strategy instruction is to place strategic behavior under automatic control.

REFERENCES

Ausubel, D. P. (1960). The use of advance organizers in the learning and retention of meaningful verbal learning. *Journal of Educational Psychology,* 51, 267–272.

Ausubel, D. P., Novak, J. D., & Hanesian, H. (1978). *Educational psychology: A cognitive view.* 2d ed. New York: Holt, Rinehart & Winston.

Baker, L., & Brown, A. L. (1984). Metacognitive skills in reading. In P. D. Pearson (ed.), *Handbook of reading research.* New York: Longman.

Baron, J. (1985). *Rationality and intelligence.* Cambridge, England: Cambridge University Press.

Belmont, J. M., Butterfield, E. C., & Ferretti, R. P. (1982). To secure transfer of training instruct self-management skills. In D. K. Detterman & R. J. Sternberg (eds.), *How and how much can intelligence be increased.* Norwood, N.J.: Ablex.

Borkowski, J. G. (1985). Signs of intelligence: Strategy generalization and metacognition. In S. R. Yussen (ed.), *The growth of reflection in children.* New York: Academic.

Brainerd, C. J. (1983). Modifiability of cognitive development. In S. Meadows (ed.), *Developing thinking: Approaches to children's cognitive development.* London: Methuen.

Brown, A. L. (1974). The role of strategic behavior in retardate memory. In N. R. Ellis (ed.), *International review of research in mental retardation.* Vol. 7. New York: Academic.

———. (1977). Development, schooling, and the acquisition of knowledge about knowledge. In R. C. Anderson, R. J. Spiro, & W. E. Montague (eds.), *Schooling and the acquisition of knowledge.* Hillsdale, N.J.: Erlbaum.

Bruner, J. S. (1960). *The process of education.* New York: Random House.

Butterfield, E. C., Siladi, D., & Belmont, J. M. (1980). Validating theories of intelligence. In H. Reese & L. Lipsitt (eds.), *Advances in child development and behavior.* Vol. 15. New York: Academic.

Campione, J. C., & Brown, A. L. (1978). Toward a theory of intelligence: Contributions from research with retarded children. *Intelligence, 2,* 279–304.

Campione, J. C., Brown, A. L., & Ferrara, R. A. (1982). Mental retardation and intelligence. In R. J. Sternberg (ed.), *Handbook of human intelligence.* New York: Cambridge University Press.

Case, R. (1980a). The underlying mechanisms of intellectual development. in J. R. Kirby & J. B. Biggs (eds.), *Cognition, development, and instruction.* New York: Academic.

———. (1980b). Implications of a Neo-Piagetian theory for improving the design of instruction. In J. R. Kirby & J. B. Biggs (eds.), *Cognition, development, and instruction.* New York: Academic.

Chance, P. (1986). *Thinking in the classroom: A survey of programs.* New York: Teachers College Press.

Collins, A. (1977). Processes in acquiring knowledge. In R. C. Anderson, R. J. Spiro, & W. E. Montague (eds.), *Schooling and the acquisition of knowledge.* Hillsdale, N.J.: Lawrence Erlbaum Associates.

Covington, M. V., Crutchfield, R. S., Davies, L., & Olton, R. M., Jr. (1974). *The productive thinking program: A course in learning to think.* Columbus, Ohio: Charles E. Merrill.

Dansereau, D. F. (1978). The development of a learning strategy curriculum. In H. F. O'Neil, Jr. (ed.), *Learning strategies.* New York: Academic.

———. (1985). Learning strategies research. In J. W. Segal, S. F. Chipman, & R. Glaser (eds.), *Thinking and learning skills,* vol. 1, *Relating instruction to research.* Hillsdale, N.J.: Erlbaum.

Dansereau, D. F., Collins, K. W., McDonald, B. A., Holley, C. D., Garland, J., Diekhoff, G., & Evans, S. H. (1979). Development and validation of a learning strategy training program. *Journal of Educational Psychology, 71,* 64–73.

deBono, E. (1985). The CoRT thinking program. In J. W. Segal, S. F. Chipman, & R. Glaser (eds.), *Thinking and learning skills,* vol. 1, *Relating instruction to research.* Hillsdale, N.J.: Erlbaum.

Derry, S. J. (1985). Strategy training: An incidental learning model for CAI. *Journal of Instructional Development,* 8(2), 16–23.

Derry, S. J., & Murphy, D. A. (1986). Designing systems that train learning ability: From theory to practice. *Review of Educational Research,* 56, 1–39.

Deshler, D. D., Alley, G. R., & Carlson, S. A. (1980). Learning strategies: An approach to mainstreaming secondary students with learning disabilities. *Education Unlimited,* 2(4), 6–11.

Deshler, D. D., Warner, M. M., Schumaker, J. B., & Alley, G. R. (1983). Learning strategies intervention model: Key components and current status. In J. McKinney & L. Feagans (eds.), *Current topics in learning disabilities.* Vol. 1. Norwood, N.J.: Ablex.

Ennis, R. H., & Millman, J. (1985). *Cornell critical thinking tests: Levels X and Z.* Pacific Grove, Calif. Midwest.

Feuerstein, R., Rand, Y., Hoffman, M. B., & Miller, R. (1980). *Instrumental enrichment: An intervention program for cognitive modifiability.* Baltimore: University Park Press.

Flavell, J. H. (1979). Metacognition and cognitive monitoring: A new area of cognitive-developmental inquiry. *American Psychologist,* 34, 906–911.

Gagne, R. M. (1985). *The condition of learning and theory of instruction.* 4th ed. New York: Holt, Rinehart & Winston.

Ginsburg, H. P. (1981). Piaget and education: The contributions and limits of genetic epistemology. In I. E. Sigel, D. M. Brodzinsky, & R. M. Golinkoff (eds.), *New directions in Piagetian theory and practice.* Hillsdale, N.J.: Erlbaum.

Haywood, H. C. & Switzky, H. N. (1986). The malleability of intelligence: Cognitive processes as a function of polygenic-experimental interaction. *School Psychology Review,* 15, 245–254.

Howe, M. L., & O'Sullivan, J. T. (1990). Development of strategic memory: Coordinating knowledge, metamemory, and resources. In D. F. Bjorklund (ed.), *Children's strategies: Contemporary views of cognitive development.* Hillsdale, N.J.: Erlbaum.

Kohlberg, L., & Mayer, R. (1972). Development as the aim of education. *Harvard Educational Review,* 42, 449–496.

Lavatelli, C. S. (1970). *Early childhood curriculum: A Piagetian program.* Boston: American Science and Engineering.

————. (1971). *Piaget's theory applied to an early childhood curriculum.* Boston: American Science and Engineering.

Lipman, M. (1985). Thinking skills fostered by Philosophy of Children. In J. W. Segal, S. F. Chipman, & R. Glaser (eds.), *Thinking and learning skills,* vol. 1, *Relating instruction to research.* Hillsdale, N.J.: Lawrence Erlbaum.

Lipman, M., Sharp, A. M., & Oscanyan, F. S. (1980). *Philosophy in the classroom.* 2d ed. Philadelphia: Temple University Press.

Lodico, M. G., Ghatala, E. S., Levin, J. R., Pressley, M., & Bell, J. A. (1983). The effects of strategy monitoring training on children's selection of effective memory strategies. *Journal of Experimental Child Psychology,* 35, 263–277.

Mulcahy, R. F., & Marfo, K. (1987). Assessment of cognitive ability and instructional programming with native Canadian children: A cognitive processes perspective. In L. L. Stewin & S. J. H. McCann (eds.), *Contemporary educational issues: The Canadian mosaic.* Toronto: Copp Clark Pitman.

Mulcahy, R. F., Marfo, K., Peat, D., & Andrews, J. (1986a). *A strategies program for effective learning and thinking (SPELT): Teachers' manual.* Edmonton: Cognitive Education Project, University of Alberta.

Mulcahy, R. F., Marfo, K., Peat, D., Andrews, J., & Clifford, L. (1986b). Applying cognitive psychology in the classroom: A learning/thinking instructional program. *Alberta Psychology,* 13(3), 9–11.

Mulcahy, R. F., Peat, D., Andrews, J., Clifford, L., Marfo, K., & Cho, S. (1989). *Cognitive education final report.* Alberta Education, Government of Alberta, Edmonton.

Nisbet, J., & Shucksmith, J. (1986). *Learning strategies.* London: Routledge & Kegan Paul.

Norris, S. P. (1985, May). Synthesis of research on critical thinking. *Educational Leadership,* 40–45.

Norris, S. P., & Ennis, R. H. (1989). *Evaluating critical thinking.* Pacific Grove, Calif. Midwest.

Norris, S. P., & King, R. (1984). *The design of a critical thinking test on appraising observations.* St. John's, Newfoundland: Institute for Educational Research and Development, Memorial University of Newfoundland.

Norris, S. P., & Phillips, L. M. (1987). Explanations of reading comprehension: Schema theory and critical thinking theory. *Teachers' College Record,* 89, 282–306.

Palincsar, A. S. (1986). Metacognitive strategy instruction. *Exceptional Children,* 53, 118–124.

Palincsar, A. S., & Brown, A. L. (1984). The reciprocal teaching of comprehension fostering and comprehension monitoring activities. *Cognition and Instruction,* 1, 117–175.

Paris, S. G. (1986). Teaching children to guide their reading and learning. In T. Raphael (ed.), *The contexts of school-based literacy.* New York: Random House.

Paris, S. G., & Oka, E. R. (1986). Children's reading strategies, metacognition, and motivation. *Developmental Review,* 6, 25–56.

Paris, S. G., Cross, D. R., & Lipson, M. Y. (1984). Informed strategies for learning: A program to improve children's reading awareness and comprehension. *Journal of Educational Psychology,* 76, 1239–1252.

Paris, S. G., Saarino, D. A., & Cross, D. R. (1986a). *Australian Journal of Psychology,* 38, 107–123.

Paris, S. G., Wixson, K. K., & Palincsar, A. S. (1986b). Instructional approaches to reading comprehension. In E. Rothkopf (ed.), *Review of research in education.* Washington, D.C.: American Education Research Association.

Pressley, M., Borkowski, J. G., & O'Sullivan, J. T. (1984). Memory strategy instruction is made of this: Metamemory and durable strategy use. *Educational Psychology,* 19, 94–107.

Pressley, M., Goodchild, F., Fleet, J., Zajchowski, R., & Evans, E. D. (1987, June). *What is good strategy use and why is it hard to teach? An optimistic appraisal of the challenges associated with strategy instruction.* Paper presented at the 15th Annual Conference of the Canadian Society for the Study of Education, Hamilton, Ontario.

Resnick, L. B. (1984). Toward an applied developmental theory. In B. Gholson & T. L. Rosenthal (eds.), *Applications of cognitive-developmental theory.* Orlando, Fl.: Academic.

Rigney, J. W. (1978). Learning strategies: A theoretical perspective. In H. F. O'Neil, Jr. (ed.), *Learning strategies*. New York: Academic.

———. (1980). Cognitive learning strategies and dualities in information processing. In R. E. Snow, P. Federicod, & W. E. Montague (eds.), *Aptitude, learning, and instruction*, vol. 1, *Cognitive process analyses of aptitude*. Hillsdale, N.J.: Erlbaum.

Rothkopf, E. Z. (1976). Writing to teach and reading to learn. In N. L. Gage (ed.), *The psychology of teaching methods (75th Yearbook of NSSE)*. Chicago: University of Chicago Press.

Rothkopf, E. Z., & Bisbicos, E. E. (1967). Selective facilitative effects of interspersed questions on learning from written material. *Journal of Educational Psychology*, 58, 56–61.

Schumaker, J. B., & Clark, F. L. (1982). *An approach to learning strategies training for groups of secondary students*. Research Monograph No. 11. Lawrence: University of Kansas Institute for Research in Learning Disabilities.

Shuell, T. J. (1980). Learning theory, instructional theory, and adaptation. In R. E. Snow, P-A. Federico, & W. E. Montague (eds.), *Aptitude, learning, and instruction*, vol. 2, *Cognitive process analyses of learning and problem solving*. Hillsdale, N.J.: Erlbaum.

———. (1986). Cognitive conceptions of learning. *Review of Educational Research*, 56, 411–436.

Sternberg, R. J. (1980). Sketch of a componential subtheory of human intelligence. *Behavioral and Brain Sciences*, 3, 573–584.

———. (1985). *Beyond IQ: A triarchic theory of human intelligence*. New York: Cambridge University Press.

———. (1986). *Intelligence applied: Understanding and increasing your intellectual skills*. San Diego: Harcourt Brace Jovanovich.

Sternberg, R. J., Ketron, J. L., & Powell, J. S. (1982). Componential approaches to the training of intelligent performance. In D. K. Detterman & R. J. Sternberg (eds.), *How and how much can intelligence be increased*. Norwood, N.J.: Ablex.

Wasserman, S. (1986, April). Teaching for thinking: The principal's role. *Canadian School Executive*, 3–10.

Watson, G., & Glaser, E. M. (1980). *Watson–Glaser critical thinking appraisal: Forms A & B*. Cleveland: Psychological Corporation.

Weikart, D. P., Rogers, L., Adcock, C., & McClelland, D. (1971). *The cognitively oriented curriculum: A framework for preschool teachers*. Urbana, Ill.: University of Illinois Press.

Weinstein, C. E. (1978). Teaching cognitive elaboration strategies. In F. O'Neil, Jr. (ed.), *Learning strategies*. New York: Academic.

———. (1982). A metacurriculum for remediating learning strategies deficits in academically underprepared students. In L. Noel & R. Levitz (eds.), *How to succeed with academically underprepared students*. Iowa City: American College Testing Service, National Center for Advancing Educational Practice.

Weinstein, C. E., & Underwood, V. L. (1985). Learning strategies: The how of learning. In J. W. Segal, S. F. Chipman, & R. Glaser (eds.), *Thinking and learning skills*, vol. 1, *Relating instruction to research*. Hillsdale, N.J.: Erlbaum.

Whimbey, A., & Lockhead, J. (1982). *Problem solving and comprehension*. 3d ed. Philadelphia: Franklin Institute Press.

Wittrock, M. C. (1974). Learning as a generative process. *Educational Psychologist,* 11, 87–95.

———. (1986). Students' thought processes. In M. C. Wittrock (ed.), *Handbook of research on teaching.* New York: Macmillan.

Yussen, S. R., & Santrock, J. W. (1982). *Child development: An introduction.* Dubuque, Iowa: W. C. Brown.

7

Knowledge Maps as Tools for Thinking and Communication

Selby H. Evans and Donald F. Dansereau

A common activity in business and academic settings is the communication of ideas in briefings, lectures, and writing. Producing these communications requires decision making, problem solving, and other activities generally described as thinking. Understanding and using the communications also requires thought.

In this chapter we will describe our efforts to explore and improve the thinking processes involved in producing and receiving communications. We have chosen this arena for a number of reasons. First, there is a strong need to improve formal communications in businesses, government, and schools. Second, the public nature of communication makes the process and products of thinking available for examination.

As part of these efforts, we have been exploring an information-processing tool for examining and enhancing the production, comprehension, and use of communication. This tool, knowledge mapping, represents information in two-dimensional box-link displays. The boxes, or nodes, contain key ideas. The links express the relationship among these ideas. (See figure 7.1 for an example of a knowledge map and figure 7.2 for the set of links used in map construction.) Knowledge mapping can be used as a tool for preparing communication as a information-presentation device, or as a technique for understanding traditional forms of communication.

Knowledge maps have advantages over displays such as flowcharts and hierarchies in that maps can represent a variety of relationships and structures in a single display. The flexibility inherent in these maps allows for the representation of a wide range of abstract and concrete knowledge domains.

Figure 7.1
Knowledge Map Overview

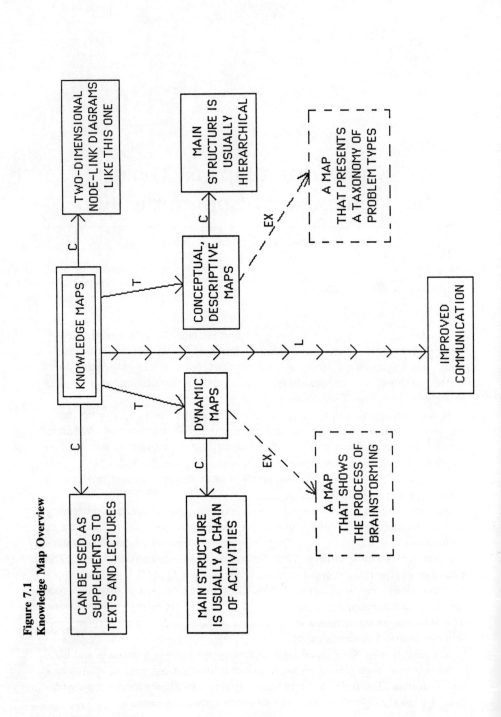

Figure 7.2
Link Types Used in Knowledge Mapping

DYNAMIC
--Generic/Canonical

    INFLUENCES

    NEXT

    LEADS TO

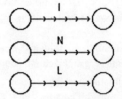

STATIC

--Generic/Canonical

    TYPE

    PART

    CHARACTERISTIC

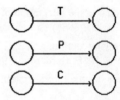

INSTRUCTIONAL

    ANALOGY

    EXAMPLE

    COMMENT

An examination of the general literature on mapping reveals a bewildering array of map types that are only loosely related to one another (e.g., concept maps—Novak & Gowin, 1984; webs—Cleland, 1981; mind maps—Buzan, 1974; networks—Holley et al., 1979; graphic organizers—Moore & Readence, 1984; idea maps—Armbruster & Anderson, 1984; cognitive maps—Diekhoff, 1982). The research with these maps has focused primarily on either map generation by students or student processing of expert maps.

Versions of student mapping have been used with students ranging in age from grade school (e.g., Bean et al., 1986; Pehrsson & Robinson, 1985) to college (e.g., Holley & Dansereau, 1984). Mapping has been used with special populations such as deaf students (Long & Addersley, 1984) and learning disabled students (Hagen-Heimlich & Pittelman, 1984; Sinatra et al., 1985). Student mapping has been used with both narrative material (e.g., Idol-Maestas & Croll, 1985), and expository text (e.g., Dansereau et al., 1979).

Writers in this field have claimed that the student production of knowledge maps can be valuable in

- examining the students' cognitive structures following presentation of traditional materials (e.g., Naveh-Benjamin et al., 1986)
- facilitating vocabulary development both before and after reading traditional text (e.g., Johnson & Pearson, 1984; Laurich, 1983)
- improving group discussion of a knowledge domain (e.g., Davidson, 1982; Diekhoff, 1982)
- enhancing learning from traditional text (Armbruster & Anderson, 1984; Barron, 1980; Cleland, 1981; Gillis, 1985; Hanf, 1971; Holley & Dansereau, 1984; Moore & Kirby, 1985)
- facilitating the integration of information from multiple texts (Bean et al., 1986; Readence et al., 1985)
- improving outlining (e.g., Hansell, 1978) and writing techniques (Draheim, 1983; Henry, 1986; Herrstrom, 1984)
- enhancing the representation of problems (e.g., McGuinness, 1986; Spurlin, 1982)

Students can also be provided with prepared knowledge maps as substitutes for typical academic and technical presentations or as supplements to texts and lectures. In comparison to purely verbal approaches, the use of expert maps has a number of potential advantages in the teaching/learning process:

- Map development assists the teacher (communicator) in understanding the nuances of the knowledge domain and helps in identifying portions of the domain that may pose learning difficulties (Camperell & Smith, 1982).
- Teacher-prepared maps provide an effective way of signaling the main ideas and macrostructure of a knowledge domain (Alvermann, 1986; Boothby & Alvermann, 1984; Darch et al., 1986).
- Expert maps inform students about the interrelationships of ideas and the logical connections between higher-order and lower-order concepts (Armbruster & Anderson, 1984).
- Presentation of maps leads to the formation of visual images that can be subsequently used to guide retrieval of verbal propositions (Amlund et al., 1985).
- The use of expert knowledge maps may help compensate for poorly developed verbal skills by engaging the students' spatial skills in the acquisition process (Hagen-Heimlich & Pittelman, 1984; Pehrsson & Robinson, 1985; Sinatra et al., 1985).

In spite of these potential advantages, the use of expert-generated knowledge maps has received little attention. Until recently, the cost of producing these nonlinear instructional materials was prohibitive. Laser printers and computer graphic capabilities have remedied this situation by providing effective ways to develop spatial presentations. The use of expert-produced knowledge maps has become practical, reasonable, and desirable.

The few published reports of the use of expert-generated maps generally indicate that they have some promise as prestudy aids (Alvermann, 1981; Camperell & Smith, 1982; Sinatra et al., 1984), poststudy aids (Moore & Readence, 1984), substitutes for typical text (Darch et al., 1986; Sinatra et al., 1985), and instructional aids (Horn, 1985; Stewart, 1984). But positive map effects have not been found for all materials (Alvermann, 1981) or under all learning conditions (Darch et al., 1986; Tyler et al., 1983).

This prior work suggests the potential of knowledge maps for enhancing communication, teaching, and learning. But most of the research is loosely controlled, relies primarily on self-report data, and has not examined important parameters such as map formats and individual differences. What is needed is a systematic program of research and development that will provide the necessary information for using maps in a real-world setting.

The mapping systems have not typically used the variety of "signaling" or knowledge-conveying capabilities available in node-link displays. These capabilities include distinguishable links, nodes, spatial configurations, and map unit organizations. Thus, the previously cited systems may not be exploiting the full potential of this spatial/verbal approach to communication and thinking.

We believe that the Texas Christian University (TCU) knowledge-mapping system and its accompanying research program respond to these shortcomings. This hybrid system incorporates all of the knowledge-conveying characteristics mentioned above. The research with this system has been well controlled and programmatic. Our recent research (Hall et al., 1989; Rewey et al., 1989; Skaggs et al., 1988) has focused on expert-produced knowledge maps as substitutes for and supplements to traditional text and lectures. The participants in these studies are college freshmen and sophomores, and the study materials are scientific and technical excerpts (e.g., circulatory system, digestive processes, experimental design issues) presented in knowledge map or traditional text format. (The information in these excerpts is equivalent to approximately 1,800-word text segments.) Delayed free-recall measures, supplemented by consumer satisfaction and processing questionnaires, serve as dependent measures. A sampling of results of these experiments follows:

1. Students are able to acquire more effective metaknowledge about the domain to be studied from a brief exposure to a map (4 min.) than from a brief exposure to text. They appear to have a better idea of how to budget their study time and are able to predict their subsequent free-recall performance more accurately.

2. Procedural/process maps (e.g., the flow through the digestive system) appear to be more effective than conceptually descriptive maps (e.g., a hierarchical description of

the renal system). The predominant processing route in the procedure/process maps may reduce confusion and nonproductive processing.

3. The procedural/process maps are generally more effective than their text counterparts, especially for the main ideas and structure of a knowledge domain. The parts of the maps that are visually more salient appear to be recalled better.

4. Maps may inhibit the processing of content-related pictures. The visual processing of the maps may interfere with the visual processing of the pictures.

5. Students with low prior knowledge about a subject area benefit greatly from the use of maps during lectures.

6. Maps facilitate cooperative interactions among students with high verbal ability.

HOW TO READ MAPS

The basic component of knowledge map (K-map) construction is the map unit, an organized set of maps on a specific topic. The map unit is analogous to a chapter or a chapter subsection in a typical text. A map describing a map unit, in sandwich form, is given in figure 7.3.

An *overview* map shows connections among main items. The overview map for problem solving is presented in figure 7.4. *Detail* maps elaborate on items that need elaboration (see figures 7.5, 7.6, and 7.7). *Alternative view* maps present overviews from different viewpoints judged by the author to be important in developing an understanding of the topic (see figure 7.8). A *Summary* map serves the traditional roles of a summary (see figure 7.9).

To use a map sandwich, first survey the overview map. Then decide what you want to get out of the material. Some common options are finding out what information is present in case you want to use it; understanding the information well enough to explain it to people, answer questions about it, or use it as background for something you have to do later; or carrying out the procedure it describes.

The main steps in the procedure march down the midline or spine (see figure 7.4). To get a general idea of what the map is about, you need only to look down the spine. The items in the spine are abstract terms denoting events. In a procedure, the terms refer to things you do to carry out the procedure. As you look down the list, note that some of the items are familiar. For example, "Recognize there is a problem" is obvious. Other items are sufficiently familiar that you have a general idea about the meaning but would need more information to carry out the actions. For example, "Generate solutions" is clear enough about the products of the step, but most people would feel that it is not helpful by itself. A natural reaction to this item is "Tell me how." In other cases, the item may be quite unfamiliar. This overview does not use technical terms, but it does use common expressions in a technical sense. "Specify the problem" and "Develop action plan" may be uninformative unless the reader known the meanings of the key terms in this context. Natural reactions would

Figure 7.3
The Map Sandwich

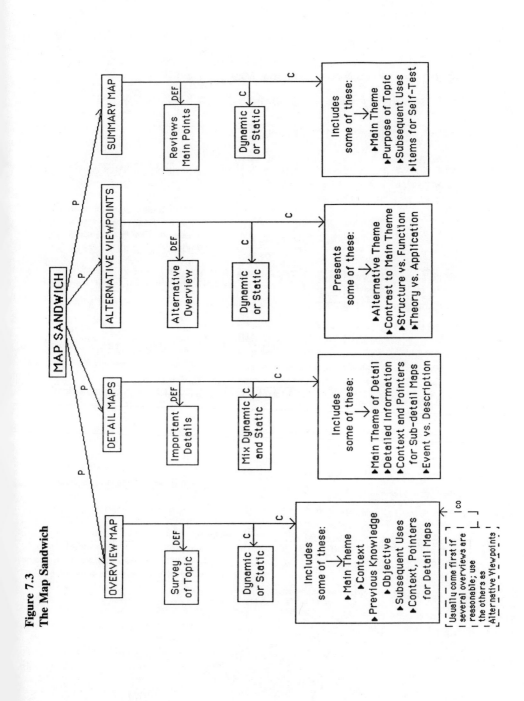

Figure 7.4
Elementary Problem Solving: Overview Map

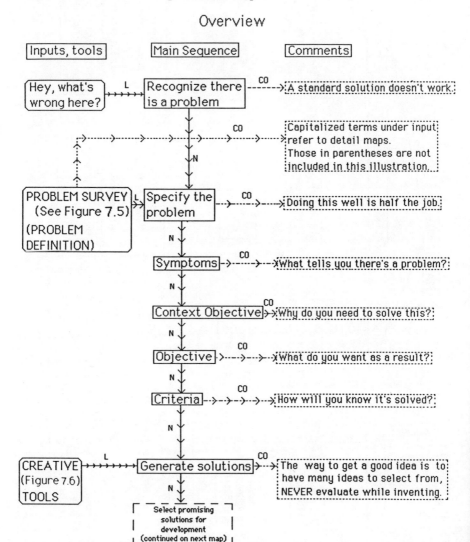

Figure 7.4—*Continued*

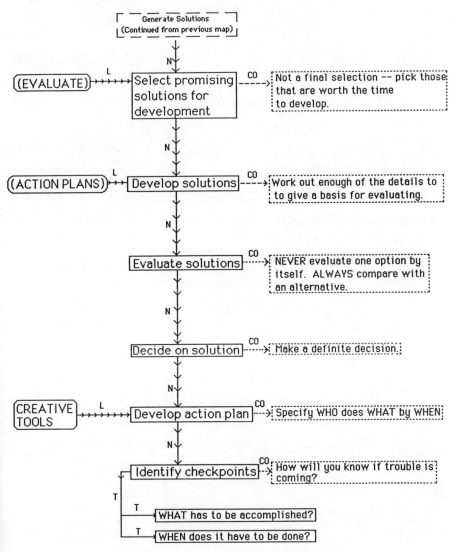

Figure 7.5
Detail Map: Problem Survey

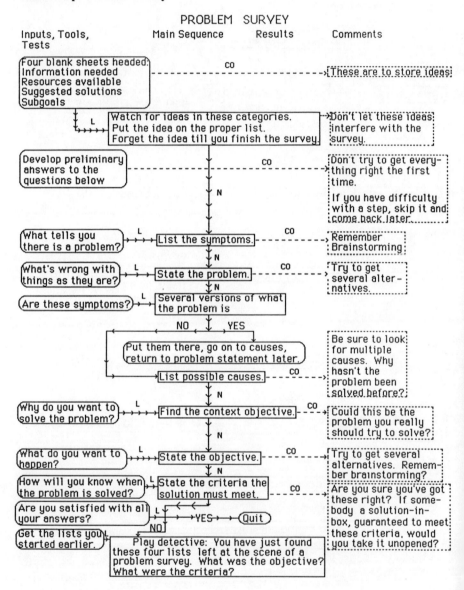

PROBLEM SURVEY

Inputs, Tools, Tests	Main Sequence	Results	Comments

Four blank sheets headed:
Information needed
Resources available
Suggested solutions
Subgoals

co

These are to store ideas

Watch for ideas in these categories.
Put the idea on the proper list.
Forget the idea till you finish the survey.

Don't let these ideas interfere with the survey.

Develop preliminary answers to the questions below

co

Don't try to get everything right the first time.

If you have difficulty with a step, skip it and come back later.

N

What tells you there is a problem?

List the symptoms.

co

Remember Brainstorming

N

What's wrong with things as they are?

State the problem.

co

Try to get several alternatives.

N

Are these symptoms?

Several versions of what the problem is

NO   YES

Put them there, go on to causes, return to problem statement later.

List possible causes.

co

Be sure to look for multiple causes. Why hasn't the problem been solved before?

N

Why do you want to solve the problem?

Find the context objective.

co

Could this be the problem you really should try to solve?

N

What do you want to happen?

State the objective.

co

Try to get several alternatives. Remember brainstorming?

N

How will you know when the problem is solved?

State the criteria the solution must meet.

co

Are you satisfied with all your answers?

YES   Quit

NO

Get the lists you started earlier.

Play detective: You have just found these four lists left at the scene of a problem survey. What was the objective? What were the criteria?

Are you sure you've got these right? If somebody a solution-in-box, guaranteed to meet these criteria, would you take it unopened?

106

Figure 7.6
Detail Map: Creativity Tools

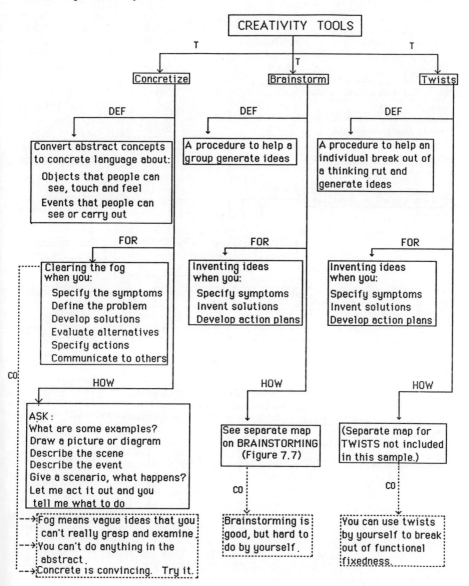

CREATIVITY TOOLS

T   T   T

Concretize   Brainstorm   Twists

DEF   DEF   DEF

Convert abstract concepts
to concrete language about:

Objects that people can
see, touch and feel

Events that people can
see or carry out

A procedure to help a
group generate ideas

A procedure to help an
individual break out of
a thinking rut and
generate ideas

FOR   FOR   FOR

Clearing the fog
when you:

Specify the symptoms
Define the problem
Develop solutions
Evaluate alternatives
Specify actions
Communicate to others

Inventing ideas
when you:

Specify symptoms
Invent solutions
Develop action plans

Inventing ideas
when you:

Specify symptoms
Invent solutions
Develop action plans

CO

HOW   HOW   HOW

ASK:
What are some examples?
Draw a picture or diagram
Describe the scene
Describe the event
Give a scenario, what happens?
Let me act it out and you
tell me what to do

See separate map
on BRAINSTORMING
(Figure 7.7)

(Separate map for
TWISTS not included
in this sample.)

CO   CO

Fog means vague ideas that you
can't really grasp and examine

You can't do anything in the
abstract.

Concrete is convincing. Try it.

Brainstorming is
good, but hard to
do by yourself.

You can use twists
by yourself to break
out of functional
fixedness.

Figure 7.7
Detail Map: Brainstorming

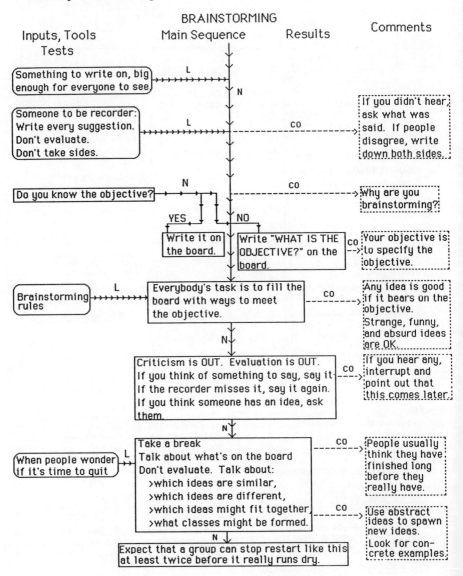

BRAINSTORMING

Inputs, Tools Tests	Main Sequence	Results	Comments

Something to write on, big enough for everyone to see. — L

N

Someone to be recorder: Write every suggestion. Don't evaluate. Don't take sides. — L — co → If you didn't hear, ask what was said. If people disagree, write down both sides.

Do you know the objective? — N — co → Why are you brainstorming?

YES / NO

Write it on the board. | Write "WHAT IS THE OBJECTIVE?" on the board. — co → Your objective is: to specify the objective.

Brainstorming rules — L — Everybody's task is to fill the board with ways to meet the objective. — co → Any idea is good if it bears on the objective. Strange, funny, and absurd ideas are OK.

N

Criticism is OUT. Evaluation is OUT. If you think of something to say, say it. If the recorder misses it, say it again. If you think someone has an idea, ask them. — co → If you hear any, interrupt and point out that this comes later.

N

When people wonder if it's time to quit — L — Take a break. Talk about what's on the board. Don't evaluate. Talk about:
>which ideas are similar,
>which ideas are different,
>which ideas might fit together,
>what classes might be formed. — co → People usually think they have finished long before they really have.

co → Use abstract ideas to spawn new ideas. Look for concrete examples.

N

Expect that a group can stop restart like this at least twice before it really runs dry.

Figure 7.8
Elementary Problem Solving: Alternative View

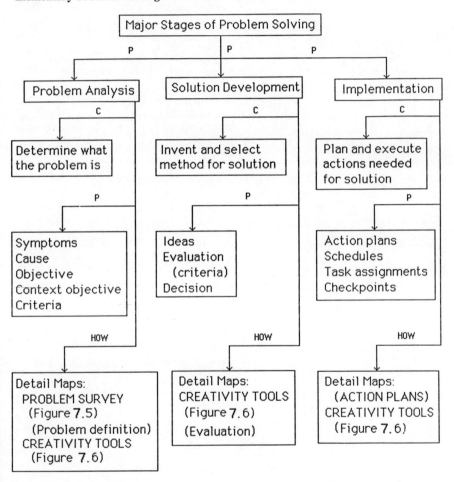

Figure 7.9
Elementary Problem Solving: Summary Map

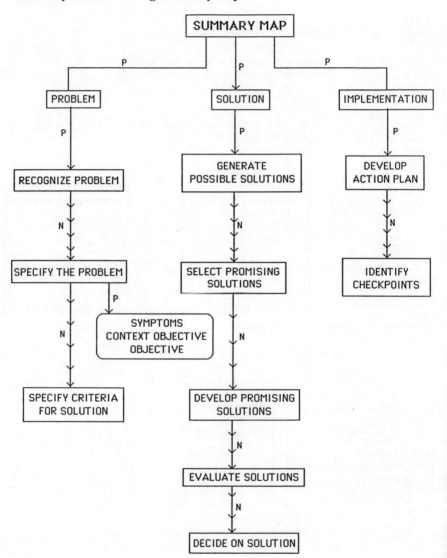

be: "What do you mean by *specify?*" and "What do you mean by *action plan?*"

After deciding what you want to get out of the material, trace through the overview map. Decide how familiar the information in each node is (quite familiar; generally familiar, but not in detail; unfamiliar, technical, or specialized concepts). You may want to mark the nodes to record your decision.

Next, check the supporting comments. All dynamic K-maps have supporting comments coming in from the right. These comments should not carry details essential to understanding the information, but they should provide support that particular readers may need to interpret the map. If you were wondering what is meant by an action plan, for example, you could look to the right and find the supporting comment, "Specify WHO does WHAT by WHEN." That does not tell you how to produce an action plan, but it does give an idea of what the author has in mind as a product.

At this point, some people will be thinking, "Why do I have to go down the spine first? Why couldn't I read the comments along with the spine?" You could. Perhaps you did, especially when the spinal item seemed a little vague. On the items that you found obvious, however, you may have ignored the comment.

One advantage of a map is that you can read it either way. In text, the comments are usually interleaved with the main items. You have to read the comments to get to the next main item. And if you forget something, you may have to scan through the whole thing again to find one comment.

For example, on this map there is a comment about capitalized terms in the input column and something about why a few are in parentheses. That is not relevant to the topic. You only need to know it if you start looking for detail maps. Some people would read it and remember it, but speaking for ourselves, we would remember it only when we noticed something like *(ACTION PLAN)* in parentheses. Then we would think, "Oh, yes. There was something about these terms in parentheses. Where was it?"

Check the inputs. All procedural K-maps have inputs coming in from the left. These inputs generally refer to tools or observations that contribute to the nodes they feed. If the tools are not already familiar to the reader, they will be included in the unit as detail maps. For any element in the spine that is familiar to you, there should be an input that tells you where to go for more information—a detail map, a reference source, or a commonsense operation.

In examining this overview, for example, "Specify the problem" might be unfamiliar. The expression obviously refers to some specialized product the author has in mind. The comments suggest that the step is important. Some elements of the activity are given and their comments provide an idea of what the author has in mind.

In this procedure, however, you expect some detailed instructions on how to specify the problem. The input "PROBLEM SURVEY" on the left indicates there is a detail map for that topic.

At this point you have a general idea of what is provided by the unit. You can select your strategy on the basis of what is there and what your objectives are. If you are just trying to get a general idea of what is provided in the unit, you might have all you need from the overview map. If not, or if your objective calls for learning in greater depth, go to the next step.

Survey any alternative view maps in the same way you did the overview. Note any items that you need more information about. Does any one of them present a view more compatible with your interests than the overview map? If so, treat that one as your overview map for subsequent work.

In the problem-solving example, one alternative view is given (see figure 7.8), a descriptive map presenting parts. A descriptive K-map presents major parts or types under the main subject. Below each part a K-map gives definitions, characteristics, and included elements as needed. This alternative view identifies three major stages, the things that go into them, and the detail maps that elaborate on them. Although a process map may be a more natural way to present the process of problem solving, the descriptive alternative view probably presents an organization that is easier to remember. Since it skips the time dimension, it invites examination either vertically or horizontally. It is inherently more abstract. That may help separate the woods from the trees.

On the basis of the overview and the alternative views, decide what further information you need to meet your objective.

•The first maps that deserve careful attention are those that present things that are generally familiar. Take them in whatever order interests you. If you do not have a preference, follow the general pattern of top to bottom and left to right on the map you are using as overview.

In the problem-solving example, the general pattern brings us to problem survey as the first detail map. Only a glance is needed to tell that it is another procedure. Again, the main sequence is down the middle. This time the inputs are specific instructions about what to do at each step. Again, the comments to the right offer assistance in case you want it.

In this map, the procedure includes results and tests on results. In some procedures, the main sequence is adequate to designate results. When results need to be described in more detail, or when there are tests on results, a position can be allowed for them at the right of the spine. Test questions, like other inputs, are put on the right.

Since the reader would come to this map with questions formulated from the survey of the overview map in mind, the obvious strategy is to look through it for the answers to the questions. The questions are probably "How do you do a problem survey?" and "Does this tell me enough so that I could actually do it?" You may want to examine the map with these questions in mind. If a person were to use the procedure in a real problem-solving situation, the map would be a convenient, step-by-step reference.

The next map suggested by the overview is creative tools (figure 7.6). This is a descriptive map with three types of tools. The link names show at a glance that the map gives essential characteristics for each type: definition, what it is used for, and how to use it. Those are probably just the questions the reader would have in mind.

Note that the characteristics are laid out in parallel. This layout lets you read the map either vertically, to find out about types, or horizontally, to compare characteristics. Most people would probably mix the two. A quick glance across to see what tools are presented, then a scan down each to see what it is and what it is used for.

If you are considering a set of tools, however, one question that comes to mind quickly is "How are these different?" You probably expect information to help select the right tool for the right job. A horizontal reading across the for nodes in the tool map proves for quick comparison among the tools.

The for nodes show immediately that concretize is used in more places than the others, that all three are used to specify the symptoms, and that concretize is not for inventing solutions. This parallel arrangement in a descriptive map allows for convenient access by attribute, as in answering the question, "What tools do I need for inventing solutions?"

For a simple procedure like concretize, the descriptive map can tell how in the node itself. If the instructions do not fit, the descriptive map can point to a lower level of detail map, as it does in the case of brainstorming (see figure 7.7).

The map on brainstorming is another procedural map. You already know how to read these. Look it over and decide whether it would offer advantages to someone who wanted to find out about brainstorming—or to someone who wanted to use it as a guide in a brainstorming session.

Those are all the detail maps we included in this illustration. That leaves the summary map (see figure 7.9). Usually the layout of a summary map will match the overview or one of the alternative views. Only the main points are mentioned. As a device for review, the summary map invites the reader to check recall. Any needed information should be easy to locate on the matching view map.

STRUCTURAL PROPERTIES
OF THE TCU KNOWLEDGE-MAPPING SYSTEM

There are two important components of the TCU knowledge-mapping system: (1) the structural properties of the resulting maps; and (2) the dynamic processes used to produce, comprehend, and use the maps. The links, nodes, spatial configurations, and unit organizations determine the structure of the maps produced by the TCU system.

Links

The links convey the relational information in the maps. They are arrows with names; they can be modified with adjectival symbols; they are directed by arrowheads; and they can be made virtually distinct with different lines.

The naming system is composed of a standard, canonical set of links that we have found useful in the mapping of most academic and technical domains (see figure 7.2). We have chosen to limit the number of canonical links to three groups of three, an arrangement favorable for short-term memory. That limit should ease the burden on both map authors and readers. This canonical system is supplemented by specialized links that are idiosyncratic to particular knowledge domains (e.g., a "proves" link that might be useful in mapping mathematical proofs).

Although educators and researchers may never agree on a single set of link names, systematically named links appear to enhance a knowledge-mapping system. They allow the map developer to use the links or relationship names to guide the search for information relevant to the domain. Named links on a finished map help the reader to interpret ambiguous relationships. The named links can also help the map user quickly find categories of information about a topic (e.g., "List all the characteristics of concept X"). Maps without named links lack these advantages.

For more precise specification of relationships, the TCU system uses link modifiers. For example, questionable relationships are modified by a question mark next to the link name. Positive and negative relationships are specified by + and − modifiers. These modifiers appear to be particularly useful in complex domains, such as science and mathematics, where students must make precise discriminations among relationships.

Arrowheads give the links direction. These arrowheads typically lead the reader from central to peripheral nodes and from one part of a process to another. In addition to specifying the relationship more precisely, the arrowheads give the reader suggested processing routes. When students are first exposed to maps, one of their main complaints is that they have difficulty arriving at a plan for studying the maps. Directional links, along with the spatial configuration, help to select appropriate paths.

Different kinds of links are represented by lines of distinctive appearance. For example, dynamic links such as "leads to" are represented by $\rightarrow\!\!\rightarrow\!\!\rightarrow\!\!\rightarrow$. These distinctive appearances help the reader rapidly locate classes of information. Other ways of creating link distinctiveness, such as the use of color and thickness, also have potential as signaling devices.

At this point, it is not clear which are the best ways of communicating link classes. One can easily overdo this signal system, however, and create maps that are aesthetically unpleasant and intimidating.

Nodes

The two most important aspects of nodes are their visual appearance and their content. As with the links, the appearance of the nodes (e.g., shape and color) is used to signal importance and to indicate the type of content they contain. This feature helps the reader in locating certain types of information.

Although the majority of the nodes contain domain-specific information (key ideas, propositions), some nodes are designed to serve placekeeping, encoding, and pointing functions. These nodes have the same function as headings, footnotes, and references in traditional text.

Spatial Configurations

The TCU system uses the spatial properties of maps to clarify the organization of a domain and to provide easy access to subcategories of information. "Gestalt" perceptual principles are used where possible to indicate symmetry, similarity, continuation, parallelism, and information gaps. Knowledge prototypes (i.e., structural schemas) are also used to organize the domain. These prototypes include descriptive hierarchies, logic and action chains, and concept clusters. The prototypes are emphasized by manipulating the appearance of the links and nodes.

Map Units

A map unit covers a delineated domain and is analogous to a chapter in a textbook or a lecture. In the TCU system, a map unit can be presented in a single, large map, or as a hierarchical set of interlocked maps. The large map may have advantages in providing an overall view of a domain and in providing easy reference during task performance. But size and complexity reduce the usefulness of these "whole" maps for instruction. An alternative is a cross-referenced set of maps to cover a domain, or a "map sandwich."

As described earlier, the map sandwich consists of an overview map that uses names and pointer nodes to refer to detail. The detail maps, next in the sandwich, elaborate the subtopics and can be extended by pointers to still more detailed maps if necessary. Alternative view maps may be included next. These survey the topic from a different viewpoint, showing structure, for example, if the overview map presented function. Finally, there is a summary map designed to help readers review the topic and their grasp of it.

This method produces less information per map. The resulting maps fit more easily on standard pages, overhead projectors, and computer screens. They may also be less intimidating and more easily treated as information chunks by the reader.

PRODUCING TCU KNOWLEDGE MAPS

The structural features described in the previous section provide a large array of potential combinations. But the practical and empirical evidence about these devices is so limited that most production decisions must be based solely on "face" validity. Just as writing styles in traditional language have evolved over hundreds of years, knowledge-mapping styles and conventions may be in flux for many years to come.

As a starting point, however, we have developed a systematic procedure for making maps. It is intended to help people get started in making a map and to provide a basic map-making procedure for research and development. While it may not fit everyone's style of authoring or every topic for maps, it does provide a frame of reference for preparing maps and for specifying the preparation as part of research on maps.

With its emphasis on named relationships, the K-map system naturally leads to a production plan based on relationships as a guide. This relationship- or link-guided search may follow a top-down or bottom-up approach.

Relationship-guided search (RGS) starts with a key node and a set of relations that the author considers relevant to the topic. The author uses the relations to generate additional nodes from the start nodes. The author asks, for example, "What are the characteristics of concept X? What does it lead to? Are there different types of X? Are there different parts?" As other key nodes emerge, the RGS is applied to them recursively.

To use a top-down path, the developer must know enough about the topic to anticipate a likely overall structure. That structure becomes the overview map. Once the overview is complete, the author can use RGS to identify the supplementary information needed for a complete presentation. In this approach, the author will usually start with a good idea of the appropriate set of relations.

The bottom-up approach would normally be used by novices in a particular domain. In this approach, the author selects a few obvious ideas (concepts) and applies the canonical relations shown in figure 7.2. This process will generate other nodes and also suggest the particular relations that are most suited to the objective and topic. As the appropriate link types become evident, the author selects an appropriate organizational structure (knowledge prototype) for the domain. The map is reorganized and fleshed out with further RGS.

USING KNOWLEDGE MAPS

Two main questions arise in connection with using maps: What kind of information is best suited to maps? In what contexts are they best applied?

Information Suited to Maps

Research cited earlier suggests that maps are particularly well suited to the presentation of processes or procedures—perhaps of any topic in which a clear sequential flow stands out as the main theme. A number of the maps in this chapter illustrate this use, as does the general use of flow charts in computer programming.

Hierarchies are another obvious application. Maplike presentations are routinely used in organizational charts and in the presentation of classification taxonomies. Presumably these choices attest to the applicability of maps for topics like these.

Descriptions of classes in an attribute space (illustrated in the map on creativity tools) seem to benefit substantially from the two-dimensional aspect of map presentation, although we have no direct evidence on the issue.

Diagnosis or decision methods lend themselves quite naturally to the use of maps, as illustrated in the map on "Is mapping suitable?" Again, the common use of flow charts for such presentation suggests recognition of this suitability.

Application Contexts

Maps may be of use either as part of a presentation or as a device to aid in preparing a presentation to appear in some other form.

As illustrated here, maps may be used as a supplement to printed text. We do not recommend them as a replacement for text, at least not with readers who are unfamiliar with reading maps. Readers may note, however, that by the time we got to the topic of producing maps, we were relying primarily on maps for presenting the information.

Maps fit quite well into a lecture format, where they may be displayed with an overhead projector or provided as lecture notes. We have information assessments from a limited sample of lecturers indicating considerable satisfaction with this application.

Maps may also be used as learning aids, either for individuals or peer groups. In such applications, maps may be presented with parts deleted to induce the active participation of the learners.

Aside from direct presentation to the learner, maps may be useful as tools for preparation of lectures or text. They may be particularly helpful in organizing the sequential presentation of material that is difficult to arrange in a single ordering.

REFERENCES

Alvermann, D. E. (1981). The compensatory effect of graphic organizers on descriptive text. *Journal of Educational Research, 75,* 44–48.
———. (1986). Graphic organizers: Cueing devices for comprehending and remembering main ideas. In J. F. Baumann (ed.), *Teaching main idea comprehension.* Newark, Del.: International Reading Association.
Amlund, J. T., Gaffney, J., & Kulhavy, R. W. (1985). Map feature content and text recall of good and poor readers. *Journal of Reading Behavior, 17,* 317–330.
Armbruster, B. B., & Anderson, T. H. (1984). Mapping: Representing informative text diagrammatically. In C. D. Holley & D. F. Dansereau (eds.), *Spatial learning strategies.* Orlando, Fla.: Academic.
Barron, R. F. (1980, December). *A systematic research procedure, organizers, and overviews: An historical perspective.* Paper presented at the National Reading Conference, San Diego, Calif.

Bean, T. W., Sorter, J., Singer, H., & Frazee, C. (1986, May). Teaching students how to make predictions about events in history with a graphic organizer plus options guide. *Journal of Reading,* 30, 739–745.

Boothby, P. R., & Alvermann, D. E. (1984). Classroom training study: The effects of graphic organizer instruction on fourth grader's comprehension. *Reading World,* 23, 325–329.

Buzan, T. (1974). *Using both sides of the brain.* New York: Dutton.

Camperell, K., & Smith, L. L. (1982, November). *Improving comprehension through the use of networking.* Presentation, Southeastern Regional Conference of the International Reading Association, Biloxi, Miss.

Cleland, C. J. (1981). Highlighting issues in children's literature through semantic webbing. *Reading Teacher,* 34, 642–646.

Dansereau, D. F., Collins, K. W., McDonald, B. A., Holley, C. D., Diekhoff, G., & Evans, S. H. (1979). Development and evaluation of an effective learning strategy training program. *Journal of Educational Psychology,* 71, 64–73.

Darch, C. B., Carnine, D. W., & Kameenui, E. J. (1986). The role of graphic organizers and social structure in content area instruction. *Journal of Reading Behavior,* 18, 275–295.

Davidson, J. L. (1982, October). The group mapping activity for instruction in reading and thinking. *Journal of Reading,* 26, 52–56.

Diekhoff, G. M. (1982). Cognitive maps as a way of presenting the dimensions of comparison within the history of psychology. *Teaching of Psychology,* 9, 115–116.

Draheim, M. E. (1983). *Facilitating comprehension and written recall of exposition through DRTA instruction and conceptual mapping.* Paper presented at the annual meeting of the National Reading Conference, Austin, Tex., November 29–December 3. ERIC Document #ED 246–406.

Gillis, M. K. (1985). *Strategies for mapping content texts.* Paper based on a workshop presented by M. K. Gillis and Bonnie Longnion, 13th Annual Meeting of the Texas State Council of the International Reading Association, Dallas, March.

Hagen-Heimlich, J., & Pittelman, S. D. (1985). *Classroom applications of the semantic mapping procedure in reading and writing.* Program Report 84-4. Madison: Wisconsin Center for Education Research, University of Wisconsin.

Hall, R. H., Dansereau, D. F., & Skaggs, L. P. (1989, April). *Knowledge maps and the presentation of related information domains.* Presented at the annual meeting of the American Educational Research Association, San Francisco, Calif.

Hanf, M. B. (1971). Mapping: A technique for translating reading into thinking. *Journal of Reading,* 14, 225–230, 270.

Hansell, T. (1978). Stepping up to outlining. *Journal of Reading,* 22, 248–252.

Henry, L. H. (1986). Clustering: Writing (and learning) about economics. *College Teaching,* 34, 89–93.

Herrstrom, D. S. (1984). Technical writing as mapping description onto diagram: The graphic paradigms of explanation. *Journal of Technical Writing and Communication,* 14, 223–240.

Holley, C. D., & Dansereau, D. F. (1984). *Spatial learning strategies.* New York: Academic.

Holley, C. D., Dansereau, D. F., McDonald, B. A., Garland, J. C., & Collins, K. W.

(1979). Evaluation of a hierarchical mapping technique as an aid to prose processing. *Contemporary Educational Psychology,* 4, 227–237.

Horn, R. E. (1985). Results with structured writing using the information mapping writing service standards. In T. M. Duffy & R. Waller (eds.), *Designing usable texts.* Orlando, Fla.: Academic.

Idol-Maestas, L., & Croll, V. J. (1985). *The effects of training in story mapping procedure on the reading comprehension of poor readers.* Tech. Rep. #352, Champaign, Ill.: Center for the Study of Reading.

Johnson, D. D., & Pearson, P. D. (1984). *Teaching reading vocabulary.* 2d ed. New York: Holt, Rinehart & Winston.

Laurich, S. M. (1983). The effects of mind mapping with average and above average readers. Unpublished master's seminar paper, University of Maryland.

Long, G., & Addersley, S. (1984). Networking: Application with hearing-impaired students. In C. D. Holley & D. F. Dansereau (eds.), *Spatial learning strategies.* Orlando, Fla.: Academic.

McGuinness, C. (1986). Problem representation: The effects of spatial arrays. *Memory & Cognition,* 14, 270–280.

Moore, D. W., & Readence, J. E. (1984). A quantitative and qualitative review of graphic organizer research. *Journal of Educational Research,* 78, 11–17.

Moore, P. J., & Kirby, J. R. (1985). *The effects of spatial organizers on text comprehension.* Presentation, 30th annual meeting of the International Reading Association, New Orleans, La., May.

Naveh-Benjamin, M., McKeachie, W. J., Lin, Y., & Tucker, D. G. (1986). Inferring students' cognitive structures and their development using the "Ordered Tree Technique." *Journal of Educational Psychology,* 78, 130–140.

Novak, J. D., & Gowin, D. B. (1984). *Learning how to learn.* New York: Cambridge University Press.

Pehrsson, R. S., & Robinson, H. A. (1985). *The semantic organizer approach to writing and reading instruction.* Rockville, Md.: Aspen.

Readence, J. E., Bean, T. W., & Baldwin, R. S. (1985). *Content area reading: An integrated approach.* Dubuque, Iowa: Kendall/Hunt.

Rewey, K. L., Dansereau, D. F., Skaggs, L. P., Hall, R. H., & Pitre, U. (1989, April). *Effects of knowledge maps and scripted cooperation on the recall of technical material.* Presented at the annual meeting of the American Educational Research Association, San Francisco, Calif.

Sinatra, R. C., Berg, D., & Dunn, R. (1985). Semantic mapping improves reading comprehension of learning disabled students. *Teaching Exceptional Children,* Summer, 310–314.

Sinatra, R. C., Stahl-Gemake, J., & Berg, D. N. (1984). Improving reading comprehension of disabled readers through semantic mapping. *Reading Teacher,* 37, 22–29.

Skaggs, L. P., Dansereau, D. F., & Hall, R. H. (1988). *The effects of knowledge maps and pictures on the acquisition of scientific information.* Presented at the annual meeting of the American Educational Research Association, San Francisco, Calif., April.

Spurlin, J. E. (1982). Utility of networking procedure for personal problem solving: Mapping of text anxiety. Ph.D. diss., Texas Christian University.

Stewart, J. H. (1984). The representation of knowledge: Curricular and instructional implications for science teaching. In C. D. Holley & D. F. Dansereau (eds.), *Spatial learning strategies: Techniques, applications, and related issues*. Orlando, Fla.: Academic.

Tyler, S. W., Delaney, H., & Kinnucan, M. (1983). Specifying the nature of reading ability differences and advance organizer effects. *Journal of Educational Psychology, 75,* 359–373.

PART 2

SPECIFIC APPLICATIONS TO SCHOOL CONTENT

In this section the role of learning and thinking skills is discussed in relation to specific content. In chapter 8, Robert S. Patterson and Sharon I. Jamieson present the view that courses in the history of education for university students can be used to teach thinking skills as well as content. Because history is not just fact but also interpretation, they designed an approach to instruction that is characterized by student inquiry and investigation. They discuss the development and implementation of this approach, which is intended to promote a student's ability to think about history in a meaningful way, facilitating thinking skills such as judging, analyzing, reasoning, decision making, and evaluation.

In chapter 9, Dan G. Bachor discusses the role of thinking skills in arithmetic word problems with particular reference to instruction and assessment. Central to Bachor's discussion is the fact that both the problem and problem solver must be taken into consideration when determining how students think and behave and in making decisions about appropriate instructional strategies. In terms of instruction, Bachor stresses the importance of strategy competence over content coverage, and discusses an instructional procedure that moves from the student tentatively acquiring and applying effective problem-solving strategies to eventually becoming confident and in control of learning. In terms of assessment, Bachor stresses the importance of using a variety of assessment techniques to obtain a reasonable estimate of a student's thinking skills and describes a number of techniques that can provide information about a student's strategic behavior under a variety of conditions.

The next two chapters focus on the role that thinking plays in reading ability.

In Chapter 10, Che Kan Leong presents the acquisition of reading proficiency and language comprehension in relation to a multilevel, multicomponent model that emphasizes the cognitive processes involved. Leong briefly describes some of the componential subskills considered to be important in skilled reading performance as well as some of the tasks used to measure these subskills. The findings of some of the studies reviewed in this chapter support the view that reading involves the concurrent evaluation and computation of different kinds of cognitive and linguistic information in a relatively short amount of time and suggest that reading skills can be aided by the teaching of learning strategies.

In chapter 11, Gabriel J. Mancini, Robert F. Mulcahy, Robert H. Short, and Seokee Cho focus on metalinguistic awareness and its relationship to reading ability. After providing a review of metalinguistic awareness and its influence on reading acquisition, production, and development, these authors present information from one of their studies that investigated metalinguistic awareness across two age groups and four subgroups of reading ability. Some of their findings support the view that metalinguistic awareness is a cognitive construct that interacts with other cognitive activities in the reading process and that reading proficiency might be aided with instruction that encourages readers to reflect on what they do and do not know.

In the last chapter in this section, Gabriel J. Mancini, Robert H. Short, Robert F. Mulcahy, and Jac Andrews discuss the role of social cognition in child development with particular attention to assessment and instruction. Social competence is an area of concern for many teachers and parents, as witnessed by a rapidly growing body of research and increased support for including the training of social skills as part of standard school curriculum. The authors indicate that social competence is a multifaceted and complex concept. They also suggest that for individuals to be considered socially competent, they must demonstrate appropriate and adaptive levels of cognitive, affective, and behavioral performance in the context of their age and culture. They further suggest that social competence is probably determined by the interaction of numerous factors, such as personality, ability and level of development, the situation, and the social task, in addition to the manner in which social information is processed. Therefore, as with the assessment of social competence, intervention to improve it is complex and must take into consideration the interaction of behavioral, affective, and cognitive states.

8

Exploring the Teaching
of Thinking Skills in History

Robert S. Patterson
and Sharon I. Jamieson

History of education courses were among the first teacher education courses offered in Canadian universities and teacher education programs. Although they have fallen upon ''rough'' times in many institutions and programs, they still occupy a prominent place in the preparation of teachers. Initially, such content was viewed as essential in helping prospective teachers develop a sense of professionalism, including a commitment to teaching, an appropriate ethical sense, and an understanding of the issues and developments that contributed to the current status of the profession. More recently, where these courses remain in the teacher education curriculum, they are more likely to be justified on the grounds that they make a valuable contribution to the general education background of the student.

Throughout this evolutionary process, courses—regardless of their status in teacher education programs—have been taught with a primary emphasis on content mastery. While students may have been encouraged to think by examining conditions and events of the past, methods of instruction and evaluation have not been systematically focused on using history of education to teach thinking skills. Over the years students have criticized such courses as uninteresting and irrelevant to their goals as future teachers.

Years of experience in teaching and researching the history of education have led the authors to consider ways of teaching this content so students will find it both more interesting and more relevant to their eventual role as classroom teachers. Our investigations were guided by the belief that the continuous increase in historical information calls for a process rather than a content-mastery focus; and history is made more interesting if the student is expected to develop individual interpretations from close encounters with historical data. The belief that all courses taken in a teacher education faculty should illustrate and inform effective and imaginative teaching was also central to this undertaking.

Instructors of history could well afford to reflect on the reasons they are interested in history and the experiences that helped them acquire the essential skills in this field of study. The authors' examination of this matter led them to conclude that it is the formulation, investigation, and reflection on a research question that makes the study of history appealing. By learning how to pose significant questions, search and evaluate relevant documents of sources, and construct plausible accounts of the past, the student of history comes to understand and appreciate the significance of the enterprise. It is not so much the *product* as the *process* that evokes student interest and contributes to the development of valuable skills.

This process of reconstruction involves sifting through pictures, documents, newspapers, and personal diaries and making decisions about what these mean in the context of the period. For the historian there is excitement, romance, and risk in this reconstruction process. There is also an understanding that the task is never completed and that the answers given are subject to reinterpretation by others. The historian knows history is not fact, but interpretation.

Unfortunately, most undergraduate courses tend to direct students more to the products of historical research than involvement in the labor itself. Granted, there are places where reliance on the insight of others and their recounting of the past is sufficient for students. Given the amount of historical knowledge and the impossibility of mastering all of it, however, there is reason to argue for an emphasis on skill development, thinking like a historian, rather than on content mastery.

USING HISTORY TO TEACH THINKING SKILLS

Our project is founded on the belief that teacher education curricula should include courses that develop a sense of professionalism, commitment to teaching, ethical behavior, and an understanding of the issues and developments that influence the role of the teacher. We believe, however, that focusing on content mastery, while important, should not be the primary goal for a course on educational history. The primary goals should be to capture the interest of the student and to develop thinking skills related to history that will allow the student to use history as a basis for understanding the present. Inherent in this process is the development of thinking skills related to analyzing, judging, and reasoning.

Over a period of approximately ten years our project has evolved from a focus on the student's direct access to primary historical materials to a focus on teaching thinking through history. Initially, we were anxious to heighten student interest in the course content by enabling them to have access to photographs, documents, textbooks, interview data, and numerous other historical sources. Collecting, cataloguing, and storing materials were the major preoccupations of our lives. The size and variety of the collection expanded, eventually including over 12,000 visual images, several thousand questionnaire responses, and hundreds of documents, papers, and books. This rapid expansion and the richness and variety of the collection led us to explore other, more innovative uses of the materials. We knew, by this time, we were correct in our hypothesis that student interest is increased by direct access to original historical sources. Students in our classes responded very positively to the collection of materials used to illustrate our teaching. They welcomed the chance to delve into the materials for purposes of their own investigations into the past. When asked to comment on the course one student indicated:

I have learned a lot when I think about it because there was no pressure. I didn't have to sit down and memorize names and dates, etc., for hours. I think I retained a lot more information and a lot more important information because I was reading all of the materials. I was interested and I wanted to learn not because I had to memorize all the information to pass an exam. I think that the approach used has enabled me to have a much more positive attitude towards history. I could read the materials without having to memorize names and dates—this is not to say though that I haven't remembered these names and dates—surprisingly enough I think I have. But with this approach it has allowed me to enjoy what I have learned rather than seeing it as a chore or an annoyance.

This success encouraged us to consider ways of reorienting our teaching from a more traditional content-mastery approach to one characterized by student inquiry and investigation. The central purpose was learning skills essential to the historian's task. At the same time, we were eager to package and present the materials in a readily available form so students could access them quickly and conveniently. The answer we settled on was to prepare a series of curriculum kits made up of original materials relevant to selected historical themes associated with the course. Considerable effort and expense helped ensure that these kits were attractive, appealing, and filled with informative and useful resources.

It was one thing, albeit a very demanding assignment, to collect, catalogue, and store the materials and then to present them to the students in ways that would help ensure their interest. It was an even more challenging task to rethink and reshape our teaching so that skill mastery replaced fact learning as the primary focus of the course. We had to direct our attention, as instructors, to an understanding of the skills we were pursuing and to the methods of instruction and evaluation that would be in harmony with this pursuit.

There was a need to find ways of assessing historical thinking skills levels prior to and following our instruction. We needed to remind ourselves and our students, constantly, of the inquiry-centered focus of our teaching. The students, who were almost totally without any personal learning experiences of this nature, required considerable support and encouragement to continue in this endeavor.

The approach this course is taking seems to be foreign to most of us. It is extremely difficult to adjust to not having generalizations spelled out for us. In most courses that we have been exposed to, we are expected to view material, store it, then regurgitate it at a later date, but for this course, we are on our own for the most part. It is our job to explore, discover and to draw conclusions from the material at our disposal. During the outset of our dealings with the topic, I felt intimidated and insecure by the activities we participated in. It seemed that nothing concrete was developing, that the course was set up only to test our skills to think quick under pressure. Still I stuck with it because I felt that maybe I wasn't giving this foreign approach its full credit. I am glad I stuck with it, because I am beginning to think more carefully about the issues.

They did persist, however, and at the conclusion of the course provided very positive feedback for both the curriculum kits and the unique purpose and methods of the course.

In the beginning, I did not have an adequate understanding of the nature of the skill-centered objectives but have since come to a greater understanding in a rather unique way. I am also taking a curriculum course in social studies right now, and the instructor is very enthusiastic about the new curriculum in that area and the point of view which it takes. While it is not labelled overtly "progressive" many of the elements are so similar as to be almost indistinguishable. What happened to really give me a jolt was that I started questioning and analyzing the material much the same way we had been questioning our material in class. My critical thinking skills have been developed to the point that I don't just passively receive information but immediately begin to question such things like validity, consider the source, look at time frames, etc., etc. Again I must say that this process happened almost on an unconscious level. For a long time I didn't even realize I was doing it until all of a sudden it hit me, because I was always asking questions! Great!

Rather than refine and consolidate the insights associated with this initial thinking skills project, we decided to extend our experimentation to include use of videodisk and computer technology in both aspects of our project: effective and interesting presentation of the historical collection and the teaching of the skills of analyzing, judging, and reasoning. The shift to technology reopened many of the concerns we had addressed in another form during the curriculum kit phase of our experiment. We needed to familiarize ourselves with the new technology, add team members who could provide the needed expertise, and consider ways of cataloguing and accessing materials stored on the disks or in the computer files. We also had to prepare new materials such as video vi-gnettes and computerized tutorials. The use of technology required a greater clarity in our course objectives, methodologies, and evaluation systems. This was essential for communication with the instructional design team and the programmers who would translate our ideas into computer-based instructional packages.

COURSE OBJECTIVES

We designed our course with the belief that history as a subject of study should provide the learner, first and foremost, with the power to reason, analyze, and judge historical events. Rather than be mere uncritical consumers of other people's observations about the past, students of history need to acquire the skills necessary to make intelligent judgments of their own. The problems related to the educational system within an information society led us to a rationale that learner strategies should focus on the development of thinking skills rather than on straight content acquisition. The focus of course content is teacher education, reform movements, progressive education, immigrant education, and native education. The overall objectives are:

1. To interest the student in the study of educational history.

2. To have the student experience history as directly as possible through presentation of historical sources.

3. To develop the student's ability to think about history in a meaningful way; specifically, to focus on judging, reasoning, and analyzing.

4. To prove a broad enough context for the experience so that it transcends the specific course and is applicable in other learner experiences.

5. To increase the learner's literacy in the use of information technologies. (This fifth objective was added as we moved from the traditional classroom instructor delivery mode to a technology-mediated mode.)

THE METHODOLOGY

In developing the methodology for meeting the course objectives we identified four significant aspects: the structure of the classroom, the processes, levels of learner development, and the evaluation strategies. We discovered a need to reconceptualize the learner environment to accommodate a different presentation mode: the interactive videodisk.

Instructor-mediated learner environments allow the instructor to bring a whole repertoire of instructional strategies to the classroom. Instruction in an inquiry-based course is very much an interactive process between the instructor and the students and among the students. Questioning, discussing, responding, critiquing, turning an idea or position over and looking at the other side, folding the sometimes loosely connected ideas and interests of the student into the overall goals of the course, are all instructional strategies used in the inquiry-based classroom.

The instructor offers an invitation and encouragement for students to develop the ability to question and critically evaluate or, as specified in this particular course, analyze, judge, and reason. There are no right or wrong answers, just the increasing ability to analyze, judge, and reason. How could the yes/no architecture of computer technology deal with this type of learner environment?

We do not pretend to know the answer to this question yet. We have discovered that in a technologically mediated learner environment it is easier to set up a self-paced structure that allows students to move at their own speed and ability level through the materials. This has challenged us to develop course segments at more than one level of ability. We are still seeking a balance between classroom interaction time and technologically mediated time. We have tended to take the position that the technology should be brought in at times but does not constitute the total course experience.

There are many inquiry-based methods. Fenton's six-step methodology provided a useful model for our instructional design:

1. Identification of a problem or issue from examination of data. This entails asking questions based on analysis of materials.
2. Formulating hypotheses from the data analysis thereby intelligently shaping further study by application of reason and analysis.
3. Recognizing the logical implications of hypothesis thinking through alternatives and consequences.
4. Gathering data.
5. Analyzing, evaluating, and interpreting data.
6. Evaluating the hypothesis in light of the data.

The thinking skills we have focused on—analyzing, judging, and reasoning—operate, to varying degrees, in each of the six steps. The steps have been presented in a linear sequential way. The process is, in fact, recursive with a continuing evaluation of extant understandings based on new knowledge.

For the purposes of our work we have defined the skills of judging, reasoning, and analyzing, as follows.

Analyzing implies an ability to separate or isolate constituent parts or elements by asking pertinent questions. Thus students developing and refining this skill when confronted with historical source materials will be able to identify relevant and significant pieces of information from among numerous alternatives, so as to be able to use these elements in understanding and describing the whole.

Judging is comparable to evaluating. It operates both at the level of determining the importance and validity of the source as well as at the content level within the source, wherein decisions must be made as to relevance and significance. Those exhibiting this skill will be able to determine quality of evidence for specific conclusions.

Reasoning as a skill implies the ability to interrelate, to trace consequences, to make sound inferences, and to build a defensible argument established through reference to evidence.

We have struggled over whether these three skills can be dealt with separately or whether they must be dealt with as a total package when assessing the ability of the student. Our definitions suggest they can be dealt with separately. Our attempts to conceptualize evaluation strategies that identify each of the skills separately have indicated that the problem is more complex than the definitions suggest.

LEVELS OF MASTERY

The objectives of the course are not only to teach the skills of analyzing, judging, and reasoning but to take the student to increasing levels of ability in using these skills. Our ideal is to position each student at some level in a thinking ability hierarchy and to bring that student to a higher level. This requires an ability to individualize instruction and to allow students to move through the course at their own pace. Clearly, if we can develop the computer courseware, we will be more able to tailor the course activities to the individual levels of the student than the standard classroom instructional mode.

As indicated earlier, the process of organizing the content for the course has meant we have not yet attended to some aspects of the course development. Identifying and assessing the stages of development that a student will move through in developing the ability to analyze, judge, and reason is rooted in an understanding of cognitive theory and the emergent area of teaching thinking. While we have not yet established a taxonomy of thinking skills that will enable us to assess student abilities, our course structure is based on a notion of increasing demand on the student's thinking abilities.

While our suggested taxonomy (see table 8.1) should be considered tentative, it is an attempt to reflect on and lay out what we understand to be the levels of complexity that a student will go through within the course structure. The student's experience moves through a very structured, limited utilization of historical sources and skills to an opening out of the world of history both in terms of the sources available as well as the critical perspectives possible for arriving at a position. The activities in the classroom will have four components: lectures, individualized instruction using the interactive videodisk, self-directed instruction with the computer tutorials, and group interactions (small group discussions, debates, and presentations).

ADAPTATIONS

It is important to understand that our project is developmental in nature. As we moved through different stages we adapted our goals to reflect what we have learned. Also, as different people have participated in the project they

Table 8.1
A Hierarchical Organization of Course Structure

LEVEL	ACTIVITIES	SOURCES
I.	Student is asked to: 1. read a single document. 2. identify the constituent parts. 3. judge on the relevance, importance of the constituent parts.	Limited in length, quantity and variety. A single one-page newspaper article.
II.	Student is: 1. given a focusing question. 2. asked to select from a variety of sources. 3. asked to identify the constituent parts of each source selected. 4. asked to judge on the relevance, importance, and comprehensiveness of sources. 5. asked to formulate a position. 6. asked to substantiate position based on the constituent parts selected.	Contextualizing documentary. Simulation of period to engage student interest. Increase in variety of sources. Less control on length. Increase in number of sources.
III.	Student is asked to: 1. reflect on alternative positions to the one taken in the previous exercise. 2. review materials. 3. formulate an alternative position. 4. substantiate alternative position based on evidence drawn from sources. 5. assess the relative merit of the two positions.	Same resources as in II. Additional contextualizing information. Tutorials on political systems.

Table 8.1—*Continued*

LEVEL	ACTIVITIES	SOURCES
IV.	Student is asked to: 1. pose their own questions regarding a specific educational issue. 2. identify and select relevant sources. 3. formulate a position. 4. present and debate their position in classroom context.	Sources provided both in a structured way within the classroom and in an unstructured way—moving the student out into libraries, archives, etc. Tutorials on the skills of a historian are provided.
V.	Student is asked to: 1. investigate a critical perspective such as Marxism, feminism, etc. 2. identify and select relevant sources. 3. formulate a position situated in the critical perspective chosen. 4. substantiate the position based on the sources and critical perspective.	Increasing removal of structure from sources. Tutorials on critical perspectives.

have brought their own perspective to the endeavor. At times this has been an uncomfortable and painful experience.

The decision to bring the student as close to real source material as possible and to use an inquiry method in the classroom meant the incorporation of a tremendous amount of information into a methodological structure that attempts to work on the individual interests of the students and to fold these interests into the goals of the course.

Visions of students buried under the massive weight of historical sources and the instructor attempting to shovel them out are not unrealistic. Obviously, the instructional design model had to be carefully worked out and, as we moved through the project, technology became an increasingly useful tool for managing massive amounts of information and controlling student access until they had the ability to deal with increasing amounts of information. The first phase of the project, which involved the development of curriculum kits, was not too difficult because the materials were still under direct instructor control. It was when we moved from the curriculum kits to the use of more advanced technologies that we encountered increasing difficulty.

We discovered that the impact of the instructional design model and the use of technology on the role of the instructor is significant. This is where we have had the most difficulty in furthering the course development. It seems we have embarked on a project that requires a role change for the instructor.

Our problem was to imagine how we could create the same type of interaction necessary in the inquiry method while using an interactive videodisk computerized instructional delivery. Our inability to conceptualize how a system could deal with this stems from two factors: (1) we continued to construct our course around the traditional classroom lecture model; and (2) we had no models to show us how to do otherwise. We have been fortunate to have a leading instructional designer work with us on the project. But this has, at times, been a source of frustration as we have tended to stubbornly resist changing our world from the classroom to the unknown, and the different structures and models introduced by the instructional designer are not easily understood.

We have at times faced circumstances where the evident limitations of the technology have required us to make a choice between what is technologically sound as opposed to what makes sense to use in the teacher-learner environment. An example of this was our attempt to place the student in a historical context through simulation strategies. Here was an example of the technology setting up a problem that would not have occurred in the "traditional" classroom context. When we designed the first lesson we provided some information that students could not possibly know if they were actually in situ. We faced the problem of compromising a "pure" simulation strategy in the face of the knowledge that we had an opportunity to create a curiosity in the student that would provide a hook for future instructional objectives. The debate still rages over this particular problem.

AN EXAMPLE

The shift to the use of videodisk and computer technology necessitated considerable rethinking of our instructional strategies and materials. There were new challenges to face, such as how and when to prepare the students for use of the equipment. There was also a need to consider whether we should expect students to begin working on some of the more encompassing questions that we had employed with the curriculum kits.

One alternative was to prepare an introductory unit designed to orient students to the skills, equipment, methodology, and evaluation system associated with the course. We opted for this latter alternative in the belief that this approach would help to reduce student frustration and confusion and that it could be used to stimulate interest in the overall endeavor through the use of interesting materials and tasks.

We searched for a historical incident within the time frame of our course to use as a "hook" on which to capture student interest. The result was the selection of an incident that occurred in 1939 in Alberta. Candidates in a Calgary municipal election challenged the content of a newly published intermediate school textbook. According to one or two of the aldermanic candidates, the textbook material was biased in favor of nazism and communism and needed to be altered or removed.

Having selected our focal topic, we next gave consideration to the ways in which we wanted to employ the subject matter to attract student interest and to teach the skills of analyzing, judging, and reasoning. It was decided that we would engage the students by creating a video simulation, supposedly in the office of the deputy minister of education, Mr. McNally. In the simulation the deputy minister appears to be speaking directly to the student about an assignment. The student is asked to investigate the allegations about the textbook and to report back in a week with a recommended course of action.

In the process of investigating students are given a choice of a limited number of resources. These choices are presented on a computerized menu screen.

SOURCES MENU

WHICH OF THE FOLLOWING WOULD YOU SELECT?

Newspapers

Books

Interviews

Department of Education Files

The students make their selection by touching one of the capitalized letters. If, for example, they choose *N* a new screen is presented that offers a choice of newspapers to consult.

NEWSPAPER MENU

WHICH OF THE FOLLOWING NEWSPAPERS WOULD YOU LIKE TO CONSULT?

Calgary Herald	Edmonton Bulletin
Calgary Albertan	Edmonton Journal
Lethbridge Herald	Red Deer Advocate
High River Times	Vegreville Observer

If students select, for example, the *Calgary Albertan,* a query screen comes up asking students to identify the time period they are interested in. A selection of November 16, 1939, would result in the following information presented on the screen.

The CALGARY ALBERTAN for November 16, 1939 contains 5 related articles:

Article one

Article two

Article three

Article four

Article five

The students are asked to select as many of these articles for study as they feel are necessary or critical to a sound understanding of the textbook issue from the perspective of the newspapers. There may be different viewpoints expressed because of regional interest, the time the article was written, or the political or ideological leaning of a paper. Part of this lesson is to help students recognize these possible differences and enable them to see how sampling techniques can be employed to lessen the need to review all the articles.

The other central thrust of this exercise is aimed at helping students identify key ideas or opinions expressed in the articles that might assist them in the recommendation they are to make to the deputy minister or that they need to investigate further through other sources. The students are asked to review the articles viewed on a computer screen and to select significant segments within the article. These segments are "remembered" by the instructional system and collected into an investigation file.

The students are allowed to make as many newspapers and segment selections as they feel are warranted. They are then asked to review their investigation file. They are asked to consider whether the items in the file are significant to the matter under review and they are given the opportunity to discard irrelevant segments.

The students are then asked to consider the reliability and credibility of the segments selected and to identify any problems related to personal or group bias, ideological or political leanings, or ambiguity in meaning. The students will be asked to make a recommendation to the deputy minister and to substantiate the recommendation from the segments selected. The students are given a choice of four possible recommendations: (1) withdraw the text, (2) edit the text, (3) do nothing, or (4) continue to investigate. They are asked to select one option and assess the items in their investigation file as strongly supporting, moderately supporting, or not supporting the position they have chosen.

The students' choices will be evaluated in a combination of ways. A group of educational historians were asked to review the materials used and identify substantiating segments for each of the four positions. They were also asked to identify any problems regarding credibility and ambiguity of the material. The student choices are compared with the "expert" opinion and feedback is provided, not necessarily as the right answer, but to show students how historians might deal with the problem. A cautionary note is provided to students at the time they are asked to make a recommendation that acknowledges the sources as too limited to justify a recommendation.

The students' choices are also evaluated in terms of the number of items selected and their choices of substantiating segments compared with their identification of problems related to ambiguity or credibility. A segment identified by students as either ambiguous or of doubtful credibility should not be identified as strongly substantiating their recommendation.

Up to this point students work on their own with the computerized instructional system. Once they have come to a point where they have made a recommendation they are drawn back into classroom discussion. This provides an opportunity for students who share the same view to enrich their support or justification for their stance. Once the position is articulated, including any observations the instructor might wish to add, an opportunity is extended to class members to challenge, question, or refute it. In addition, students of differing viewpoints have the opportunity to debate one position with another.

The purpose of the interaction is primarily to teach students to break down or analyze the news items with sufficient care and intelligence, to note differing arguments or similar concerns, and to observe that some reporters are not dealing with a common point of information.

An effort is made to have the class note readily observable differences such as those in the editorials of the *Lethbridge Herald,* the *Edmonton Journal,* or the *Vegreville Observer.* When these items are juxtaposed, time is spent trying to account for the differences, looking for regional biases, if known, or quality of argument. This highlighting of differences and examination of possible reasons not only teaches the students to analyze content, but to reason with related information and to make judgments about the relative value of the statements.

Another part of this exercise is aimed at recognizing that most of the information in the articles is a report of what was said or written. The task in relation to this information is to decide if it is reliable information and, if it is, how it affects the recommendation. For example, it is reported that the Alberta Teachers' Association endorsed the textbook. Numerous other people are cited in opposition to the book. A person trying to make a decision about the textbook needs to know who is in favor and who is opposed and for what reasons.

This extended examination of the newspapers in the collection is aimed at four objectives:

1. drawing out major differences of opinion and trying to account for why these differences exist.

2. noting the information reported in the various articles that illuminates supporting and dissenting voices because the credibility or the reliability of some of these sources may be critical to the way one decides this matter.

3. helping students discover the specific items of controversy leading to the criticism that needed to be investigated further.

4. helping the students see how values of the period may have led to the opinions whereas a contemporary or modern interpretation would not be warranted.

The students would be helped to see that only one or two items of study would not suffice using these sources and would be instructed on the richness of the documents for clues or leads to a conclusion.

One of the major issues we have faced is trying to sort out whether the instructional process has made a difference. We had a number of choices here. We could accept the position that greater learning is achieved if students are more interested and attempt to establish the perceived interest of students. Our other alternative was to attempt to place students in some sort of relative position in terms of a hierarchical notion of historical thinking skills at the beginning of the course. We could then measure achievement throughout the course and make decisions when they are ready to move on to the next level of complexity.

In a sense, we have chosen both of these alternatives. We do assume that students learn better when they are interested and our post-test on the curriculum kits supports an increased interest on the part of the students. But we have gone beyond that in an attempt to establish levels of complexity for thinking and in evaluating student achievement as they move to increasing ability to think historically.

At this stage in our project we believe we have considerable evidence to support the significance and value of the undertaking. Unfortunately, we have yet to develop, test, and evaluate the whole enterprise sufficiently to offer conclusive, definitive statements about the value or limitations of the technology in this instructional approach, and uniqueness and interrelationships of these three skills and how they are mastered. Notwithstanding the stages of uncertainty at which we are currently operating, we believe there are some insights from our experience that may help others who are interested in similar concerns. More important, we hope by revealing our experiences, assumptions, and beliefs, our findings and our areas of uncertainty, and our questions that there will be those more experienced and informed in the field of thinking skills teaching who will help to advise and, where needed, reorient us.

We have come to our interest and involvement in thinking skills instruction as novices in the area. Our preoccupation with the acquisition and preparation of the materials has further limited our time to acquire a more sophisticated understanding of thinking skills and how they are acquired and taught. We wish, from our limited, yet apparently successful experience, to add our voices to the growing number who support and advocate skills-centered learning. We believe it should be a vital part of teacher education experiences.

9

Thinking Skills or Strategic Behavior and Arithmetic Word Problems: Research, Assessment, and Instruction

Dan G. Bachor

The manner in which children manifest thinking has remained a topic of interest for a considerable period of time, having been investigated under the rubrics of learning, intelligence, cognition, learning strategies, self-regulated behavior, and cognitive science (Case, 1985; Derry & Murphy, 1986; Ferguson, 1956; Gagné, 1980; Pressley, 1986; Vernon, 1969). In a more applied context, thinking has been examined as a component of reading comprehension (e.g., Palincsar & Brown, 1984, 1989; Peterson & Swing, 1983; Raphael & Wonnacott, 1985), science instruction (e.g., Anderson, 1987; Carey, 1986), and problem solving in mathematics (e.g., Garofalo et al., 1987; Gick, 1986). In the majority of these investigations into the manifestation of thinking, at least two conundrums remain. First, measuring how children think requires the use of indirect assessment techniques (Bachor, 1990; Sternberg & Martin, 1988). Second, the methodology of thinking skills instruction is open to debate (e.g., Biggs & Collis, 1982; Perkins & Salomon, 1989; Sternberg, 1983).

Within mathematics one key in investigating thinking has been to examine the problem-solving processes and other strategic behavior demonstrated by children when faced with arithmetic word problems. In this chapter, some research methods, assessment procedures, and instructional techniques for arithmetic word problems are examined.

THE WORD PROBLEM

The word problem has served as the focus of much of the thinking skills research in arithmetic, and such problems are employed widely as a vehicle to represent children's thinking and understanding in mathematics learning (Nesher 1986). Four general tactics have emerged to investigate arithmetic word problems and to examine any related problem-solving behavior: (1) factors contributing to problem difficulty of word problems either found in mathematics curricula (e.g., Carpenter et al., 1980; Jerman & Rees, 1972; Linville, 1976) or written explicitly for the investigation (e.g., Caldwell & Goldin, 1979) have been analyzed; (2) word problems designed to reflect individual differences in problem-solving ability have been selected or constructed (e.g., Cawley, 1984; Cawley et al., 1979); (3) "expert" problem-solving models using controlled text (De Corte et al., 1985; Kintsch & Greeno, 1985; Riley et al., 1983) have been designed; and (4) problem-solving models based on generalized learner characteristics, such as affective traits or developmental stages, have been developed (Threadgill-Sowder et al., 1985; West et al., 1969). Of these four general tactics used to examine word problems, the arithmetic word problem itself has been the impetus for investigation to address the first two, while the person solving the problem has been the starting point in the latter two cases.

Adopting either the task or the person as the primary focus of arithmetic word problem investigations has resulted in variations in the manner in which word problems have been designed or selected and the nature of the sample of individuals chosen for study. The viewpoint advanced in this chapter is that both the word problem and the problem solver must be considered when the goal is to understand how children think and behave. An example will illustrate this point.

Jake is a grade 7 student (aged twelve years, two months) who was referred to the Learning Assistance Center at the University of Victoria for assistance in mathematics. At the same time, due to his facility in composing and his overall intellectual ability, Jack was being considered for placement in the school-based gifted program. Typically he has been a positive, contributing member of his class. This description must be tempered slightly when it comes to mathematics. Jake does not especially enjoy doing mathematics, nor is he especially successful at it, although he has been more favorably disposed to arithmetic word problems. In completing several of his mathematics assignments, Jack often would engage delaying tactics, such as working slowly, or avoidance techniques, such as talking about a book he was reading. In the two questions given below the interaction between the problem and the problem solver is apparent. It should be noted that Jake did obtain correct answers to all three questions and enjoyed reading the problems he was assigned.

When doing the first word problem, which required multiplication (280×19), he took five minutes to complete the question. As he was working, Jake sighed and tried to think of ways to avoid doing the problem, his favorite being to ask questions, such as "Why do people keep these sleeves on the erasers?" In the second problem, Jake used a different strategy, employing comparison and repeated subtraction rather than division. The problem read: "Joe scored 19 on one spelling test, 15 on a second test, and 17 on a third test. What was his average score?" Jake approached this problem differently again, answering 17 almost immediately. He explained his speed by pointing out that "two each way is 17." In completing these problems, the logic necessary to disembed the arithmetic operations was not problematic for Jake. As suggested earlier, his difficulty appeared to have occurred, in part, because he has had a negative attitude toward arithmetic. In addition, Jake has had a tendency to invent more complex solution strategies than necessary. To reiterate, the interaction between the problem and the child must be considered rather than attending solely to one of these components.

Word problems themselves have been an interesting source of study and debate. Originally efforts at understanding word problem difficulty were directed at identifying the independent contribution of various constituents of arithmetic word problems (e.g., Caldwell & Goldin, 1979; Linville, 1976). As a result of investigations of this type, the major categories of variables that can shift the difficulty of word problems have been identified. Arithmetic variables, such as the relative difficulty of operations (Carpenter et al., 1980) or the importance of computation level (Reys et al., 1984; Washburne, 1931), and language factors, such as vocabulary level and the total number of words used (Jerman & Rees, 1972) or syntactic complexity (Barnett, 1979; Larson et al., 1979), were typical of the word problem constituents investigated.

While isolating elements included in the problem space has resulted in the identification of specific characteristics that may add to, or subtract from, problem difficulty, less progress has been made in considering what combinations of elements may result in an adequate set of word problems for classroom or individual assessment. The unresolved question is quite straightforward to state but has been difficult to solve. How does one best write word problems to facilitate the investigation of thinking (problem-solving) skills? The most commonly advanced solution has been that real-life problems must supplant those word problems currently being written so that problem solving can be better understood as it applies to daily concerns (Sharma, 1984). Regardless of the procedures used to construct or select problems, some aspect must be deemphasized, for example, either the language surface or semantic structure or the mathematical semantic structure. If this argument is accepted, no one set of problems will suffice. Rather, a wide variety of problem types (such as varying in form [text, graphic, pictorial, or tabular], length, or number and complexity of operations) will be necessary if any adequate conceptualization of the full range of children's strategic behaviors is to be identified. One addition would be to build a set of problems that would allow the role of language in arithmetic word problems to be explored and that would assist researchers and practitioners in identifying individual differences in word problem-solving skills.

Toward a Language-Based Item Pool

Following a technique suggested by Cawley and his associates (Cawley et al., 1979; Cawley, 1985), a word problem grid or a matrix of item characteristics has been developed (see the appendix). This is a technique similar to constructing a table of specifications when constructing classroom tests (Bachor, 1989). When building a table of specifications, the purpose is to ensure that the content to be measured is adequately and fairly sampled, whereas the objective of constructing a word problem matrix is to allow any selected item characteristics or word problem elements to be carefully sampled. In addition to systematically specifying item characteristics within such a matrix, it also is necessary to attend to other aspects of item development, such as the specific wording of each item and the operationalization of the selected item characteristics. Based on this analysis, the following rationale emerged and has been used as a basis for problem development: To unravel the enigma of word problems, task variables must be incorporated in a typology in which the included problems are to be considered simultaneously as requiring language manipulation, logical analysis, and mathematical computation (Bachor, 1987).

In addition, in examining elementary mathematics curriculum, it has been noted that the potential influence of question type has been ignored in the development of word problems. Following the theory of Pearson and Johnson (1978) and the subsequent research of Raphael and her associates (Raphael & Wonnacott, 1985), Bachor (1985, 1987) has proposed that question type also be reconsidered when designing and assessing performance on arithmetic word problems. The three types of questions suggested by Pearson and Johnson are text explicit (TE), text implicit (TI), and script implicit (SI). Text explicit questions can be answered directly from any text, that it, without requiring integration of information across statements or prior declarative or procedural knowledge. Text implicit questions require that students be able to gather and synthesize information, but does not require prior background knowledge. Script implicit questions demand that information be integrated across text and that prior knowledge assumed within text be utilized.

From the perspective of mathematical word problems, the three types of questions can be seen to vary in the number of assumptions made about the potential problem solver. With TE problems the assumption made is that the respondent can read the text and locate the required answer, neither selecting an operation nor completing any computation. With TI problems the respondent may be required, depending on problem construction, to integrate information from more than one statement and then to complete at least one operation. While problem solvers may need to integrate information, the semantic knowledge required to complete the problems as given is summarized in classification statements in the actual problem. With SI problems any required prior learner knowledge of the semantic relationships between the subordinate and superordinate categories of nouns also is assumed. It should be noted that as a result of this assumption, SI problems contain less text than TI problems. Drawing from the reading research on the role of question type cited in the last paragraph, it has been hypothesized that the inclusion of different question types would influence differently performance on arithmetic word problems.

Bachor (1988), in beginning to test this hypothesis, has investigated the role of question type in interaction with easy and hard vocabulary on word problem performance with a wide range of normally achieving intermediate grade elementary students. A sample of eighty-four grade 6 and fifty-three grade 7 students were administered thirty-two word problems that varied in the type of question posed and in the difficulty of the language incorporated. For grade 6 students questioned that required prior knowledge were more difficult than those which did not require such prerequisite knowledge. This finding did not hold for grade 7 students. Changing the complexity of the language used in the preparation of the word problems resulted in poorer performance for both grade 6 and grade 7 students.

The next as yet incomplete step is to describe the strategic response patterns of individuals, who vary in overall achievement, as they complete various word problems. This information would appear to be useful in determining where children face difficulty with such problems. In addition, the strategies children use in answering can be compared to accumulated descriptions of typical performance patterns of other students of varying word problem proficiency.

The Problem Solver

When the starting point of research has been the problem solver, emphasis has been placed on describing how the normally achieving individual solves problems. Models representing students' conceptualization of problem fields and solution procedures have been developed, which form the basis for typing both problems and learners (Carpenter & Moser, 1982; De Corte et al., 1985; Kintsch & Greeno, 1985).

Starting with the typical performance of normally achieving students has been quite useful in developing a conceptual model of problem solving. Such models seem to be helpful if the purpose is to compare all individuals to an expected theoretical standard of performance. Such theoretical driven models of problem solving, however, have at least one limitation when comparison to standards are desired. Surface structures have been allowed to vary within any given conceptually determined model of problems, resulting in a high probability that when a diverse sample of students is investigated, problem-solving performance will not conform to prediction. Clements and Del Campo (1987), for example, found that the 1978 Heller and Greeno model of problem solving for addition and subtraction did not fit the performance of a diverse sample of over one thousand elementary school students, a sample that included some individuals who did not have English as a first language. De Corte and Verschaffel (1987) reported that grade 1 students demonstrated considerable differences in solution strategies as a function of variations in word problem task characteristics, such as the order of information presentation. While these efforts to understand the nature of problem solving are both valid and important, the evidence from these two articles would provide further support for the suggested expansion in the variety of types of word problems investigated.

Disregard for Learner Background

Students come to any teaching and learning situation with a variety of characteristics that might be expected to affect their individual performances (e.g., Case, 1985; Garofalo et al., 1987). Strategy awareness and deployment may be influenced by some of the following learner characteristics: (1) aspects achievement or attainment, such as reading (Conca, 1987), mathematical abilities (Jerman & Rees, 1972; Threadgill-Sowder et al., 1985), experiential background (Bachor et al., 1980; Kifer, 1987), and overall intellectual attainment (Bilsky & Judd, 1986); (2) factors related to cognitive capabilities, such as functional short-term memory span (Case, 1985; Case et al., 1982; Chi, 1976; Pascual-Leone et al., 1978), and strategy repertoire (Case, 1978; De Corte et al., 1985; Pressley, 1986; Mulcahy & Marfo, 1987); and (3) variables linked to affect, such as test anxiety (Dusek, 1980; Wine, 1980) and academic self-concept (Kistner et al., 1987; Winne et al., 1982).

Few of the above characteristics have been extensively researched with respect to learning strategies. The first characteristic described has received the most attention and is the most readily translated into implications for strategic behavior research. A wide discrepancy in subjects' reading level, for example, will be observed as variability in text processing and restricted world knowledge (Kintsch, 1988). Thus, at a minimum, steps should be taken to observe subjects' reading levels and to describe their reading strategies across a variety of word problems (for example, text only or with graphic, pictorial, or tabular support). Similarly, students' ability to remember material may influence their strategy knowledge and utilization, as will their confidence in approaching such tasks. Following this argument, the following principle has been suggested as a frame of reference for further research (Bachor, 1987). In order to understand strategic behavior, a process-structural theory of development and instruction (e.g., Case, 1978, 1985; Pascual-Leone et al., 1978) is needed so that students who vary in age, strategy awareness, and strategy deployment can be compared. Associated with this principle are three corollaries: (1) students' memory span will influence their strategic behavior; (2) affective markers, such as anxiety and self-concept, will influence students' strategic behavior; and (3) students' existing general knowledge will influence their strategic behavior.

As an initial step in investigating the usefulness of above principle, Steacy and Bachor (1987, 1988) have begun to consider individual differences among learners in relation to strategy awareness deployment. In both studies, individuals' strategic behavior in solving word problems was compared when memory span (as measured by the counting span task; Case et al., 1982) and academic self-concept (as measured by the students' perception of ability scale; Boersma & Chapman, 1977) were considered. In the first study, they argued that the roles of memory span in rule adoption were differentiated. Memory span was more indicative of first-trial performance and academic self-concept was more predictive of later trial performance. In the second follow-up study, twelve students were randomly sampled from stratified performance groups employed in the first study. These students were interviewed after they had solved a set of problems to obtain post hoc talk-aloud summaries and were asked if they had developed a rule (rule induction) while solving a number of arithmetic word problems and, if so, if they could describe it. These patterns were then compared to the oral descriptions provided by the subjects as to the nature of the problems and their specific solution strategies utilized. Looking over the commonalities, we suggested that there are interactions between memory and academic self-concept in determining effective performance. The combination of a memory span of four or five along with a high self-concept resulted, in most cases, in immediate rule induction. When a low academic self-concept is combined with a functional memory span of three, the result for any subject would seem to have been a reduction in the probability of learning. Considering the results of both investigations, the combination of grade 6 students' academic self-concept with their functional memory span appears to have had an impact on word problem strategic behavior.

Rule induction then would appear to be a pivotal component of thinking skills. Having a rule allows the student to recognize any analogous relationships among the relevant elements in the problem space. Once induced, an appropriate rule may be applied to any problem recognized as having the same isomorphic relationship among essential elements. The concept of "isomorphic" word problems is an adaptation of the term suggested by Reed (1987) in his investigation of algebraic word problem solving among high school students. Problems are isomorphic if, and only if, the relationship among the relevant elements within the problem space, and, therefore, the rule(s) dictating the manipulation of those elements, are identical across problems. The attributes of the specific elements themselves are irrelevant to the isomorphic relationship among problems; thus, word problems with similar surface contexts are not isomorphic if they require different solution procedures (e.g., different rules).

Suggesting the importance of rule induction may have important theoretical consequences as to the relative importance of problem solving in completing any set of word problems. Problem solving is only necessary when a person is determining what to do to resolve an unknown. After a solution strategy has been selected and verified, problem solving is no longer necessary. Instead rule application (employing what has been learned) is required. This logic would lead to the conclusion that problem solving is only a small part of completing any set of world problems. This pattern is especially noticeable in some elementary mathematics curricula, where word problems usually require the use of one operation and directly follow the presentation of material on that specific operation.

Strategy Use

To summarize, there are two critical limitations in current paradigms to address children's strategies. These procedures may restrict further conceptualization of how children think, learn, and behave. The first one is that researchers are selecting tasks completed over short durations. Strategies usually are observed on a single occasion or at most two occasions. As a next step in arithmetic word problem research, it is necessary to observe over time while comparing children of varying ability. Further, strategy use typically has been observed when children are completing addition and subtraction problems (e.g., Clements & Del Campo, 1987; De Corte et al., 1985; De Corte & Vershchaffel, 1987). Second, comparisons typically have not been made with respect to how different students, varying in ability and achievement, proceed to identify, apply, evaluate, and adjust how they approach and complete a variety of assignments outside the domain of mathematics. These limitations have not allowed researchers to identify and differentiate the relative effectiveness of children's strategies as applied to mathematics or to determine if differences exist among students in their strategy proficiency.

The methodology used to examine children's cognitive strategies typically involves having children complete individually an assigned task while indicating in some manner the strategies deployed and utilized to complete that task. The most common procedure employed to investigate strategy deployment has been to have children talk aloud as they work (e.g., Hutchinson, 1987; Simons, 1987). Proficiency in strategy use typically is estimated by comparing novices and experts as they complete some task (Simon, 1975, 1978). An unanswered question, which is related to strategy use and proficiency, is the degree to which students' descriptions or think-aloud protocols match their performance patterns across specified problem sets.

An alternative procedure objective is to observe and record strategy knowledge and deployment in a variety of situations. To date, there is considerable debate as to which types of strategies are more effective in instructional situations (Pressley et al., 1987; Sternberg & Martin, 1988). More specifically, two different perspectives are offered consistently as explanations of children's and adolescents' cognitive learning strategies. Identification and training of effective task-specific strategies or tactics is the first focus. For example, a number of text comprehension strategies such as summarizing (Brown & Day, 1983), monitoring comprehension and "backtracking" (Garner et al., 1984; Scardamalia & Bereiter, 1984), and looking for main ideas (Kieras, 1982; Meyer et al., 1980) have been identified as differentiating between good and poor readers. Reluctant readers seem to have demonstrated success in developing strategic behavior (Garner et al., 1984; Palincsar & Brown, 1984). Similarly, effective strategies have been identified in learning and problem solving in specific subject matters, such as mathematics (e.g., Hiebert & Wearne, 1986; Kintsch & Greeno, 1985). General, content-free strategies that may be used across tasks or subject matter domains have been the second common approach to learning strategy research (Derry & Murphy, 1986; Mulcahy & Marfo, 1987; Sternberg, 1983). The goal in this case is to identify and train executive intellectual skills to allow children to identify task demands and to implement content- or task-specific strategies as required.

Several common themes in both the methodology and outcomes of the research just described illustrate that a more thorough description of the strategies naturally used by learners in various learning situations is needed. First, in nearly every study reviewed in which executive or content-specific strategies that are used spontaneously by learners have been examined, the research was conducted within the context of a single subject area and incorporated a limited set of experimenter-provided stimulus materials. Moreover, in these studies, students' strategic learning behaviors typically have been sampled in only a single task or instructional sequence. Typically a single instrument or method for collecting data on students' cognitive processing has been incorporated into such studies, which limits the confidence that can be placed in the validity and reliability of their findings (Ericsson & Simon, 1980; Nisbett & Wilson, 1977). Second, the argument has been made (e.g., Corno, 1988; Hiebert & Wearne, 1986) that students' ability to apply strategies for learning vary considerably across tasks and subject areas, at least partly as a result of variations in their existing knowledge. Third, a common stumbling block in research on strategic behavior is that of helping learners to identify the task situations in which various strategies would promote learning or problem solution. This is a problem that has pervaded strategy training programs both at the executive skill level and with content-specific strategies (Derry & Murphy, 1986; Gagné, 1980; Paris et al., 1983). Some of this debate may be resolved by observing and recording how subjects plan and use strategies in a variety of school subjects. Thus, data are needed on the variation of individual learners' strategic behaviors across a variety of contexts. It is only through our understanding of such variations in naturally occurring approaches to tasks that instructional interventions can be designed to directly address and adapt to learners' existing strategic knowledge and skill levels.

ASSESSMENT

Assessment Accuracy

A major difficulty facing researchers and applied professionals who are interested in thinking skills is assessment accuracy. If one administers a series of arithmetic word problems with the intention of establishing strategic behavior, to some lesser, or greater, extent such performance must be inferred. Even if the goal is to establish children's arithmetic procedural knowledge in such tasks as adding single digit numbers, inference is necessary. For example, Nesher (1986) argues that even if young children always execute answers using calculators, assuring they understand the underlying principles involved in learning mathematics remains important, as their conceptualization of number and the principles of counting still are represented in thought. Further, any observed strategic behavior is only a sample of what might have been obtained.

As a result, assessment always requires inference and is subject to error.

There are at least two potential errors that influence the accuracy of any procedure designed to estimate thinking skills. First, there is the error of the measurement that accompanies obtaining a time-bound sample. Gathering such data provides only an estimate of what a person did, not what he or she may have done on a different occasion. Second, there is the error associated with administering each instrument or procedure selected to obtain an estimate of strategic behavior. No single procedure, regardless of the attractiveness of the assessment technique, can stand alone. In sum, the application of all assessment techniques, regardless of validity, can never result in more than a situation-specific estimate of a child's thinking skill performance pattern.

Assessment Procedures

The logical shift implied in collecting different types of data over time has been incorporated into the decision-making model developed by Bachor and Crealock (1986). Assessment, when using this model, changes to a multifaceted process designed to reflect a child's continuum of strengths and weaknesses in the awareness, and use, of strategies. To obtain a reasonable estimate of thinking skills, a number of assessment techniques (interviewing, observing, testing) must be employed that yield information about strategic behavior under a variety of conditions (such as when receiving instruction, when working independently, when doing something enjoyed, etc.). By following such procedures, information will be obtained that will allow a more thorough description of strategy awareness, deployment, and utilization. As well, when all the measures are taken together the probability of making either of the two errors in measurement are reduced.

In applying the decision-making model to solving word problems, assessment should start with an examination of students' prior achievement and other relevant personal history. The purpose is to obtain a general viewpoint of students' approach to school and to note any previous comments on the type of strategies they have employed. This tactic of reviewing past school records likely will have a low information yield for students who are achieving in the average range for any age group or grade placement; it usually is helpful when considering students who have learning or emotional problems or those individuals who are receiving instructional enrichment.

Comparative observation (Bachor, 1990) is a technique in which students' classroom performance is examined, for example, to determine their degree of organization in doing assignments or the amount and quality of work accomplished. This sample of performance is then compared to a stratified sample of three groups of students: those performing near the top of the class, those performing the average range, and those who are having difficulty. The data yields an estimate of such factors as task persistence and strategy effectiveness.

Comparative observation may be supplemented by continuous chronologues. The purpose of completing such a chronologue is to obtain a descriptive summary of the students' activities in the classroom environment. This observation should extend beyond the class time devoted to mathematics to include as wide a variety of activities as is possible across the school day. Especially germane in this case would be to observe and describe factors related to planning, implementing, monitoring, and strategy use. This would include such things as noting work habits, the planning and execution of strategies, the frequency and type of questions asked, and the nature of self-help or self-checking techniques employed (Wang et al., 1987).

Work sample analysis is a procedure utilized to obtain technically adequate samples of classroom performance that can be translated directly into instructional objectives (Bachor, 1979, 1990). Specifically the following four steps have been suggested to complete work sample analysis:

1. Select three to five assignments completed over a period of two to six weeks. The results of deploying thinking skills must be repeated in some form in each selected assignment. For each assignment, list strengths (strategies at or above grade or age level expectations), skills present (strategies mastered by the individual but not meeting grade or age level standards), and weaknesses (errors of omission or of commission in the application of strategies).
2. Look for commonalities in the pattern of strategic utilization across all obtained work samples.
3. Compare observations of strengths, skills present, and weaknesses to strategic behavior expectations set for students.
4. Repeat work sample analysis approximately once every three months.

By following these procedures the probability of the estimate being accurate increases and the error of measurement decreases.

The purpose in obtaining interview data is to obtain descriptions of the various types of strategy knowledge and deployment used by children. Such interviews can be conducted in three separate phases. First, students can be asked to explain how they plan to do any task. Second, they can be interviewed while completing a preselected standardized assignment similar to classroom-based activities. In this interview children can be asked to explain the procedures that they use to solve any problem. This is the mostly commonly employed interviewing technique and has been termed "think-aloud protocols" (e.g., Lawson & Rice, 1987; Simon, 1975, 1978). Third, they can be questioned for post hoc explanations of performance. These procedures result in a descriptive normative data base that allows differentiation of students of varying placements and ages over time and grade levels.

A final assessment procedure useful in the evaluation of strategic behavior is to conduct trial lessons. Trial lessons are carefully chosen lessons that are controlled for the amount of material given and difficulty level. The purpose of completing such lessons, in this context, is to evaluate the acquisition or application of strategic behavior to instructional tasks. A number of different objectives can be met by evaluating during instruction. First, the length of time and amount of assistance needed by children to acquire any strategy can be noted. Second, it can be noted whether students can remember the newly acquired strategy at the end of a lesson or some days later. Third, the application of previously learned, adapted, or student-generated strategies can be monitored. Fourth, students' affective responses to instruction can be observed. Finally, the degree to which students have learned to self-monitor can be checked.

Adopting a decision-making model changes the emphasis placed on any one or two measurements to the verification of strategic behavior by taking several different types of estimates of performance over time. Thus, the measurement procedure becomes one of identifying the utility of the information collected to obtain descriptions of strategy awareness, acquisition, utilization, memory, and monitoring.

INSTRUCTIONAL STRATEGIES

One of the main difficulties experienced by many students is that they proceed to solve word problems as if they could simply extract the numbers from text, identify the required operation or operations, solve the problem, and then check their answers. This belief is supported by the fact that in the vast majority of elementary curricula word problems follow instruction in some operation and those problems likely only contain that operation.

A second potential difficulty that children face is that they may be taught to solve word problems by using a key word approach to problem analysis. In this technique, they are taught that certain key words mean that a particular operation must be performed. Thus, for example, "in all" means add; "share" is taken as requiring division. The presence of other words are taught as signals of other operations. Lester et al. (1988), in interviewing children, have discovered that they cling to the key word approach even when there are no such words in the problems to be solved. Further, these authors point out that the students they interviewed used this approach instead of attempting to understand the relationships expressed in the problem.

Instruction in the application of strategies does help students in the intermediate grades of the elementary school attend to the various types of relationships they may face in any set of word problems. Yet children having difficulty in school often refuse to believe that they can succeed when completing arithmetic word problems. For some of these students, their self-doubt has become so generalized that they will not even attempt problems they believe to be too difficult. A milder form of negative attitude also is found among some normally achieving students. They may demonstrate lack of persistence due to their belief that word problems are too difficult (Lester et al., 1989).

A final concern in providing strategic instruction for word problems has been that many children do not transfer what they have learned outside the immediate context of instruction. For students with learning problems, this failure to transfer may relate to self-doubt. Often, however, such students simply have failed to recognize that the strategies they have been taught apply elsewhere. For example, Case and Harris (1988) found successful transfer from a teacher to a learning disabled child from addition to subtraction word problems only when students had a clear grasp of addition word problems; otherwise, students had some degree of difficulty.

Given the concerns addressed above, the instructional principles suggested for word problems have been designed to increase the probability that students acquire effective strategies, that they are confident in using them, and that such strategic training will transfer. The suggested strategies are designed to incorporate the principles of reciprocal teaching (Palincsar & Brown, 1984, 1990) and direct explanation (Paris & Oka, 1986, 1989), which have been developed for reading instruction but can be applied to arithmetic word problems quite readily. These two principles, when translated into instruction for arithmetic word problems, mean that the practices of reading, questioning (e.g., What do I already know about the textual information given or the operation(s) required?), clarifying (e.g., Have I misread the problem? Have I been fooled by the wording of the problem?), and checking need to be explained sufficiently, modeled by the teacher, and then practiced by students to allow them to see where any given strategy does and does not apply.

One instructional procedure for arithmetic word problems includes some of the principles of reciprocal teaching. Fleischner and O'Loughlin (1985) have included self-questioning strategies as a component of a four-phase word problem solution tactic. The student: (1) identifies the required information in the problem; (2) constructs a solution plan; (3) establishes a number sentence and performs the required operation(s); and (4) verifies the solution. This procedure, while useful, has only been partially successful in its application to students with learning problems (van Lieshout, 1986).

In the strategy instruction procedures given below, instruction has been designed around two general principles. While attention must be given to both the strategies and the content to be taught, the primary focus during the first phase of single strategy acquisition must be on strategic competence, not content coverage. The second general principle is that students' confidence follows competence; that is, they will only learn to believe that strategic behavior is useful after being successful on several occasions. The model has been divided into two phases: (1) teaching strategy acquisition and application; and (2) teaching self-regulation.

Teaching Strategy Acquisition and Application

This phase of strategic instruction is completely teacher-controlled. The teacher begins by demonstrating to students that their knowledge base needs to be enlarged, that their current procedure does not work or is insufficient. This may seem like an unnecessary step. Children with learning problems, however, often fail to recognize the relative inefficiency of their own strategic behavior. Once they acknowledge that assistance may be of benefit, instruction has a higher probability of success.

This first step is followed by the elimination of a sufficient number of task complexities (number and type of operation, for example) until students reach a success rate of 90 to 100 percent without instruction. Once this criterion has been met, the strategies of reading, modeling, questioning, clarifying, and verifying are introduced; that is, the steps of reciprocal teaching and direct explanation discussed earlier are taught and applied to those word problems the student can already solve successfully, if somewhat inefficiently.

Next, the use of this new strategic behavior is practiced on teacher-selected word problems where the level of difficulty parallels that found in the original lesson or lessons but the text and numbers involved differ. The teachers' emphasis at this point is on the acquisition, application, and review of the principles of strategic behavior to increase the probability the student will overlearn the process of strategy use. Overlearning is accomplished by reexamining the standards set for the student once mastery has occurred. The use of this principle means rejecting the 80 percent rule as being sufficient to ensure that any strategy will be remembered and encourage as close to a 100 percent success rate as is possible. Next, the level of difficulty of the teacher-selected word problems is shifted by gradually reintroducing the eliminated complexities and having the student repeat overlearning procedures.

Teaching Self-regulation

In this phase of strategy instruction the emphasis changes from the teacher to the student. The primary concern now is on learner self-regulated learning and confidence.

First, the student is taught self-instructive skills. These

are defined as students' ability to access, organize, and use relevant knowledge and skills for new learning. According to this definition, self-instructive learners are knowledgeable about the subject matter related to the criteria [sic] task to be learned and about the learning environment and its functional requirements. They also must be capable of using what they know to learn independently and deliberately through strategy planning, self-monitoring and assessment, and self-interrogation and clarification. (Wang et al., 1987, p. 4)

During this phase, two instructional guidelines have been found useful in encouraging self-regulation. First, students must learn to compare, to learn to select the best available answer and explain why it is the best, to select incorrect answers and explain why they are inappropriate. Second, controlled risk taking while answering word problems should be encouraged so that students will try to answer when they are uncertain of their solutions or their strategies.

Finally, after self-regulation has been taught, teacher support still will be necessary to increase student confidence or self-belief. This is perhaps the most frustrating component of instruction. Children will fall back to old ineffective procedures if circumstances emerge in which they doubt their strategies or, even more generally, themselves. Thus both the teacher and the student must be patient in moving toward the independent application and regulation of strategic behavior across a variety of word problems. A rough criterion of the length of time necessary for self-belief to occur is a function of the duration of students' problem history (remembering the factors involved—number, severity, frequency required, and importance attached to them).

Three general positions have been advanced in this chapter about the application of thinking skills or strategic behavior to arithmetic word problems. First, strategy research, in general, needs to be reevaluated with the goal of better determining how strategic behavior is acquired and applied. Second, assessment procedures must be modified and expanded to allow a more complete description of where and how strategies are applied. Finally, children must first be taught a combination of strategies; then, they are instructed to self-regulate their strategy use when given a variety of word problems.

APPENDIX: CRITERIA FOR, AND SAMPLES OF, WORD PROBLEMS

Major Features of Language-Based Word Problems

Arithmetic Word Problem Variables

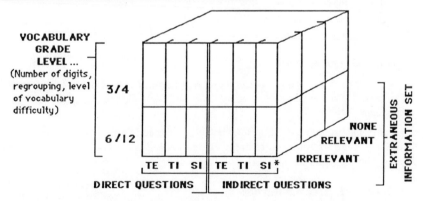

*TE = Text Explicit Questions; TI = Text Implicit Questions;
SI = Script Implicit Questions

VOCABULARY LEVEL

All the problems were written so that the answers would be whole numbers since the referent was always an intact object (such as strangers, teachers, pigs, or felines). The reason for this choice is that the emphasis has been on the language category rather than on, for example, operations involving fractional or decimal numbers.

The basic set of problems was written at the grade 3–4 level. To establish grade level, every word used in the problems was judged against both a graded Canadian spelling list (Thomas, 1979) and a graded vocabulary compilation (Dale & O'Rourke, 1976, 1981). Next, two variations in the basic set language level were constructed, either by inserting adjectives into the basic problem set or modifying nouns used in the original problems. Before any adjective addition or noun substitution was made, two criteria had to be met: (1) both the adjectives and nouns had to be rated in the Dale & O'Rourke list as falling between the grade levels of 6 and 12; and (2) the selected adjectives had to be logically consistent with the nouns incorporated into the basic problem set, and the new nouns had to fall into a logical superordinate category. In addition, some mathematical terms used in the problems were changed to increase the difficulty level; the same criterion of difficulty was applied to these terms as was used for the adjectives and nouns. Verb selection was completed in a similar manner; verbs, however, were held constant at the grade 3–4 level of difficulty. Some variations in verbs occurred among the three language levels so that the resultant word problems would read better. Sample problems of the three levels of language are given below:

Grade 3–4 Level, Basic Set

1. The stranger counted a few chickens. The stranger counted 3 geese. Chickens and geese are birds. The stranger counted 8 birds altogether. How many chickens did the stranger count?

2. 8 squirrels have 28 nuts each. 3 chipmunks have 18 nuts each. How many nuts did the squirrels and chipmunks have?

Grade 6–12, Adjective Insertion

1. The tyrannical king photographed 4 frenzied tigers. The pretentious prince photographed 9 gigantic bears. How many tigers and bears did the king and prince photograph?

2. 4 efficient nurses want the same number of spirited horses each. 7 distinguished doctors want 8 spirited horses each. The nurses and doctors want 88 horses. How many horses does each nurse want?

Grade 6–12, Noun Substitution

1. The conservationist counted a limited number of lynx. The conservationist counted 5 cougars. Lynx and cougars are felines. Considered collectively the conservationist counted 9 felines. How many lynx did the conservationist count?

2. 5 optometrists rented the same number of condominiums each. 6 pharmacists rented 3 condominiums each. The professionals rented 38 condominiums. How many condominiums did each optometrist rent?

QUESTION TYPE AND EXTRANEOUS INFORMATION

The three types of question have been defined in the body of the chapter. Examples of text explicit, text implicit, and script implicit question types are given below. These examples are illustrated with problems that contain both extraneous information and different set complexity.

Two types of extraneous information are found in the problems. They vary in the number of cues the learner will receive when determining if the information is to be excluded from the total problem set.

In the first case, the extraneous information has been termed "set irrelevant extraneous information" (SIR). It is irrelevant in that the reader is cued that the information is extraneous in two different ways: (1) a change in the noun, either in the subject or the object or in both the subject and the object; and (2) a change in the verb. In the second case, the extraneous information is referred to as "set relevant information" (SR). In set relevant extraneous information only the verb is changed, providing only one cue for the reader to determine if such information should be omitted. In the examples given below both types of extraneous information are contained in each problem. There is a third case but it does not involve any new type of extraneous information. In this third case, termed "set relevant and set irrelevant" (SR/SIR), both types of extraneous information are combined in one problem. The person answering the type of question must omit both types of extraneous information before the word problem can be solved successfully.

As was noted above, the manner in which the noun and verb is excluded changes as a function of the relationship among the elements of the problem sets. In this series of examples, exclusion occurs in both the subject and the object (in the noun case) and in the verb, in the complex object and in the verb, in the complex noun and in the verb, or in either the complex subject or the complex object (but not in both) and in the verb (a complete set of examples is only provided for script implicit questions).

Text Explicit

1. The cook ordered 69 pies. The buyer bought 76 cookies altogether (SIR). The cook prepared 78 more pies (SR). How many pies did the cook order?

2. The lawyer and doctor photographed a group of 28 cars and boats. The plumber and nurse sold a group of 89 tigers and lions. The lawyer and doctor desired a group of 75 cars and boats. How many cars and boats did the lawyer and doctor photograph?

Text Implicit

1. At first the farmer bought 44 pigs. The farmer bought 97 more pigs. The shepherd ordered 80 sheep altogether (SIR). The farmer fed 68 pigs (SR). How many pigs did the farmer buy altogether?

2. Mary desired 57 horses. Ellen desired 46 horses. Sue raced 92 horses. Jack led 76 horses. Mary, Ellen, and Sue are girls. How many horses did the girls desire?

Script Implicit

1. At first the wolf caught 41 chickens. The wolf caught 69 more chickens. The fox picked 38 ducks altogether (SIR). The wolf sighted 83 more chickens (SR). How many birds did the animal catch?

2. Tom had 78 cats. Tom had 47 dogs. Tom helped 32 seals. Tom desired 47 rabbits. How many pets did Tom have?

3. The man rented 12 houses. The woman rented 78 houses. The bank sold 86 houses. The worker fixed 63 houses. How many houses did the people rent?

4. Mrs. Green caught 35 sharks. Mrs. Brown caught 65 trout. Mrs. Smith saw 87 frogs. Mrs. Watson cooked 55 salmon. How many fish did the women catch?

MATHEMATICAL OPERATION AND COMPUTATION LEVEL

Two types of problems have been used to define the number and type of operation contained in the problems: direct and indirect. The operations in the direct problems are either addition or multiplication, or both addition and multiplication. A direct question is found when only definite quantifiers are used in the word problems. On the other hand, indirect questions have indefinite quantifiers incorporated into one of the preliminary statements. This change results in a shift in the required operation to either subtraction or division, or both subtraction and division.

Three variations in computational level are found: single digit, double digit, and single/double digit combinations. For the single digit problems, the digit 1 was omitted since it is logically impossible to have the result of one, given the plural nature of the required answers (e.g., one horses is illogical). All digits were used in the other computational levels. The difference between the last two cases was that regrouping was required at least once during the calculation of the final answer in the second case and was never necessary in the first instance.

REFERENCES

Anderson, C. W. (1987). Strategic teaching in science. In B. F. Jones, A. S. Palincsar, D. S. Ogle, & E. G. Carr (eds.), *Strategic teaching and learning: Cognitive instruction in the content areas.* Elmhurst, Ill.: North Central Regional Educational Laboratory.

Bachor, D. G. (1979). Using work samples as diagnostic information. *Learning Disabilities Quarterly,* 2, 45–52.

———. (1985). Questions for and by the learning disabled student. In J. F. Cawley (ed.), *Cognitive strategies and mathematics for the learning disabled.* Rockville, Md.: Aspen.

———. (1987). Towards a taxonomy of word problems. In J. Bergeron, N. Herscovics, & C. Kieran (eds.), *Proceedings of the Eleventh Conference of the International Group for the Psychology of Mathematics Education.* Vol. 2. Montreal: PME.

————. (1988, June). The influence of question type on grade six and seven students' performance on arithmetic word problems. Paper presented at the Canadian Society for Studies in Education Conference, Windsor, Ont.

————. (1989). The importance of shifts in language level and extraneous information in determining word problem difficulty: Beginning steps towards individual assessment. *Diagnostique*, 14, 94–111.

————. (1990). Towards improving assessment of students with special needs: Expanding the data base to include classroom performance. *Alberta Journal of Educational Research*, 36, 65–77.

Bachor, D. G., & Crealock, C. (1986). *Instructional strategies for students with special needs.* Scarborough, Ont.: Prentice-Hall.

Bachor, D. G., Sitko, M., & Slemon, A. G. (1980). Information processing demands of questions on the student with special needs. In G. M. Kysela (ed.), *The exceptional child in Canadian education: Canadian Society for the Study of Education seventh yearbook.* Edmonton: CSSE.

Barnett, J. (1979). The study of syntax variables. In G. A. Goldin & C. E. McClintock (eds.), *Task variables in mathematics problem solving.* Columbus, Ohio: ERIC Clearinghouse for Science, Mathematics, and Environmental Education.

Biggs, J. B., & Collis, K. F. (1982). *Evaluating the quality of learning: The SOLO taxonomy (Structure of the Observed Learning Outcome).* New York: Academic.

Bilsky, L. H., & Judd, T. (1986). Sources of difficulty in the solution of verbal arithmetic problems by mentally retarded and non-retarded individuals. *American Journal of Mental Deficiency*, 90, 395–402.

Boersma, J. W., & Chapman, F. J. (1977). *The students' perception of ability scale.* Edmonton, Alberta: PsiCan.

Brown, A. L., & Day, J. D. (1983). Macrorules for summarizing text: The development of expertise. *Journal of Verbal Learning and Verbal Behavior*, 22, 1–14.

Caldwell, J. H., & Goldin, G. A. (1979). Variables affecting problem difficulty in elementary school mathematics. *Journal for Research in Mathematics Education*, 10, 323–336.

Carey, S. (1986). Cognitive science and science education. *American Psychologist*, 41, 1123–1130.

Carpenter, T. P., & Moser, J. M. (1982). The development of addition and subtraction problem-solving skills. In T. P. Carpenter, J. M. Moser, and T. A. Romberg (eds.), *Addition and subtraction: A cognitive perspective.* Hillsdale, N.J.: Erlbaum.

Carpenter, T. P., Corbitt, M. K., Lindquist, M. M., & Reys, R. E. (1980). Solving verbal problems: Results and implications from national assessments. *Arithmetic Teacher*, 28(2), 8–12.

Case, L. P., & Harris, K. R. (1988, April). Self-instructional strategy training: Improving the mathematical problem solving skills of learning disabled students. Paper presented at the American Educational Research Association, New Orleans, La.

Case, R. (1978). A developmentally based theory and technology of instruction. *Review of Educational Research*, 48, 439–469.

————. (1985). *Intellectual development: Birth to adulthood.* New York: Academic.

Case, R., Kurland, D. M, & Goldberg, J. (1982). Operational efficiency and the growth of short-term memory span. *Journal of Experimental Child Psychology*, 33, 386–404.

Cawley, J. F. (1984). An integrative approach to needs of learning-disabled children: Expanded use of mathematics. In J. F. Cawley (ed.), *Developmental teaching of mathematics for the learning disabled*. Rockville, Md.: Aspen.

―――. (1985). Learning disability and mathematics appraisal. In J. F. Cawley (ed.), *Practical mathematics appraisal of the learning disabled*. Rockville, Md.: Aspen.

Cawley, J. F., Fitzmaurice, A. M., Shaw, R. A., Kahn, H., & Bates, H. (1979). Math word problems: Suggestions for LD students. *Learning Disability Quarterly, 2*, 35–41.

Chi, M. T. H. (1976). Short term memory limitations in children: Capacity or processing deficits? *Memory and Cognition, 23*, 266–281.

Clements, M. A., & Del Campo, G. (1987). Linguistic and pedagogical factors influencing elementary schoolchildren's processing of arithmetic word problems. Unpublished paper, Catholic Education Office of Victoria and Association of Independent Schools of Victoria, Victoria, Australia.

Conca, L. (1987, April). A naturalistic study of strategy choice in learning disabled children with good and poor naming skills. Paper presented at the American Educational Research Association, Washington, D.C.

Corno, L. (1988). The study of teaching in mathematics learning: Views through two lenses. *Educational Psychologist, 23*, 181–202.

Dale, E., & O'Rourke, J. (1976, 1981). *The living word vocabulary, the words we know: A national vocabulary inventory*. Elgin, Ill.: Dome.

De Corte, E., & Vershchaffel, L. (1987, April). The influence of some non-semantic factors on solving addition and subtraction word problems. Paper presented at the annual meeting of the American Educational Research Association, Washington, D.C.

De Corte, E., Vershchaffel, L., & De Win, L. (1985). Influence of rewording verbal problems on children's representations and solutions. *Journal of Educational Psychology, 77*, 460–470.

Derry, S. J., & Murphy, D. A. (1986). Designing systems that train learning ability: From theory to practice. *Review of Educational Research, 56*(1), 1–39.

Dusek, J. B. (1980). The development of test anxiety in children. In I. G. Sarason (ed.), *Test anxiety: Theory, research, and applications*. Hillsdale, N.J.: Erlbaum.

Ericsson, K. A., & Simon, H. A. (1980). Verbal reports as data. *Psychological Review, 87*, 215–251.

Ferguson, G. A. (1956). On transfer and the abilities of man. *Canadian Journal of Psychology, 10*, 121–131.

Fleischner, J. E. & O'Loughlin, M. (1985). Solving story problems: Implications of research for teaching the learning disabled. In J. F. Cawley (ed.), *Cognitive strategies and mathematics for the learning disabled*. Rockville, Md.: Aspen.

Gagné, R. M. (1980). Learnable aspects of problem solving. *Educational Psychologist, 15*, 84–92.

Garner, R., Macready, G. B., & Wagoner, S. A. (1984). Readers' acquisition of the components of the text-lookback strategy. *Journal of Educational Psychology, 76*, 300–309.

Garner, R., Hare, V. C., Alexander, P., Haynes, J., & Winograd, P. (1984). Inducing use of a text lookback strategy among unsuccessful readers. *American Educational Research Journal,* 21, 789–798.

Garofalo, J., Kroll, D. L., & Lester, F. K. (1987). Metacognition and mathematical problem-solving: Preliminary research findings. In J. Bergeron, N. Herscovics, & C. Kieran (eds.), *Proceedings of the Eleventh Conference of the International Group for the Psychology of Mathematics Education.* Vol. 2. Montreal: PME.

Gick, M. L. (1986). Problem-solving strategies. *Educational Psychologist,* 21, 99–120.

Hiebert, J., & Wearne, D. (1986). Procedures over concepts: The acquisition of decimal number knowledge. In J. Hiebert (ed.), *Conceptual and procedural knowledge: The case of mathematics.* Hillsdale, N.J.: Erlbaum.

Hutchinson, N. L. (1987). Teaching representation and solution for three types of algebra word problems: A study with learning disabled adolescents. In J. Bergeron, N. Herscovics, & C. Kieran (eds.), *Proceedings of the Eleventh Conference of the International Group for the Psychology of Mathematics Education.* Vol. 3. Montreal: PME.

Jerman, M., & Rees, R. (1972). Predicting the relative difficulty of verbal arithmetic problems. *Educational Studies in Mathematics,* 4, 306–323.

Kieras, D. E. (1982). A model of reader strategy for extracting main ideas from simple technical prose. *Text,* 2, 47–81.

Kifer, E. (1987, April). Background characteristics related to the opportunity for mathematics instruction: An international perspective. Paper presented at the American Educational Research Association, Washington, D.C.

Kintsch, W. (1988). The role of knowledge in discourse comprehension: A construction-integration model. *Psychological Review,* 95, 163–182.

Kintsch, W., & Greeno, J. G. (1985). Understanding and solving word arithmetic problems. *Psychological Review,* 92, 109–129.

Kistner, J., Haskett, M., White, K., & Robbins, F. (1987). Perceived competence and self-worth of LD and normally achieving students. *Learning Disability Quarterly,* 10, 37–44.

Larson, S. C., Parker, R., & Trenholme, B. (1979). The effects of syntactic complexity upon arithmetic performance. *Learning Disability Quarterly,* 1(4), 80–85.

Lawson, M. J., & Rice, D. N. (1987). Solving word problems: A detailed analysis using think aloud data. In J. Bergeron, N. Herscovics, & C. Kieran (eds.), *Proceedings of the Eleventh Conference of the International Group for the Psychology of Mathematics Education.* Vol. 2. Montreal: PME.

Lester, F. K., Garofalo, J., & Kroll, D. L. (1989). Self-confidence, interests, beliefs and metacognition: Key influences on problem-solving behavior. In D. B. McLeod & V. M. Adams (eds.), *Affect and mathematical problem-solving: A new perspective.* New York: Springer-Verlag.

Linville, W. J. (1976). Syntax, vocabulary, and the verbal arithmetic problem. *School Science and Mathematics,* 76, 152–158.

Meyer, B. J. F., Brandt, D. M., & Bluth, G. J. (1980). Use of top-level structure in text: Key for reading comprehension of ninth-grade students. *Reading Research Quarterly,* 16, 72–103.

Mulcahy, R. F., & Marfo, K. (1987, April). Two years of cognitive education: Some preliminary results for the Alberta cognitive education project. Paper presented at the American Educational Research Association, Washington, D.C.

Nesher, P. (1986). Learning mathematics: A cognitive perspective. *American Psychologist,* 41, 1114–1122.

Nisbett, R. E., & Wilson, T. D. (1977). Telling more than we can know: Verbal reports on mental processes. *Psychological Review,* 84, 231–259.

Palincsar, A. S., & Brown, A. L. (1984). Reciprocal teaching of comprehension-fostering and comprehension-monitoring activities. *Cognition and Instruction,* 1, 117–175.

————. (1990). Classroom dialogues to promote self-regulated comprehension. In J. Brophy (ed.), *Teaching for understanding and self-regulated learning.* Vol. 1. Greenwich, Conn.: JAI.

Paris, S. G., & Oka, E. R. (1986). Children's reading strategies, metacognition, and motivation. *Developmental Review,* 6, 25–56.

————. (1989). Strategies for comprehending text and coping with reading difficulties. *Learning Disability Quarterly,* 12, 32–42.

Paris, S. G., Lipson, M. Y., & Wixson, K. K. (1983). Becoming a strategic reader. *Contemporary Educational Psychology,* 8, 293–316.

Pascual-Leone, J., Goodman, D., Subelman, I., & Ammon, P. (1978). Piagetian theory and Neo-Piagetian analysis as psychological guides in education. In J. M. Gallagher & J. A. Easley (eds.), *Knowledge and Development,* vol. 2, *Piaget in education.* New York: Plenum.

Pearson, P. D., & Johnson, D. D. (1978). *Teaching reading comprehension.* New York: Holt, Rinehart & Winston.

Perkins, D. N., & Salomon, G. (1989). Are cognitive skills context-bound? *Educational Researcher,* 18, 16–25.

Peterson, P. L., & Swing, S. R. (1983). Problems in classroom implementation of cognitive strategy instruction. In M. Pressley & J. Levin (eds.), *Cognitive strategy research: Educational applications.* New York: Academic.

Pressley, M. (1986). The relevance of the good strategy user model to the teaching of mathematics. *Educational Psychologist,* 21, 139–161.

Pressley, M., Goodchild, F., Fleet, J., Zajchowski, R., & Evans, E. D. (1987, June). What is good strategy use and why is it hard to teach?: An optimistic appraisal of the challenges associated with strategy instruction. Paper presented at the Canadian Society for Studies in Education Conference, Hamilton, Ont.

Raphael, T. E., & Wonnacott, C. A. (1985). Heightening fourth-grade students' sensitivity to source of information for answering comprehension questions. *Reading Research Quarterly,* 20, 282–296.

Reed, S. K. (1987). A structure-mapping model for word problems. *Journal of Experimental Psychology: Learning, Memory, and Cognition,* 13, 124–139.

Reys, R. E., Suydam, M. N., & Lindquist, M. M. (1984). *Helping children learn mathematics.* Englewood Cliffs, N.J.: Prentice-Hall.

Riley, M. S., Greeno, J. G., & Heller, J. I. (1983). Development of children's problem-solving ability in arithmetic. In H. P. Ginsburg (ed.), *The development of mathematical thinking.* New York: Academic.

Scardamalia, M., & Bereiter, C. (1984). Development of strategies in text processing. In E. H. Mandl, N. L. Stein, & T. Trabasso (eds.), *Learning and comprehension of text.* Hillsdale, N.J.: Erlbaum.

Sharma, M. C. (1984). Mathematics in the real world. In J. F. Cawley (ed.), *Devel-*

opmental teaching of mathematics for the learning disabled. Rockville, Md.: Aspen.

Simon, H. A. (1975). The functional equivalence of problem solving skills. *Cognitive Psychology,* 7, 268–288.

———. (1978). Information-processing theory of human problem solving skills. In W. Estes (ed.), *Handbook of learning and cognitive processes.* Vol. 5. Hillsdale, N.J.: Erlbaum.

Simons, P. R. J. (1987, April). Individual differences in self-regulation of learning, emerging from thinking aloud protocols. Paper presented at the annual meeting of the American Educational Research Association, Washington, D.C.

Steacy, N., & Bachor, D. G. (1987, June). Learner characteristics and task variables as predictors of rule induction ability on word problems. Paper presented at the Canadian Society for Studies in Education Conference, Hamilton, Ont.

———. (1988, June). A description of selected grade 6 rule induction behavior when solving arithmetic word problems. Paper presented at the Canadian Society for Studies in Education Conference, Windsor, Ont.

Sternberg, R. J. (1983). Criteria for intellectual skills training. *Educational Researcher,* 12, 6–12.

Sternberg, R. J., & Martin, M. (1988). When teaching thinking does not work, what goes wrong? *Teachers College Record,* 89, 555–578.

Thomas, V. (1979). *Teaching spelling. Canadian word lists and instructional techniques.* 2d ed. Toronto: Gage.

Threadgill-Sowder, J., Sowder, L., Moyer, J. C., & Moyer, M. B. (1985). Cognitive variables and performance on mathematical story problems. *Journal of Experimental Education,* 54, 56–62.

van Lieshout, E. C. D. M. (1986, April). Developing a computer-assisted strategy training procedure for children with learning deficiencies to solve addition and subtraction problems. Paper presented at the American Educational Research Association, San Francisco, Calif.

Vernon, P. E. (1969). *Intelligence and cultural environment.* London: Methuen.

Wang, M. C., Levine, L. J., & McGill, A. M. (1987, April) The use of observational data for analysis of student use of the self-instructional process in classroom learning contexts. Paper presented at the American Educational Research Association, Washington, D.C.

Washburne, C. (1931). Mental age and arithmetic curriculum: A summary of the committee of seven grade placement investigations to date. *Journal of Educational Research,* 23, 210–231.

West, C. K., Lee, J. F., & Anderson, T. H. (1969). The influence of test anxiety on the selection of relevant from irrelevant information. *Journal of Educational Research,* 63, 51–52.

Wine, J. D. (1980). Cognitive-attentional theory of test anxiety. In I. G. Sarason (ed.), *Test anxiety: Theory, research, and applications.* Hillsdale, N.J.: Erlbaum.

Winne, P. H., Woodlands, M. J., & Wong, B. (1982). Comparability of self-concept among learning disabled, normal, and gifted students. *Journal of Learning Disabilities,* 15, 470–475.

10

Modeling Reading as a Cognitive and Linguistic Skill

Che Kan Leong

Downing and Leong (1982) consider reading as a skill subsuming a hierarchy of interrelated subskills. The main subskills of decoding at the word level and comprehending at the sentence and paragraph level are also affected by the readers' world knowledge. In taking this line of approach they were influenced by general observations of motor skill development, and made suggestions for reading with considerable trepidation. They were, however, encouraged by the conceptualization of skill acquisition and development in cognitive psychology in terms of the declarative stage and the procedural stage (Anderson, 1980, 1982). The declarative stage refers to the interpretation or cognitive aspect of the skill domain; with practice knowledge is transformed into a procedural form in performing the skill.

Drawing from the observations of general skill development and the formalism of cognitive psychology, Downing and Leong (1982) view reading as a complex behavior with cognitive, mastering, and automaticity phases of development. The development of proficient reading is accompanied by certain characteristics: (1) smooth performance, (2) proper timing, pacing, and flexibility, (3) anticipation of future events, (4) consciousness of the reading activities and their functions, (5) sensitivity to shifts from external to internal cues, (6) use of increasingly larger units of processing, (7) automaticity beyond mere accuracy for flexible resource allocation for various subskills, and (8) integration of these cascading subskills.

MODELING READING PROCESSES

Assumptions of the Study

Certain mutually facilitating processes are emphasized in fluent reading: (1) word analysis, (2) discourse analysis above the word level, and (3) integrative analysis (Frederiksen, 1982). In particular, skilled reading performance derives from integrated, automatic processing of various knowledge-based subskills. The integration of the subskills operates in an orderly cascade system, enabling outputs from a particular level (e.g., word processing) feeding into adjacent levels (e.g., sentence processing), and also distant levels. The efficiency of the processing is particularly important. Mechanisms for the interaction of the components may differ for "expert" readers and for "novice" and less skilled ones. While poor readers are generally inefficient in processing component reading tasks, there are individual differences and the locus of inefficiency varies from component to component and from subskill to subskill.

For grade 4–6 readers, reading proficiency results from a complex operation of components that interact with one another: (1) the orthographic and phonological component, (2) the morphological component, and (3) the sentence and paragraph comprehension component. These components are conceptualized as latent or unobserved variables that act on some manifest variables or subskills as indicators. These parsimonious latent variables are further hypothesized as providing a "causal" link in the descriptive sense, as verified in structural equation modeling, to the latent reading competence, as represented by scores on standardized word reading and reading comprehension tests (Leong, 1988).

The sample for the study consisted of 298 children in grades 4, 5, and 6 in 12 rooms in 3 schools. The subskills or tasks subserving the latent domains were all administered via the microcomputer with reaction times as the dependent variables (Leong & Lock, 1989). The subskills are described briefly below.

Modeling Orthographic and Phonological Knowledge

The orthographic and phonological domain was subserved by the orthographic subskill, phonological subskill, and rhyme-matching subskill tasks. The orthographic subskill task required individual children to distinguish accurately and rapidly words from homophonous letter strings matched for length and pronunciation (e.g., RAIN, RANE; CLOUN, CLOWN). The assumption is that a correct lexical decision is based on knowledge of the orthographic code of the letter strings. The phonological subskill task required subjects to designate accurately and rapidly the pseudohomophonic letter strings that sound like real words in item pairs matched for length and orthographic similarity (e.g., BLOG, BLOE; KAKE, DAKE).

The rhyme-matching task tests the hypothesis that the cognitive and linguistic demand, and by inference the latency for decision, of rhyme matching is markedly increased where there is a conflict between orthographic and phonological cues. This notion was tested with matched nonrhyming word pairs that contain identical rhyme but different onsets (e.g., PAID–SAID; GOLF–WOLF). This rhyme-matching condition with conflicting orthographic and phonological cues was compared with other word pair conditions that rhyme (e.g., BLUE–FLEW), and word pairs that both rhyme and are orthographically similar (e.g., PAIR–FAIR). Statistical analyses of the response latencies show clearly the different rhyme-matching conditions vary significantly according to the cognitive and linguistic demands of the conditions and for readers of varying reading abilities in different grades (Leong, 1991).

Modeling Morphological Knowledge

The morphological domain relates to declarative knowledge of the structural composition of words with particular emphasis on derivational morphology and morphemic parsing (Leong, 1989a, 1989b). The complementary derived form morphology and base form morphology subskills examined individual subjects' automatic morphological knowledge of the derived forms and base forms of words embedded in sentence frames in relation to reading proficiency. Latency results of the automatic processing in vocalizing the appropriate derived or base words from the target base or derived forms and the sentence frame contexts show clearly the increased cognitive and linguistic demand from the no change (e.g., WARM#TH; ENJOY#MENT) through the orthographic change (e.g., SUN–SUNNY), phonological change (e.g., DRAMA–DRAMATIC) to the orthographic and phonological change (e.g., EXPLAIN–EXPLANATION) processing conditions (Leong, 1989a, 1989b).

The morphological decomposition subskill relates the basic orthographic syllabic structure (BOSS) principle and its corollaries of Taft (1987) to reading proficiency in the present study. This task is based on the logic that the parsing mechanism conserves the underlying morphological relationship among semantically related words. For example, ACTOR is accessed by ACT–OR rather than the syllabic AC–TOR and LANTERN by LANT–ERN rather than LAN–TERN. There is also a cost associated with the parsing of a word into prefix + pseudoroot or pseudoroot + suffix. The results with different reading subgroups and different grades suggest that the efficiency in lexical decision via the morphemic or syllabic division of words is a source of individual differences in reading proficiency (Leong, 1989a; Leong & Parkinson, 1990).

Modeling Verbal Comprehension

The sentence and paragraph comprehension domain was subserved by several subskills. The sentence lexical decision task is predicated on the rationale that the grammatical structure of incomplete sentences affects lexical latencies.

Modal verb contexts, followed by main verb targets, and preposition contexts, followed by plural noun targets, should lead to faster response latencies than do the opposite pairings. This principle of grammaticality and parsing procedures should differentiate response latencies and provide another indicator of reading performance. In this task the subject was asked to press a YES/NO key to denote if the target word would make the anomalous sentence "better" (but still anomalous) or "not so good." Sample couplet sentences were: "*If the ball falls, it will LAUGH" (YES); "*If the ball falls, it will CROPS" (NO).

The sentence pattern task is essentially a sentence decision task assessing subcategorization, particle movement, selection restriction, and transformations (including negation, question formation, and passivization). Examples of parallel sentences were: "The runner turned off the road" (YES); "*The runner turned the road off" (NO). Efficient access of knowledge of functional grammar is another source of individual differences in reading proficiency.

The paragraph comprehension task aimed at assessing the child's ability to detect quickly and accurately the one incongruous or inconsistent sentence embedded in running texts of six sentences each. An example was a passage with the schema of a boy going into a barber shop, waiting, and finally getting a hair cut, but the title of "Visit to a Doctor" was incongruous. It was hypothesized that the ability to detect inconsistency in connected discourse would affect reading performance.

Sentence-Picture Verification Task

The sentence verification task was predicated on the psycholinguistic processing models of sentence-picture verification of Clark and Chase (1972) and Carpenter and Just (1975), and their precursor, the processing of positive and negative information, by Wason (1959). There were two parts to the task: sixteen sentence-picture verification pairs and sixteen sentence-letter verification pairs. The rationale of the first part of this subskill and its effect on readers of varying proficiency are discussed below. Details are given elsewhere (Leong, 1990). The emphasis is on the cognitive and linguistic processing needed in what might appear to be a simple sentence verification task and yet one with implications for verbal comprehension.

In essence, typical sentence-picture pairs are constructed by taking four binary dimensions (STAR, PLUS), (IS, IS NOT), (ABOVE, BELOW), and (*, +; +, *) in all possible combinations to yield sixteen sentence-picture pairs with four truth conditions: true affirmative (TA), false affirmative (FA), true negative (TN), and false negative (FN). The sentence-picture combination is displayed simultaneously on the microcomputer screen such that individual subjects might see the sentence "Star is above plus" and a picture of a star above a + (TA condition). They are asked to verify accurately and quickly if the sentence is a true or false description of the picture combination with a key press that will terminate the timer to provide precision verification timing. This standard procedure was followed in the present study.

This type of verification task taps the cognitive process involved in holding a series of reading units in memory until their meaning is accessed, and this process is used irrespective of the linguistic or the pictorial strategy employed. The response latency thus reflects the combined time taken to encode and comprehend the sentence and the picture pair, and also to verify the match or mismatch of the TA, FA, TN, or FN truth conditions. Despite some technical differences between the Clark and Chase (1972) and the Carpenter and Just (1975) psycholinguistic models, there is general agreement that verification latencies show increasing linearity according to the degrees of match or mismatch or the number of constituent comparisons. Furthermore, the robust linearity results account for a very large proportion of the variation in latencies across truth conditions. True negative (TN) sentence-picture pairs should take the longest processing time because of the mismatch between the embedded strings of the sentence and the picture encoded in propositional forms and the embedding strings. The next longest latencies are the false negatives (FN), then the false affirmatives (FA); the true affirmatives (TA) are processed the fastest. In other words, the cognitive and linguistic demands of the truth conditions as reflected in response times can be hypothesized as: $TA < FA < FN < TN$. The information-processing mechanism of the sentence-picture verification task is shown in table 10.1.

It should be noted that the true negative (TN) condition is the most complicated in terms of the mental operations needed for verification. It is likely that in the verification process subjects mentally delete the negative, then verify the truth or falsehood of the statement, and then change the answer to accommodate the deletion of the negative. It is TN, not false negative (FN), which is a double negative in that TN denies a falsehood. Hence it is reasonable to expect TN to take the longest time to process.

The linearity of processing as a function of the number of constituent comparisons was borne out with the 298 grade 4, 5, and 6 children trichotomized into below average (BA), average (AV), and above average (AA) readers on the aggregate of standardized word reading and reading comprehension tests.

The mean and standard deviations of the verification times (TRUE/FALSE) of the correct answers after editing for outliers for the three grades by reading levels and for the four verification conditions are shown in table 10.2. The results are displayed graphically in figure 10.1.

Without going into detail and without loss of generality, the analyses of variance of the verification time measures indicate performance differences among the different grades and varying reading levels. In particular, the ANOVA results show significant differences in response latencies among the four verification conditions, and these differences vary linearly according to the levels of match or mismatch in the mental operations, as shown earlier in the robust findings with adults (Carpenter & Just, 1975; Clark & Chase, 1972).

Table 10.1
Sentence Verification Task

Truth Condition		Sentence Representation	Picture Representation	No. of Constituent Comparisons
True Affirmative (TA)	☆ + Star is above plus. / Plus is below star.	[AFF (STAR, TOP)]	(STAR, TOP)	K
	+ ☆ Plus is above star. / Star is below plus.	[AFF (PLUS, TOP)]	(PLUS, TOP)	K
False Affirmative (FA)	+ ☆ Star is above plus. / Plus is below star.	[AFF (STAR, TOP)]	(PLUS, TOP)	K + 1
	☆ + Plus is above star. / Star is below plus.	[AFF (PLUS, TOP)]	(STAR, TOP)	K + 1
True Negative (TN)	+ ☆ Star is not above plus. / Plus is not below star.	[NEG [AFF (STAR, TOP)]]	(PLUS, TOP)	K + 5
	☆ + Plus is not above star. / Star is not below plus.	[NEG [AFF (PLUS, TOP)]]	(STAR, TOP)	K + 5
False Negative (FN)	☆ + Star is not above plus. / Plus is not below star.	[NEG [AFF (STAR, TOP)]]	(STAR, TOP)	K + 4
	+ ☆ Plus is not above star. / Star is not below plus.	[NEG [AFF (PLUS, TOP)]]	(PLUS, TOP)	K + 4

Hypothesis: TA < FA < FN < TN (all in RTs)

After Carpenter & Just, 1975; Clark & Chase, 1972.

166

Table 10.2

Mean and Standard Deviations (in Parentheses) of Sentence-Picture Verification Times (Msec) by Condition and Reading Level for Grade 4, 5, and 6 Children (N=298)

Reading Level

Truth Conditions	Grade 4 Below Average (BA)			Grade 5 Average (AV)			Grade 6 Above Average (AA)		
	BA	AV	AA	BA	AV	AA	BA	AV	AA
True Affirmative (TA)	4692 (1386)	4428 (1230)	3521 (1091)	4494 (1104)	3710 (788)	3498 (743)	4014 (1121)	3054 (640)	2757 (705)
False Affirmative (FA)	5232 (1561)	4304 (1512)	3764 (1246)	4708 (1153)	3559 (919)	3438 (790)	4336 (1185)	3245 (610)	3088 (759)
True Negative (TN)	6302 (2184)	5667 (1728)	5021 (1765)	5902 (2227)	4850 (1034)	4827 (1596)	4985 (1415)	4206 (919)	3894 (1043)
False Negative (FN)	5499 (1789)	5181 (1908)	4842 (1710)	5592 (1702)	4494 (1501)	4178 (1291)	4896 (1513)	3934 (1220)	3565 (960)
Sample Size	35	34	34	27	30	31	36	34	37

Figure 10.1
Sentence-Picture Verification Times (Msec) for Grade 4, 5, and 6 Children (N = 298) by Reading Level and Truth Condition

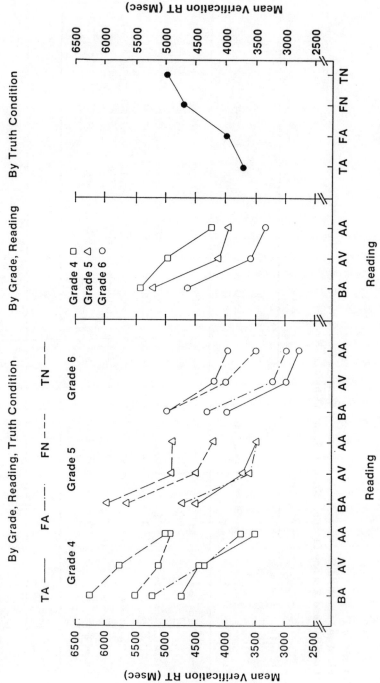

Reading level: below average (BA), average (AV), above average (AA); truth condition: true affirmative (TA), false affirmative (FA), false negative (FN), true negative (TN).

Of the four verification conditions, the true affirmative (TA) condition involves no mismatch between the sentence and picture representation and should be processed the fastest. The base number of constituent comparison (denoted by K) is incremented by one mental operation in the false affirmative condition where there is a mismatch between the sentence and picture propositions. Similarly, for the false negative (FN) condition the number of constituent comparison is $K + 4$; and for the true denial of a falsehood or true negative (TN) condition the number of constituent comparisons is $K + 5$. The ANOVA results show clearly that the response latencies among the four verification conditions vary linearly according to the levels of match or mismatch in the mental operations. More precisely, overall latencies collapsing across grades and reading levels increased by 177 msec. between FA and TA, 711 msec. between FN and NA, and 384 msec. between TN and FN. In sum, the above results show that the verification of truth conditions as a form of verbal comprehension is not so much a function of affirmation or negation per se, but of the number of constituent comparisons among the mental representations.

IMPLICATIONS FOR INSTRUCTION

Verbal Efficiency

One of the purposes of the longitudinal two-cohort study outlined in this chapter was the modeling of reading processes with a number of laboratory reading tasks sampling interrelated reading subskills under rather stringent experimental conditions. The administration of all the experimental tasks via the microcomputer with response time measures as the dependent variable aims at capturing the on-line, real-time nature of reading. In analogy with other complex skills, reading involves the concurrent computation of different kinds of cognitive and linguistic information in a relatively short period of time. The immediacy nature of reading is best represented in the latency measures derived from the various lexical and sentence decision tasks and the vocalization tasks. The computerized tasks also encourage automaticity (due care being taken to guard against speed-accuracy tradeoffs) at "lower" levels of processing so that resources can be devoted to "higher" levels of processing. The underlying notion is the promotion of verbal efficiency (Perfetti, 1985).

Interrelated Components of Reading

Details of the interrelatedness of the three latent components of reading (orthographic and phonological; morphological; and sentence and paragraph comprehension) and their "causal" effects on grade 4, 5, and 6 readers' reading performance as measured by standardized word reading and reading comprehension tests have been reported elsewhere (Leong, 1988). Briefly, linear structural equation modeling with LISREL (Joreskog & Sorbom, 1984) shows that the three-component, nine to ten independent variables modeling seems to provide a good fit for grade 4 data, a reasonable fit for grade 5 data, but was less unambiguous for grade 6 data. This "loose" fit suggests that the model and its variant forms need to be formulated more rigorously, and "clean" manifest tests should enhance the contribution of the interrelated domains to school reading performance. It should be pointed out that for the second cohort of about three hundred children in phase 2 of the longitudinal study, the manifest or indicator tests were in fact "purified" on the basis of item analysis using the Rasch model. Furthermore, initial results from the multisample structural equation modeling using LISREL suggest resonable stability over time and across cohorts in terms of the fit of the model and its variants with the data.

Results of the analyses of variance of the experimental tasks (Leong, 1989a, 1989b, 1991) and the LISREL analyses should add to the argument for the multilevel and multicomponent model of reading proposed by Frederiksen (1982) and Olson et al. (1985). Conscious awareness of the knowledge of phonology as represented by the orthographic and phonological component in the study has been shown to be important in the early reading (see Leong, 1987, 1991, n.d.), and phonological processing of lexical access is not diminished with age or with familiar words (Van Orden, 1987). At the same time, knowledge of the compositional and relational nature of lexical items as reflected in the morphological component is also important. This is shown by the finding in multiple regression analyses that the derived morphology task accounted for 32, 34, and 44 percent of the variance of the criterion of reading performance for grade 4, 5, and 6 readers, respectively (Leong, 1988). Verbal comprehension as subserved by the sentence decision, sentence pattern, paragraph comprehension, and sentence verification tasks is equally important, because reading evolves around the learning of concepts from texts in addition to acquiring and developing word knowledge. As shown by the classic studies of Carpenter and Just (1975), Clark and Chase (1972), and Wason (1959), and as can be inferred from the heuristic values of my results with children summarized here (see tables 10.1 and 10.2, figure 10.1), the basic mental processes involved in sentence verification are part of a larger system of mental operations used in verbal comprehension in general. In comprehending linguistic materials readers (and for that matter listeners) need to encode the lexical and syntactic information, access the concepts, and simultaneously compute the interpretations on the basis of previous knowledge.

Training of Components of Reading

The delineation of functionally defined information-processing domains and their interactions as suggested by Frederiksen (1982) and Perfetti (1985), among others, emphasizes the linking of the components and the possibility of training individual subskills. The cognitive framework and actual training procedures are well stated by Frederiksen and his colleagues (Frederiksen & Warren, 1987;

Frederiksen et al., 1985a, 1985b). The underlying notion is that "tasks high in a skill hierarchy (e.g., the inference task) depend on the effective, integrated operation of a number of skills that are functionally linked, either through shared data structures or shared processing resources, to the skills explicitly acquired to perform such tasks." (Frederiksen et al., 1985b, p. 334).

Frederiksen and his colleagues have developed microcomputer training environments focusing on individual components of reading and have carried out training studies to evaluate transfer effects to other functionally linked components. These "enabling" processes in word analysis and parallel, frame-based analysis of text demonstrate the feasibility of the componential approach to instruction and remediation. Our efforts following on the phase 2 study of the second cohort of children were much more modest. Two twin training projects extending over five consecutive weeks on a daily basis and involving poor readers identified in the study and their controls were carried out (Leong et al., 1990). The emphasis was on verbal efficiency and its interaction with the underlying mental representation systems (Beck & Carpenter, 1986). Study 1 stressed the development of the word knowledge component in poor readers through multiple exposures and multiple sources of information (McKeown & Curtis, 1987; Miller & Gildea, 1987). Study 2 aimed at elaboration training in the prose comprehension component (see Palincsar & Brown, 1984; Wong, 1985). Analyses of the quantitative and qualitative data show some measure of success in the modest five-week training program in promoting word knowledge and efficient self-questioning among poor readers. Both study 1 and 2 also suggest that direct, explicit teaching with discussion of learning strategies and feedback could go some way in helping not only less skilled, but also skilled, readers.

ACKNOWLEDGEMENT

The research summarized in this chapter was assisted by S.S.H.R.C. of Canada through S.S.H.R.C. grant #410-87-0058 and #410-89-00128. I am grateful for their assistance.

REFERENCES

Anderson, J. R. (1980). *Cognitive psychology and its implications*. San Francisco: Freeman.

———. (1982). Acquisition of cognitive skill. *Psychological Review, 89*, 369–406.

Beck, I. L., & Carpenter, P. A. (1986). Cognitive approaches to understanding reading: Implications for instructional practice. *American Psychologist, 41*, 1098–1105.

Carpenter, P. A., & Just, M. A. (1975). Sentence comprehension: A psycholinguistic processing model of verification. *Psychological Review, 82*, 45–73.

Clark, H. H., & Chase, W. G. (1972). On the process of comparing sentences against pictures. *Cognitive Psychology, 3*, 472–517.

Downing, J., & Leong, C. K. (1982). *Psychology of reading*. New York: Macmillan.

Frederiksen, J. R. (1982). A componential theory of reading skills and their interactions. In R. J. Sternberg (ed.), *Advances in the psychology of human intelligence*. Vol. 1. Hillsdale, N.J.: Erlbaum.

Frederiksen, J. R., & Warren, B. M. (1987). A cognitive framework for developing expertise in reading. In R. Glaser (ed.), *Advances in instructional psychology*. Vol. 3. Hillsdale, N.J.: Erlbaum.

Frederiksen, J. R., Warren, B. M., & Rosebery, A. S. (1985a). A componential approach to training reading skills, pt. 1, Perceptual units training. *Cognition and Instruction*, 2, 91–130.

———. (1985b). A componential approach to training reading skills, pt. 2, Decoding and use of context. *Cognition and Instruction*, 2, 271–338.

Joreskog, K. G., & Sorbom, D. (1984). *LISREL VI: Analysis of linear structural relationships by the method of maximum likelihood*. Chicago: Scientific Software.

Leong, C. K. (1987). *Children with specific reading disabilities*. Lisse, The Netherlands: Swets & Zeitlinger.

———. (1988). A componential approach to understanding reading and its difficulties in preadolescent readers. *Annals of Dyslexia*, 38, 95–119.

———. (1989a). The effects of morphological structure on reading proficiency—A developmental study. *Reading and Writing: An Interdisciplinary Journal*, 1, 357–379.

———. (1989b). Productive knowledge of derivational rules in poor readers. *Annals of Dyslexia*, 39, 94–115.

———. (1991). From phonemic awareness to phonological processing to language access in children developing reading proficiency. In D. J. Sawyer & B. J. Fox (eds.), *Phonological awareness in reading: The evolution of current perspectives*. New York: Springer-Verlag.

———. (n.d.) *Sentence verification as a source of reading comprehension in children*. Manuscript.

Leong, C. K., & Lock, S. (1989). The use of microcomputer technology in a modular-approach to reading and reading difficulties. *Reading and Writing: An Interdisciplinary Journal*, 1, 245–255.

Leong, C. K., & Parkinson, M. E. (1990, June). *Understanding of orthotactic rules in visual word recognition by poor readers*. Paper presented at the annual convention of the Canadian Psychological Association, Ottawa, Canada.

Leong, C. K., Simmons, D. R., & Izatt-Gambell, M.-A. (1990). The effect of systematic training in elaboration on word meaning and prose comprehension in poor readers. *Annals of Dyslexia*, 40.

McKeown, M. G., & Curtis, M. E. (eds.). (1987). *The nature of vocabulary acquisition*. Hillsdale, N.J.: Erlbaum.

Miller, G. A., & Gildea, P. M. (1987). How children learn words. *Scientific American*, 257, 94–99.

Olson, R. K., Kliegl, R., Davidson, B. J., & Foltz, G. (1985). Individual and developmental differences in reading disability. In G. E. Mackinnon & T. G. Waller (eds.), *Reading research: Advances in theory and practice*. Vol. 4. New York: Academic.

Palincsar, A. S., & Brown, A. L. (1984). Reciprocal teaching of comprehension-fostering and comprehension-monitoring activities. *Cognition and Instruction*, 1, 117–175.

Perfetti, C. A. (1985). *Reading ability*. New York: Oxford University Press.

Taft, M. (1987). Morphograhic processing: The BOSS reemerges. In M. Coltheart (ed.), *Attention and performance 12: The psychology of reading.* London: Erlbaum.

Van Orden, G. C. (1987). A rows is a rose: Spelling, sound, and reading. *Memory & Cognition,* 15, 181–198.

Wason, P. C. (1959). The processing of positive and negative information. *Quarterly Journal of Experimental Psychology* 11, 92–107.

Wong, B. Y. L. (1985). Self-questioning instructional research: A review. *Review of Educational Research,* 55, 227–268.

11

Metalinguistics and Reading Ability

Gabriel J. Mancini, Robert F. Mulcahy,
Robert H. Short, and Seokee Cho

There are few who would debate that language development is an integral part of human development. Language can be viewed as being inextricably and reciprocally related to all aspects of human development. The unconscious ease with which language is acquired provides an additional source of impetus to the notion that it is central to the very nature of human beings. Chomsky (1972, p. 4) emphasizes that "language is a mirror of mind in a deep and significant sense. It is a product of human intelligence, created anew in each individual by operations that lie far beyond the reach of will or consciousness."

Understanding the nature of language—its acquisition, development, and vagaries—is of interest to epistemologists, psychologists, sociologists, and anthropologists alike.

To the educator, language is not only a medium of communication but a catalyst to individual learning and academic success. The importance placed on the role of language is witnessed by the unprecedented proliferation of research designed to investigate the relationship between language and reading, particularly in the area of reading disability. Despite this diversity of research in the field of reading problems, however, little attention has been directed to the important area of metalinguistic awareness, the knowledge that an individual possesses about language and its implications for reading acquisition.

A review of the most recent literature on learning disabilities stresses the importance of using a metalinguistic approach to facilitate a better understanding of the nature of reading disability.

Metalinguistic awareness has been defined, in information-processing terms, as "the ability to perform mental operations on the products of mental mechanisms involved in sentence comprehension; that is, the systematic phones, the words and their association meanings, the structural representation of sentences, and the sets of interrelated propositions'' (Tunmer & Fletcher, 1981, p. 175). Metalinguistic awareness has also been defined as ''reflective understanding of language and awareness of the nature of language'' (Dejarlais & Lazar, 1976, p. 11).

Research is accumulating that suggests that the development of metalinguistic abilities may be related to reading ability (Ehri, 1979; Tunmer & Bowey, 1980). Furthermore, since most researchers in the area of reading regard spoken language as a fundamental cornerstone to reading acquisition, the basic task in acquiring reading is to transcribe the printed language onto the existing spoken language. This requires the ability to manipulate the structural features of spoken language. The metalinguistic awareness of spoken language should, therefore, correlate highly with learning to read since weakness in the former would hinder the discovery of the properties of spoken language. These properties bridge written and spoken language forms.

There appears to be considerable individual variation in the development of metalinguistic skill. Some individuals are not only conscious of the linguistic patterns but also take considerable pleasure in exploiting this consciousness into verbal jokes, punning, and linguistic analysis. On the other hand, others seem to be quite unaware of the intricacies of language and seem quite surprised when obvious linguistic patterns are presented to them. This variation provides a marked contrast to the relative consistency with which language develops in individuals. It seems that the ''synthesis of an utterance is one thing; the awareness of the process of synthesis is quite another'' (Mattingly, 1972, p. 140).

Metalinguistic awareness is by no means a passive phenomenon. Individuals can utilize this awareness to control, in a conscious way, their linguistic activities by appreciating, for example, that words are not only part and parcel of their referents but also can be used to denote abstract concepts. Furthermore, metalinguistic awareness can facilitate the understanding of different meanings within written texts or language such as in the appreciation of ambiguities in spoken or written sentences.

Research on metalinguistic development has been rather scant and has focused mainly on young children (preschoolers, first and second graders). Nevertheless, some experimenters have reported that metalinguistic awareness plays an integral role in reading acquisition (e.g., Ehri, 1979), while others have reported that metalinguistic awareness encompasses ''not so much awareness but access to the individual's knowledge of the grammatical structure of sentences'' (Mattingly, 1979, p. 2). These suggestions, however, have been made with little empirical evidence. To date, investigators have not yet arrived at a common consensus as to which tasks make up the framework and measures of metalinguistic awareness. Therefore, if one wishes to discover how metalinguistic awareness develops, and what relationship it has to the acquisition of academic skills (reading), one must know what it is that is being acquired.

Thus, achieving a suitable description of the phenomenon called metalinguistic awareness is the first responsibility of investigators in this area.

Very little research has specifically investigated the relationship between metalinguistic awareness and reading acquisition. A major emphasis in research has been one of investigating metalinguistic development within young populations, not with reading disabled children or older age groups. Consequently, there is scant evidence available for understanding the development of metalinguistic awareness and its relationship to reading acquisition.

The relationship between metalinguistic ability and reading proficiency is supported by a growing body of research. For the last several years, researchers have come to believe that a child's understanding of language and ability to treat language analytically may be more important to the acquisition of reading than the child's language itself. Read's (1978) appreciation of the relationship between language and reading is reflected by his statement that

the performance of adapting, manipulating, segmenting, correcting and judging language seems to play an important role in at least three processes: learning to read and write, learning a nonnative language, and responding to social expectations. In short, they have a great deal to do with using language effectively under varied circumstances. Whether they are conscious, or can appear to be brought to consciousness appears to be of secondary importance. (p. 66)

Why is it that a child who knows the alphabetic characters and their sounds may still not be able to read the word or the syllable they compose? This is, of course, the riddle of the reading process, and the entire history of teaching reading pivots around this riddle. Results of investigations in the United States and Russia have revealed a striking relationship between cognitive development and reading disability. For example, cognitive problems may not be due primarily to insufficient practical knowledge, but rather a disability in voluntarily "representing" that which is known. Representational competence is inextricably related to the proficiency of using symbolic systems such as language.

Reading disabled children have been found to function at a preoperational level of thinking, using figurative aspects of thought rather than operative thinking (Klees & Le Brun, 1972). Pursuant to the above evidence, it is not surprising that language difficulties pose considerable problems for reading. For example, the transformation of a sentence into an interrogative or imperative form, using a passive tense, necessitates a rather complex mental operation. Thus reliance on figurative thought hinders the successful manipulation of complex structures that require a number of manipulations to be performed. While some investigators have studied populations with generalized reading disability, others have focused upon the specific interrelationship between language and reading.

Reading has been described as a "psycholinguistic guessing game in which the readers sample only a minimal number of visual signals, relying heavily on the redundancy of language to predict structures" (Gerber, 1981, p. 93). Consequently, it is reasonable to suggest that the process of reading requires readers to utilize their knowledge of language and the world, for example, thinking. Thus, weaknesses in the linguistic system would be directly translated to difficulties in reading/thinking. For example, ineptitude in word retrieval in spoken language would mirror a disability in reading, since "reading like picture naming requires ready elicitation of spoken equivalents" (Jansky & de Hirsch, 1972, p. 40). Similarly, syntactic deficiency has been found to correlate with a disability in reading comprehension since "meaning is conveyed primarily through the systematic structure rather than individual words" (Vogel, 1975, p. 36).

Denner (1970) and Farnham-Diggory (1967), in investigating the relationship between syntactic ability and reading, presented their subjects with groups of three logographs and required them not only to cut out the sentences composed of these logographs, but also to perform the appropriate responses. The results revealed that the reading disabled experienced considerable difficulty in translating and synthesizing the meaning of the sentence as a whole, an operation that develops between the ages of six and nine. These children consistently attempted to perform the act of each logograph (e.g., "block," "jump," and "over" instead of "jump over block"). Denner (1970) reports that the inability to synthesize the logographs into a meaningful string of words is directly related to syntactic incompetence. Furthermore, Denner (1970) suggests that "these children do not read sentences, but a series of individual words, and the sentence meaning is some conglomerate of individual words rather than a unified contextual conception" (p. 882). Wallach (1978) characterized this phenomenon as the inability to "hold together grammatical frames and abstract meaning from larger contexts" (p. 181). This difficulty occurs largely due to inappropriate understanding and misapplication of linguistic rules and strategies that are important in language comprehension and, more specifically, reading. Thus, reading can be described not as a purely perceptual act, but as a "language-based activity" requiring the orchestration of both knowledge of language and the world.

It is rather interesting that a number of investigators have come to believe that reading requires a linguistic awareness of greater magnitude and sophistication than that required for speaking. This awareness reflects a high degree of variability within the population (Mattingly, 1972; Shankweiler & Liberman, 1972). Gerber (1981) maintains that

it is highly possible, although not as yet thoroughly researched, that part of the learning disabled child's deficits lie not solely in his linguistic systems themselves, which functions out of wariness, but in the inadequacy of this secondary linguistic awareness or what might be labelled meta-linguistic skills." (p. 93)

This argument is convincing when consideration is given to the phonological domain and to the phonetic skills of word segmentation that, according to Kinsbourne and Coplan (1979), "calls for an analytical listening attitude and requires deliberate effort'' (p. 123). Vygotsky (1962) claims that ''consciousness and control appear only at a stage in the development of a function, after it has been used and practiced unconsciously and spontaneously'' (p. 43). Thus, it seems reasonable to assume that language may be conceived of as functioning at different levels of complexity and that language and reading are closely related. Furthermore, it may be argued that a necessary condition for proficient reading is the existence of language awareness or metalinguistic awareness.

Developmentally, linguistic awareness unfolds after the individual has learned to speak and understand. It is also closely related to the type of linguistic representation that is required to successfully perform the task. That is to say, deep representations are easier to access and report than are less processed (superficial) representations since the latter are limited in their conscious reflection.

Because metalinguistic awareness emerges relatively late in comparison with general language development (Dale, 1976; Mattingly, 1972; Slobin, 1978), and because of the inconsistencies and variability with which it is found in adults, metalinguistic awareness may not be directly connected with early language acquisition.

Reading, like language development, requires metacognition to be a conscious act and, like metalinguistic awareness, is an inconsistent skill. Moreover, reading is also wholly ''responsive'' to the type of script or schema used. These are knowledge representations that facilitate the making of inferences about concepts and aid in reading comprehension. Scripts that are ''deep representations'' are easiest to appreciate and learn since they facilitate conscious reflection.

According to Mattingly (1979), metalinguistic awareness is directly related to the ability to access the ''individual's knowledge of the grammatical structure of sentences'' (cited in Downing & Leong, 1982, p. 98). The relationship between reading and metalinguistic awareness, according to Mattingly (1980), is directly related to the degree with which the individual has actively pursued language learning. This quest would lead the individual to acquire greater grammatical knowledge and thus render reading easier.

This hypothesis at first glance seems reasonable since failure to utilize language and to strive for greater linguistic goals would weaken one's facility to use the particular linguistic awareness skills. Mattingly (1972) also suggests, however, that if children fail to ''pursue language acquisition beyond what is needed for ordinary usage, their language awareness will atrophy and that this is likely to make it difficult for them to learn how to read'' (cited in Downing & Leong, 1982, p. 100).

From a syntactical perspective, Bever et al. (1973) emphasize that grammar does not wither away since it is well entrenched in the individual. According to Bever et al., grammar becomes ''epiphenamental'' to comprehension (e.g., I understand what you are saying in spite of the fact that your grammar is terrible). Grammar is required to understand not only what you are saying and reading but also to understand what other people are saying. Moreover, it may be that the primary stumbling block for young children learning to read is that grammar is only implicitly known and often inaccessible.

A somewhat similar phenomenon has been reported with respect to language. DeVilliers and deVilliers (1979), Gleitman et al. (1972), Hirsch-Pasek et al. (1978), and Kessel (1970) have reported that children of three and four years of age are virtually unconversant with respect to reporting grammatical ambiguities. For example, children who say "Claire and Eleanore is a sister" will in fact report the sentence to be grammatically correct. This seems to indicate that speech and understanding appear early in life while ability to judge grammaticality appears later. Furthermore, it contradicts Mattingly's position that access, intuitively present, is observed at an early age and is part and parcel of language awareness.

In summary, metalinguistic awareness—the ability to think, reflect, and comment upon language—develops rather late in comparison to language acquisition.

A review of recent literature in the area of reading disability reflects a change of attitude and focus in this area. The traditional question of "Why can't Jimmy read?" has been overridden, or at least modified, to "Why *can* Jimmy read?" This reflects an intensified concern for the capacities and skills required for reading, and, most important, how the awareness of these skills may be related to the acquisition of reading proficiency.

In recent years, investigators have attributed language problems to reading disability. Most studies in this area have taken their inspiration from the classical work of Shankweiler and Liberman (1972, 1976). On the basis of a number of investigations, they conclude that poor readers lack awareness of the phonetic structure of both spoken language and printed words, and that they have a marked weakness in engaging the necessary phonological "machinery" for storing information in short-term memory. Studies in metalinguistics have recently provided a different perspective in attending to the problem of reading disability. Considerable attention has been given to understanding the development of children's linguistic and communication skills. Little research, however, has been directed toward the understanding of the child's progressive awareness of language as "language."

In addition, investigators have hypothesized a relationship between metalinguistic awareness and reading acquisition or reading proficiency (Ehri, 1979; Mattingly, 1979). These hypotheses have been proposed in the absence of research and empirical substantiations. Thus there is a need to investigate the area of metalinguistic awareness within an older population, with normal and reading disabled children, as well as to investigate the efficiency and relationship among the tasks used as measures of metalinguistic awareness.

We have utilized this approach in a major study of 340 students (170 nine-year-olds and 170 eleven-year-olds) divided into subgroups of superior, average, below average, and significantly below average readers (Mancini et al., 1990). The study utilized the following tasks:

- Five tasks subsumed under the broad component of disambiguation of ambiguities: (1) phonological ambiguity, (2) lexical ambiguity, (3) surface structure ambiguity, (4) deep structure ambiguity, and (5) morphemic boundary ambiguity.
- Five tasks assessing phonological awareness in terms of segmentation adapted from Rosner (1974): (1) final consonant elision, (2) initial consonant elision, (3) medial consonant elision, (4) medial vowel elision, and (5) final vowel elision.
- Four tasks, with a total of sixteen five-word sentences, assessing children's perception of sentences in a sentence repetition or sentence imitation format (Carrow, 1974) assessing: (1) the repetition of acceptable sentences, (2) random-word sentences, (3) unrelated-word sentences, and (4) anomalous sentences.
- Four measures assessing morphophonological knowledge encompassing a total of twenty-seven items (Berko, 1958): (1) morphology-number (2) morphology-tense, (3) morphology-case, and (4) morphology-person.

One of the aims of the study was to delineate the pattern of metalinguistic abilities in two age groups of readers and to examine if these abilities could be differentiated from specific language tasks more focused on language usage. A four-component and a two-component model were utilized to interpret the data. The two-component model accounted for 54 and 47 percent of the variance for the nine-year-olds and the eleven-year-olds, respectively. In general, there was a component subserved by the ambiguity tasks and sentence repetition tasks, although the specificity (in terms of the total variance and the indicators) varied somewhat for the two age groups. This may be termed the metalinguistic component. The specific language ability component accounted for 20 and 19 percent of the variance, respectively, for the younger and older readers. This component was subsumed by the auditory analyses and synthesis task and the tasks dealing with morphological knowledge. This cluster may be loosely termed the specific language abilities. Thus, there seems to be some differentiation, although rather blurred, between the metalinguistic and specific language ability components. However, the four-component interpretation suggested that the four-domain model, consisting of disambiguation of ambiguities, phonological awareness, understanding of syntax domain, and morphological knowledge, offers a better fit of the data. These four domains accounted for a total of 67 and 62 percent of the variance for the nine-year-old and the eleven-year-old groups, respectively.

A two-domain model was utilized to determine whether different reading ability groups could be differentiated on metalinguistic ability and/or specific language ability related to reading. Factor scores were derived for each age sample from the factor structure matrices of the two-factor model. A two-way analysis of variance was conducted for each age group. Reading comprised the first independent variable, with four levels of reading ability. The two factors, meta and specific, comprised the two levels of the second independent variable. Thus, the experimental design was a 4 × 2 ANOVA with repeated measures on the second independent variable (factor). There was a significant main effect for reading level (F = 108.33, df = 3,166, p < .001) indicating differences in factor score means among the reading level groups. As expected, because of scaling, the main effect for factor type was insignificant. The interaction effect was also insignificant, suggesting that the trends in group differences were similar for the two factors. Post hoc tests were conducted to identify those specific group differences that contributed to the significant group effect. These post hoc tests were conducted utilizing the group means for individual factors rather than a combination of the factor scores, since individual factors were of greater theoretical interest. Pairwise comparisons between group means were tested with Tukey's multiple range test.

The most important features of the patterns of pairwise comparison results were as follows. Superior readers surpassed all other groups in metalinguistic ability. Average and below average readers were not differentiated on metalinguistic skills but surpassed significantly below average readers on this ability. Superior readers surpassed all other groups in specific skills related to reading. Average readers surpassed both of the remaining two groups on specific skills related to reading and, in turn, below average readers surpassed significantly below average readers. There were no differences between mean scores on metalinguistic ability and specific skills related to reading within any one reading group.

Overall these results indicate that ability in metalinguistic awareness and specific skills related to reading are differentiated among groups of nine-year-old children of various reading ability levels.

ANOVA for eleven-year-olds indicated a significant main effect for reading level (F = 86.89, df = 3,166, p < .001). This indicates differences in factor score means among the reading level groups. The effect of factor type was insignificant. The interaction between effect for reading level and factor type was significant (F = 17.96, df = 3,166, p < .001). This indicates that the trends in group differences were not similar across the two factors.

Post hoc tests were conducted to determine the nature of the group x factor interaction. Pairwise comparisons of factor score means were tested with Tukey's multiple range test.

The main features of the pattern of pairwise comparison results are as follows. Superior readers surpassed average readers in metalinguistic abilities. Average readers surpassed both below average and significantly below average readers on this factor. The latter two groups did not differ significantly on this factor. The pattern of group differences in specific skills related to reading was identical to the pattern for metalinguistic abilities. The mean metalinguistic ability score for superior readers was significantly higher than the overall group's mean score on specific skills related to reading. In contrast, the mean metalinguistic ability score of the average readers was significantly lower than the mean score on specific reading skills for that of the overall group. Such within-group differences had not been obtained with the nine-year-old sample. The contrasting direction of these differences for the two reading ability levels suggests that this pattern of results contributed to the significant interaction effect in the main ANOVA for this age group. One further post hoc test was conducted to test this hypothesis.

Differences between the means of average and superior readers were calculated for each metalinguistic and specific reading skill and these differences were contrasted. The significance of this contrast was tested with Scheffe's test for pairwise comparisons and found to be significant ($F = 56.38$, df = 3,166, $p < .01$). Mean differences between superior and average readers on metalinguistic abilities were significantly larger than the corresponding difference on specific skills related to reading. These results indicate that superior readers are perhaps more strongly differentiated from average readers on the basis of metalinguistic ability than on the basis of specific language skills.

It is felt that children's responses to the metalinguistic tasks provide an insight into their understanding of words and language in general. Within this perspective, we utilized a word definition task, interchangeability of labels (Cummins & Mulcahy, 1981), and ambiguous sentences. Subjects were requested to respond to a number of questions through an individual interview.

Children's (seven-year-old SRs, nine-year-old BAs, nine-year-old SBAs, and eleven-year-old SBAs) responses to short and long words appear to be related to the graphic representation of the signifier. A word is "long" or "short" simply by virtue of the number of letters it contains. It is noteworthy that children, prior to dichotomizing the word/referent relationship, accompany their justifications with restrictions that focus upon the quantitative aspect of the referent. For example:

Question: "What is a long word?" (to a seven-year-old SR).

Response: "BECAUSE IT HAS LOTS OF LETTERS. FIVE OF THEM. EN-CY-CLO-PE-DIA, AND BECAUSE THE ENCYCLOPEDIA HAS SO MANY BOOKS AND SO MUCH INFORMATION THAT IT TAKES A LONG TIME TO LEARN."

It seems that these children are at the transition stage of dichotomizing or differentiating words from the physical reality they represent. A reader's facility and higher-level understanding of words is perhaps best exemplified by the following play on words:

Question: "Can you give an example of a long word?"

Response: "SMILE."

Question: "Why is smile a long word?"

Response: "BECAUSE IT HAS A MILE AT THE END."

Children were also requested to provide examples of difficult words and to justify their answer. *Question:* "Can you give an example of a difficult word?" The (7SRs, 9BAs, 9SBAs, 11SBAs) children's responses are based on the fact that they are experiencing difficulty in spelling words. For example, *Response:* "BELL, I ALWAYS FORGET TO PUT TWO 'L'S. "

While this is a very justifiable explanation, it is related to the individual's ability and may not relate to the complexity of the word itself. The complexity of the task relative to the individual's skills and abilities must be considered.

The higher-ability groups (9SRs, 9As, 11SRs, 11As) provided higher-order justifications by using grammatical terms and demonstrated an understanding that these terms are part of subsets. For example:

Question: "What is a difficult word?" (to a nine-year-old SR)

Response: "PNEUMONIA . . . IT IS DIFFICULT TO SPELL BECAUSE THE FIRST SYLLABLE "P" IS SILENT AND THE SECOND VOWEL "U" IS ALSO SILENT."

Question: "What is a difficult word?" (to an eleven-year-old SR)

Response: "WORDS LIKE 'RETURNED' BECAUSE THEY CAN BE USED AS ADJECTIVES OR VERBS."

Question: "Can you give me an example?"

Response: "ADJECTIVE: THE RETURNED BOOK SAT ON HIS DESK. VERB: HE RETURNED THE BOOK TO THE LIBRARY."

Inconsistencies are again observed within the nine-year-old SR and the nine-year-old A readers. Their definitions of a word seemed to be more abstract than those of the seven-year-old SRs. Nevertheless, remnants of concreteness were observed. By contrast, their performance on long, short, and difficult word tasks indicated a considerable degree of linguistic sophistication. These differences could be explained by the characteristic nature of the questions themselves. The question "What is a word?" is a very abstract and difficult question. In fact, in a personal communication, Peter Bryant (1982) reported that a philosopher at Oxford University had difficulty providing a definition of "word." Providing examples of a long, short, and difficult words, in comparison to defining a word, is a much easier task since it is less open-ended, more concrete, and taps physical attributes of words. Justifications for the chosen word can be abstracted from learned information. These observations provided added justification for the previously stated notion that these tasks are not pure measures of generic metalinguistic awareness.

A further aspect worthy of comment is the performance of the three superior reading groups on definition of a word task and interchangeability of labels task. These two tasks require the individual to look at language, to know and not just respond, and to use language abstractly. The responses of the seven- and nine-year-old SRs did not appear to differ significantly. Their responses on the whole tended to be somewhat unanalyzed, iconic, and situation-bound. Both

groups offered as a definition of a word: "MEANING: A WORD MEANS SOME-
THING or A WORD TELLS YOU SOMETHING." These children rejected articles
and other functors as examples of words since "THEY DON'T MEAN ANY-
THING." Similarly, when asked to respond to the question, Suppose someone
was making up names for things; could he then call the sun the moon and the
moon the sun?" the majority of the seven-year-olds responded with: "NO . . .
BECAUSE THE MOON DOES NOT SHINE LIKE THE SUN." When asked what would
night look like, their answer was invariably "BRIGHT." By way of contrast,
the nine-year-old SRs responded to the first question with such affirmative responses as "IF YOU WANT TO, I GUESS IT'S OK. BUT YOU REALLY SHOULD NOT
BECAUSE THEY ALREADY HAVE NAMES" or "IT'S OK IF YOU'RE AN INVENTOR"
or "IT'S OK TO JUST PRETEND." Their responses to what would night look like
was also "BRIGHT." It appears that the concept of "wordness" is more crys-
tallized in the nine-year-old SR than in the seven-year-old SR. When the nine-
year-olds were placed in a decision-making process that violated their experiences (e.g., attributes of night versus attributes of day), however, they fell into
the trap of not being able to separate the name of the object from its attribute.
As Vygotsky (1962) has noted, "they cling to the name when it is transferred
like possessions following their owner" (p. 129). Vygotsky's hypothesis is
perhaps best exemplified by a nine-year-old's SBA response to the question,
Could he then call a cat a dog and a dog a cat? "NO OF COURSE NOT! THE CAT
WOULD THEN HAVE TO CHASE THE DOG." Again, as evidenced above, the
seven-year-olds, similar to the nine-year-old SBA readers, are yet unable to
appreciate the semantic structure of a word since they have difficulty in distinguishing between reference and meaning. By way of contrast, the nine-year-
old superior readers have to some extent overcome this difficulty. The concepts
for them are evolving but are not fully at their command.

The eleven-year-olds (SR), on the other hand, appear to have overcome this
difficulty and can treat words abstractly and symbolically. For example, in
defining words they offered the following: "WORDS ARE PART OF A SENTENCE
AND WITHIN THE SENTENCE THEY HAVE MEANING LIKE, IT, THE, ETC. . . .
WORDS ARE ALSO PART OF GRAMMAR (ADJECTIVES, NOUNS, ADVERBS, PREPOSI-
TIONS, ARTICLES, ETC.). . . . WORDS PROVIDE INFORMATION AND DESCRIPTIONS
OF THINGS. . . . THEY HELP US TO COMMUNICATE. . . . WORDS ARE MADE UP
OF LETTERS. . . . SOME ARE VOWELS AND SOME ARE SYLLABLES." As can be
seen, words have become more differentiated, abstract, and opaque at this age.
Similar findings have also been reported by Berthoud-Papandropoulou (1978).
The average readers, however, were not able (generally speaking) to provide
such an all-encompassing definition. The general trend was to provide a defi-
nition such as: "WORDS GIVE MEANING, YOU CAN WRITE WITH THEM AND MAKE
SENTENCES, YOU CAN SPEAK WITH THEM. WORDS ARE USED FOR GRAMMAR."

Question: "Is "the" a word?"

Response: (After a long pause) "YES, BECAUSE IT'S AN ARTICLE."

The SBA and BA readers seldom provided parsimonious definitions and basically gave meaning as a definition.

Intuitive knowledge of spoken language and comprehension of that language are highly related to academic success and in particular to reading. Schooling is primarily a reading process and reading is a language-oriented skill (Vellutino, 1978). In addition, language is the primary medium in which teachers teach and children learn. Therefore, unless the individual possesses the necessary linguistic skills to understand language, schooling may be fruitless. Flood and Salus (1982) suggest that "less obvious is the fact that the ability to think and talk about language (a meta-linguistic task) is critical to successful academic achievement in terms of learning and providing evidence of this learning" (p. 57).

If the reading process is related to the process of consciously manipulating the different categories and relations in language (a metalinguistic ability) and if reading requires the individual to stand back and analyze language objectively (Menyuk & Flood, 1981) then awareness of ambiguities in sentences, word definition, and interchangeability of labels must also play a role in reading acquisition. After all, a prerequisite of reading can be thought of as a metalinguistic process in which the individual is required to extract information from visually presented materials. In addition, if the ability to read is invariably related to complete relations between the "psycholinguistic processing of printed materials and oral syntactic metalinguistic abilities, then, differences in these abilities could account for the differences in reading achievement among children" (Flood & Salus, 1982, p. 61).

It was noted, from the observational data, that the amount of time required to respond and obtain a correct response increased as ability level decreased. In addition, it was also noted that the amount of qualitative information (precise and to the point), decreased as a function of lower ability levels. The following example is indicative of the type of responses provided by poor readers (nine-year-old SBAs):

Question: "What signs should be used in a frozen food department? The best foods you ever thaw!"

Response: "FROZEN FOOD DEPARTMENT, I GUESS THAT'S A PLACE LIKE SAFEWAY, YOU KNOW WHERE YOU FIND ICE CREAM, AND PIZZA. I REALLY LIKE MCCAINS PIZZA, THEY PUT A LOT OF STUFF ON THEIR PIZZA LIKE LOTS OF CHEESE."

Question: "That's right but what does the joke mean?"

Response: "WHAT WAS THAT JOKE AGAIN?"

(The joke was repeated.)

Response: "THE FOOD IN A FROZEN FOOD DEPARTMENT IS FROZEN AND IF THE FRIDGES BREAK THE FOOD WILL THAW. RIGHT? OH! WAIT A MOMENT, SAW AND THAW ARE ALMOST THE SAME, THEY SOUND ALIKE. NO, THE JOKE WAS NOT THAT FUNNY."

The eleven-year-old significantly below average readers' responses were not as embellished with irrelevant information as were their nine-year-old counterparts. Nevertheless, the responses were not as precise and parsimonious as those of the eleven-year-old superior readers. For example: "THAW AND SAW ARE VERY SIMILAR SOUNDING WORDS; IT'S A PLAY ON WORDS."

In summary, it seems that the lower-ability groups utilize a strategic behavior of trial and error that finally leads to success. These results suggest that metalinguistic abilities are present in the lower-ability groups but may not be as "automatized" as in the higher-ability groups. The lower-ability groups may lack the awareness of how to employ, immediately, appropriate resources or strategies in order to obtain the ultimate response or level of performance. This hypothesis has received considerable attention and consistency in its findings dealing with memory (Brown, 1975; Chi, 1976) and metalinguistic awareness (Hakes, 1980). The results of the above studies indicate that over the course of development, increased performance is related to more effective use by the individual of limited resources via greater awareness and more efficient use of strategies for efficient information processing (Chi, 1976; Dennis, 1982). It is important to emphasize that all of the tasks adopted in this study were orally presented and thus emphasize oral language processing (listening/speaking). This mode of presentation, coupled with the fact that they were allotted as much time as required, might have afforded the poor readers with the opportunity to employ whatever metalinguistic ability they possess in order to provide the appropriate judgment or response. Similar findings have also been reported by Menyuk and Flood (1981).

This study attempted to identify the factors underlying a group of tasks that measured skills believed to be important to reading. Tests believed to measure metalinguistic ability and specific skills related to reading appeared on separate factors, labels generic metalinguistic ability and specific skills related to reading, for both nine- and eleven-year-old children. The evidence for the significance of a separate metalinguistic factor, however, was much weaker at the nine-year-old level than at the eleven-year-old level. In fact, there was direct evidence from principal component analysis on total scores for a single general factor underlying reading abilities.

This study indicates that researchers need to be more cognizant of the tasks they use to measure metalinguistic awareness. For example, auditory phonological segmentation and synthesis—which has been used as a metalinguistic task since it requires the child to think about the language used unconsciously everyday—was found to be a poor measure of generic metalinguistic awareness. Thus, tasks should be analyzed, and age and different ability levels should be considered.

Two distinct factors—a meta and a specific factor—emerge from this study, especially for the eleven-year-old group. This seems to suggest that metalinguistic awareness is not just an all-encompassing process with respect to reading, but is rather a cognitive construct that interacts with other cognitive activities. Thus, it can be modified and can modify other cognitive activities. In addition, a significant interaction was found between the eleven-year-old superior and average readers. It seems that for the nine-year-old both metalinguistic abilities and knowledge of specific skills are necessary for reading.

The eleven-year-old superior and average readers were differentiated only by metalinguistic ability. This may suggest that metalinguistic ability is perhaps important not only for acquiring reading but also for a higher conceptual level in reading such as comprehension. Thus, metalinguistic awareness, for this age group, would be more related to the "how" and "why" of certain interactions. This, of course, does not imply that younger children are incapable of interpreting "how" and "why" relationships. Perhaps younger children are more concerned with the "how" and "why" of specific actions and not so concerned with certain interactions (Sinclair, 1978).

Factor scores on both the metalinguistic and specific skills factors were able to discriminate children of various levels of reading comprehension abilities. At the nine-year-old level, the trend on factor score means of superior, average, below average, and significantly below average readers reflected an almost linear relationship between reading comprehension and each of metalinguistic ability and specific skills related to reading. These two factors do not differ in their ability to discriminate among reading levels, as reflected by the lack of a significant interaction in the factor type of reading level ANOVA for nine-year-olds. In contrast, the significant interaction on the corresponding ANOVA for eleven-year-old children reflects differences in the power of these factors to discriminate children of various levels of reading ability. Superior readers could be more clearly separated from average readers by metalinguistic abilities than by specific skills related to reading.

The stronger evidence for the significance of a separate metalinguistic factor and its superior power in discriminating between superior and average readers at age eleven may reflect overlearning and automaticity of the specific skills at that age level and/or cognitive maturation leading to the refinement of metalinguistic skills of superior readers. In other words, children's performance on specific tasks such as pluralizing a word may become automatized. In contrast, children's cognitive capability for such abstract tasks as metalinguistic ones becomes refined and increasingly differentiated as age increases. The rationale for this interpretation is as follows: Both specific skills and metalinguistic abilities are related to reading at both age levels as reflected by group differences on both factors at both age groups. The variance in reading ability, however, may be more strongly influenced by variance in metalinguistic abilities than by variance in specific skill at age eleven. Evidence for a stronger role played by metalinguistic abilities is supplied by the significant interaction between factor type and reading level. Support for the above interpretation is available from Messick (1972). He argues that complex tasks involve a number of components and abilities that may be executed sequentially throughout task performance. Some components are more difficult to master than other components and are thus mastered at later ages. The importance of ability on any one particular component to ability on the complex task may change as a function of practice or exposure to the component task. This phenomenon has been demonstrated in regard to the importance of applying chunking strategies to memory span tasks (Dempster, 1981) and the relative importance of visualization and physical or motor coordination to performance on psychomotor tasks (Messick, 1972).

The above interpretation of results of the present study can only be offered as hypotheses to be tested by further research. These hypotheses cannot be tested directly by the procedures used in the present study. These procedures were all essentially correlational. Consequently, causal statements about the effect of development of abilities on component skills cannot be made. Factor analysis is a procedure for simplifying patterns of correlations among variables.

Messick (1972) has argued that whereas factor analysis is valuable for identifying ability of personality traits it is not capable of specifying the nature of the trait. He suggests that factor interpretation may be aided by multivariate studies in which factors or traits are experimentally manipulated. One can either manipulate the factors or traits directly as independent variables or indirectly as dependent variables via manipulation of a true independent variable.

Further research should attempt to examine the above presented hypothesis regarding metalinguistic skills through further experimental manipulation of metalinguistic abilities and specific skills related to reading.

Prior to experimentally manipulating metalinguistic awareness and specific tasks related to reading, a number of considerations should be addressed:

1. Research should endeavor to task analyze any experimental tool or task utilized to measure metalinguistic awareness. This process should facilitate not only an in-depth understanding of metalinguistic awareness but also assist in determining the degree to which metalinguistic awareness is being measured. In addition this procedure should assist in controlling for or understanding any extraneous variables.

2. With due regard to extraneous variables or covarying factors it would be useful to investigate the influence of formal and informal educational experiences on metalinguistic awareness.

3. In order to specifically determine the relationship between metalinguistic awareness a systematic investigation would require training in metalinguistic awareness. This procedure, while adopting appropriate methodological approaches, would permit a greater understanding into the experimental variables and how they are related to the performance characteristics on various intellectual tasks (e.g., reading comprehension, understanding expressive and receptive language).

4. An additional area worthy of exploration is to examine metalinguistic awareness with different ages in both "normal" and exceptional populations. Until there is evidence of a definite relationship between reading and metalinguistic awareness and evidence for a widespread application of metalinguistic skills, the application of the concept of metalanguage will seriously be called into question

In summary, it would appear that there is some evidence for different but interrelated components of metalinguistic and specific language subskills subserving reading proficiency. From a pedagogical perspective, the present study, along with others, indicates the role of metalinguistic awareness, as measured by such tasks as ambiguities, in facilitating reading. Going beyond language awareness level is the epistemic level, where individuals reflect on what they know and what they do not know (Mancini et al., 1990). Reading proficiency, not unlike cognition, requires the interplay of metacognition in order for language representations to be brought from the implicit to the explicit level.

REFERENCES

Berko, J. (1958). The child's learning of English morphology. *Word,* 14, 150–177.

Berthoud-Papandropoulou, I. (1978). An experimental study of children's ideas about language. In A. Sinclair, R. J. Jarvella, & W. J. M. Levelt (eds), *The child's conception of language.* New York: Springer-Verlag.

Bever, T. G., Garrett, M. F., & Hurtig, R. (1973). The interaction of perceptual processes and ambiguous sentences. *Memory and Cognition,* 1, 277–286.

Brown, A. L. (1975). The development of memory, knowing, knowing about knowing and knowing how to know. In H. W. Reese (ed.), *Advances in child development and behavior.* Vol. 10. New York: Academic.

Carrow, E. (1974). A test using elicited imitation in assessing grammatical structure in children. *Journal of Speech and Hearing Disorders,* 39, 437–444.

Chi, M. T. H. (1976). Knowledge structures and memory development. In R. Siegler (ed.), *Children's thinking: What develops?* Hillsdale, N.J.: Erlbaum.

Chomsky, N. (1972). *Language and mind.* New York: Harcourt, Brace, & World.

Cummins, J., & Mulcahy, R. F. (1978). Orientation to language in Ukranian-English children. *Child Development,* 49, 1239–1242.

Dale, P. (1976). *Language development: Structure and functions.* 2d ed. Toronto: Holt, Rinehart & Winston.

Dejarlais, L., & Lazar, A. (1976). *An inquiry into the psychopathology of language acquisition in the school-age child: A study of readiness.* Final report. Canadian Ministry of Education: University of Ottawa.

Dempster, F. N. (1981). Memory span: Sources of individual and developmental differences. *Psychological Bulletin,* 89, 62–100.

Denner, F. (1970). Representational and syntactic competence of problem readers. *Child Development,* 41, 881–887.

Dennis, S. S. (1982). *Attention and levels of processing.* Unpublished Ph.D. diss. University of Alberta.

de Villiers, P. A., & de Villiers, J. G. (1979). *Early language.* Cambridge, Mass.: Harvard University Press.

Downing, J., & Leong, C. K. (1982). *Psychology of reading.* New York: Macmillan.

Erhi, L. C. (1979). Linguistic insight: Threshold of reading acquisition. In T. G. Waller & G. E. MacKinnon (eds.), *Reading research: Advances in theory and practice.* New York: Harcourt Brace Jovanovich.

Farnham-Diggory, S. (1967). Symbol and synthesis in experimental reading. *Child Development,* 38, 221–231.

Flood, J., & Salus, M. W. (1982, September). Metalinguistic awareness: Its role in language development and its assessment. *Topics in Language Disorders*, 2(4), 56–64.

Gerber, A. (1981). Problems in the processing and use of language in education. In A. Gerber & D. N. Bryen (eds.), *Language and learning disabilities*. Baltimore: University Park Press.

Gleitman, L. R., Gleitman, H., & Shipley, E. (1972). The emergence of a child as grammarian. *Cognition*, 1, 137–164.

Hakes, D. T. (1980). *The development of metalinguistic abilities in children*. New York: Springer-Verlag.

Hirsch-Pasek, K., Gleitman, L. R., & Gleitman, H. (1978). What did the brain say to the mind? A study of the detection and report of ambiguity by young children. In A. Sinclair, R. J. Jaevella, & W. J. M. Levelt, (eds.) *The child's conception of language*. New York: Springer-Verlag.

Jansky, J., & de Hirsch, K. (1972). *Preventing reading failure*. New York: Harper & Row.

Kessel, F. (1970). The role of syntax in children's comprehension from six to twelve. *Monographs of the Society for Research in Child Development*, 35(6) (Social No. 139).

Kinsbourne, M., & Coplan, P. J. (1979). *Children's learning and attention problems*. Boston: Little, Brown.

Klees, M., & Le Brun, A. (1972). Analysis of the figurative and operative processes of thought of 40 dyslexic children. *Journal of Learning Disabilities*, 5, 389–396.

Mancini, G. J., Mulcahy, R. F., & Leong, C. K. (1990). Metalinguistic and specific language abilities in nine and eleven year old good and poor readers. In G. Paulidis (ed.), *Perspectives on dyslexia*, vol. 2, *Cognition, language and treatment*. New York: Wiley.

Mattingly, I. G. (1972). Reading, the linguistic process and linguistic awareness. In J. F. Kavanagh & I. G. Mattingly (eds.), *Language by ear and by eye*. Cambridge, Mass.: MIT.

————. (1979). *Reading, linguistic awareness, and language acquisition*. Paper presented at IRA/University of Victoria International Reading Research Seminar on Linguistic Awareness and Learning to Read, June, Victoria, B.C., Canada.

————. (1980). *Reading, linguistic awareness, and language acquisition*. Haskins Laboratories Status Report on Speech Research, SR-61.

Menyuk, P., & Flood, J. (1981). Language development, reading/writing problems and remediation. *Orton Society Bulletin*, 31, 13–28.

Messick, S. J. (1972). In search of functional models of psychological processes. *Psychometrika*, 37, 357–379.

Read, C. (1978). Children's awareness of language, with emphasis on sound systems. In A. Sinclair, R. J. Jarvella, & W. J. M. Levelt (eds.), *The child's conception of language*. New York: Springer-Verlag.

Rosner, J. (1974). Auditory analysis training with pre-readers. *Reading Teacher*, 27, 379–384.

Shankweiler, D., & Liberman, I. Y. (1972). Misreading: A search for courses. In J. Kavanagh and I. Mattingly (eds.), *Language by ear and by eye*. Cambridge, Mass.: MIT.

————. (1976). Exploring the relations between reading and speech. In R. M. Knights

& D. J. Bakker (eds.), *Neuropsychology of learning disorders: Theory and approaches*. Baltimore: University Park Press.

Sinclair, H. (1978). Conceptualization and awareness in Piaget's theory and its relevance to the child's conception of language. In A. Sinclair, R. J. Jarvella, & W. J. M. Levelt (eds.), *The child's conception of language*. New York: Springer-Verlag.

Slobin, D. I. (1978). A case study of early language awareness. In A. Sinclair, R. J. Jarvella, & W. J. M. Levelt (eds.), *The child's conception of language*. New York: Springer-Verlag.

Tunmer, W. E., & Bowey, J. A. (1980). The role of linguistic awareness in a theory of reading acquisition. *Educational Research and Perspectives*, 7, 80–101.

Tunmer, W. E., & Fletcher, C. M. (1981). The relationship between conceptual tempo, phonological awareness, and word recognition in beginning readers. *Journal of Reading Behavior*, 13, 173–185.

Vellutino, F. R. (1978). Toward an understanding of dyslexia: Psychological factors in specific reading disability. In A. L. Benton & D. Pearl (eds.), *Dyslexia: An appraisal of current knowledge*. New York: Oxford University Press.

Vogel, S. A. (1975). *Syntactic abilities in normal and dyslexic children*. Baltimore: University Park Press.

Vygotsky, L. S. (1962). *Thought and language*. Cambridge, Mass.: MIT.

Wallach, G. P. (1978). The implication of different language comprehension strategies in learning disabled children: Effects of thematization. *Dissertation Abstracts International*, 38, 3647-B.

12

Social Cognition and Social Competence: Instructional Issues

Gabriel J. Mancini, Robert H. Short,
Robert F. Mulcahy, and Jac Andrews

How people learn and think is not only of interest to educators but to every-body. Everyone would like to read faster, remember better, think more logically, and become more socially adept. Traditionally, learning and thinking, or cognition, have been associated only with intellectual and academic achievement. Recently, however, cognition has been broadened to encompass all of human functioning, including intellectual, behavioral, emotional, and social domains. The same general cognitive processes are seen as subserving each of these human capabilities. Social cognition, the topic of this chapter, incorporates the underlying processes governing social competence, something that is now regarded as an essential part of intelligent functioning. For many, human cognition is regarded as social in nature (Chandler, 1977; Piaget, 1970). Much of our knowledge is a product of social contexts, colored by the norms and mores of society and shaped by ideas and representations at both the individual and societal level (Kuhn, 1962; Forgas, 1981). Vygotsky (1981) emphasizes that in order to understand psychological phenomena they have to be examined within a developmental context and within social interactions. People influence their environment and are in turn influenced by that environment, particularly when they communicate with others on a social level.

The cognitive processes underlying socially competent behavior, or social cognition, involve thinking about people—what they do or ought to do, as well as about the social relationships between people (Flavell, 1985). Flavell maintains that social cognition primarily involves a person's knowledge of "between-person" social relations, such as friendship and collegiality, as well as "within person" processes such as perceptions, feelings, and thoughts about the self and others. Conceptually, social cognition can be described as cognition within and between people, mediated by thoughts, emotions, development, experience, motivation, personality, and moral reasoning.

Research in social cognition is quite varied and includes issues such as peer difficulties that result from limited social competence and later adjustment problems (Bierman & Furman, 1984; Trower et al., 1978; Walker 1981); social skills and social status of learning disabled children (Bryan, 1974, 1976; Bryan & Bryan, 1978; Bursuck, 1981; Deshler et al., 1980); the discrepancy between the social "ideal" and social "real" self in learning disabled children (Barnett & Zucker, 1980; Bingham, 1980); and the lower self-esteem scores that result from limited social capabilities in younger children (Bingham, 1980; Black, 1974; Bryan & Pearl, 1979). Generally speaking, investigators have examined the expression of social cognition, or social competence, through discrete social skills such as pseudocommunication, eye contact, and smiling (Bellack, 1979); verbal communication (Michelson & Wood, 1980); or global cognitive behaviors such as problem solving and social role taking (Ford, 1982; Weissberg & Gesten, 1982). Research indicates that role-taking ability coupled with accuracy in social perception is highly correlated with age (Ausubel, 1952; Flavell et al., 1968), emotional stability (Taft, 1955; Solomon, 1963; Chandler, 1971), and intellectual potential (DeVries, 1970; Neale, 1966; Selman, 1971a, 1971b).

It is interesting to note that Selman (1971a) has also defined a five-stage developmental model of social role taking, paralleling it to Kohlberg's lower-level stages of moral judgment. Byrne (1975) has recognized several higher stages of role taking that are related to Kohlberg's fifth and sixth stages of moral judgment. In general, research strongly supports the central role of social cognition in social competence while emphasizing its developmental characteristics and its relationship to abilities such as moral judgment.

The scaffolding of human cognition—cognitive structure—functions in an integrated and dynamic way at all levels of development to impose regularity and conformity on knowledge, including social knowledge. Cognitive and social developmental milestones never emerge coincidentally but are determined by the same general structures and formal mechanisms of the mind. The interactive relationship between people's knowledge and the cognitive structures that support it directly influences what they will learn and think, and how they will relate to one another. Social competence may be considered to be one of the significant manifestations of successful human adaptation. As Weiner et al. (1983) note, "we are best able to predict and perhaps control what goes on around us if we can identify lawful (systematic) relationships and invariants that explain our own and other people's behavior across a variety of situations" (p. 123).

Social cognition and social competence are mutually related. As Flavell (1985) points out, "social behavior (competence) mediates cognitive growth and cognitive skills mediate social development" (p. 160). Shantz (1983) sees reasoning about other people and social situations as a major determinant of social competence, while Ford (1982) maintains that "social competence is the attainment of relevant social goals in specified social contexts, using appropriate means (cognitive strategies) resulting in positive developmental outcomes" (p. 323).

Developmentally, social competence in young children requires a range of prerequisite skills, including the ability to organize, think critically, solve problems, and control attention, as well as being self-motivated, having a healthy self-concept, and possessing a favorable attitude toward learning (Anderson & Messick, 1974). Furthermore, a socially competent child is goal-directed (Baumrind, 1975), active (Ford, 1982), independent (White, 1959), systematic and playful (Spivock et al., 1976), and empathic (Hogan, 1973). These authors also support the view that a socially competent individual must also possess a clear sense of morality. While cognition focuses on the "whys" and "hows" of social behavior, moral judgment is the "should" or "ought" component of such behavior. One further attribute required of socially competent people is empathic ability. This would appear to be a necessary component of successful role taking where interpersonal understanding is paramount. Rogers (1952) defines empathy, from a counselor's perspective, as "(possessing) the internal reference frame of the client, to perceive the world as the client sees it, to perceive the client as he is seen by himself, . . . but without himself, as a counsellor, experiencing those hates and hopes and fears" (p. 29)

Social cognition is also facilitated by the activation of cognitive strategies. These are typically defined as internally organized skills or control processes with which the individual regulates cognitive behavior (Gagne, 1977). Such regulation likely determines the expression of social competence. Social cognition strategies can be viewed as a repertoire of skills that facilitate the activation, regulation, and retrieval of information and also control activities such as self-monitoring, attention, comprehension, and the problem-solving skills required for the immediate social situation. In addition, empirical research indicates that: (1) systematic training in problem solving assists children in coping with everyday difficulties (Elias & Rothbaum, 1986); (2) the generation of alternative solutions to problem situations correlates with measures of peer interaction (Olson, 1976); (3) socially competent children are more knowledgeable about how to make friends (Gottman et al., 1975); and (4) they are more cognitively resourceful and hence more capable of recognizing problems, constructing purposeful plans, and recognizing the impact of their actions (Ford, 1982; Spivack et al., 1976). The general conclusion is that social competence and cognition are desirable qualities that are amenable to modification via systematic intervention.

Interest in social cognition has existed for many years but the recent burgeoning interest in learning and thinking ability over the last fifteen years has produced a flurry of research in these social aspects of cognition. The increased focus on social cognition and social skills is perhaps related to three factors. First, there is a heightened awareness of the relationship between inappropriate social development and later adjustment problems (Berman, 1981; Crawford, 1982). Second, the passage of Public Law 94-142 in the United States and the general trend toward mainstreaming in North America has focused attention on social cognition. It was hoped that by placing handicapped and nonhandicapped children together, the social competencies of the former would be enhanced. There has been negative reaction to this policy, however. Walker (1981) maintains that these expectations were too naive and simplistic. Gerber (1980) states that they have in fact created a restrictive social environment for all involved. This in part is probably due to the fact that extremely handicapped children may require considerable teacher supervision and direction, particularly if they are lacking in fundamental strategic skills. Where this kind of assistance is not forthcoming it often results in repeated failure and avoidance in the handicapped, leading to a further reduction in their motivation and an inability to acquire the appropriate strategies for effective problem solving. Finally, there is a heightened awareness among parents and teachers that social and behavioral variables are related to academic success (Cartledge & Milburn, 1978).

There has always been a hidden curriculum in schools that endeavors to teach children appropriate social behaviors—the coercive whipping, caning, and strapping of past years, and the more constructive current attempts at teaching social skills via formal instruction. The past decade has seen an unprecedented increase in research and program development designed to improve cognitive strategies and social skills. Some representatives of cognitive strategy programs are the SPELT program (Mulcahy et al., in press); CoRT program (deBono, 1975); Productive Thinking program (Covington et al., 1974); Instrumental Enrichment program (Feuerstein, 1980); and Philosophy for Children program (Lipman, 1982). Social skills programs, although not as numerous as cognitive strategy programs, are still plentiful. Included are the Accepts program (Walker et al., 1983); Core Social Skill program (Jackson et al., 1983); Skill Streaming program (Goldstein et al., 1980; McGinnes & Goldstein, 1984); and Social Skills in the Classroom program (Stephens, 1978).

In these programs, social skills are usually simply defined as the behavioral competencies required in social settings (Phillips, 1978). The underlying assumption is that children can be trained to use general strategies that will help them solve socially based problems. Although these programs often result in significant improvements in social skills attainment, these are several issues and problems that need to be addressed by those involved in their development and implementation.

For example, there is scant evidence showing that social skills are generalized beyond the immediate instructional setting. The danger of assuming that generalization will automatically occur has been shown by several researchers (Brown, 1980; Gagne, 1985; Perkins, 1987). Unless training encompasses planned steps to ensure generalization of the skills, it is unlikely that the actual generalization of skills will occur. Brown et al. (1981) confront this issue when they differentiate between "blind" and "informed" training. The former involves presenting strategies without an explanation of the reasons for learning them or for how to apply them appropriately. Informed training, on the other hand, involves supplying the rationale for strategy use, including how and when they should be used. Brown et al. conclude that informed training, coupled with self-control and self-monitoring, is extremely important for the generalization of skills. Bransford et al. (1987) maintain that such training should also involve the differentiation of problem type in order to select strategies that are most appropriate to the instructional process. They also believe that training should impart information about the conditions and constraints of newly learned strategies. Moreover, in order to increase their generalizability, the problems presented during training should not be simply procedural but should reflect real-life situations and be dialectical in nature.

The teaching of social skills to improve social competence is often carried out in group settings. Generally speaking, the group reinforces the individual members, encouraging shared responsibility and collaborative efforts to solve the problem at hand. It is unlikely, however, that individuals will use collaborative efforts outside of the group training setting or use the strategies learned in the protective group environment when dealing with everyday problems unless they are trained to do so. Often, natural social situations are ill-defined, unstructured, and complex, and may be lacking in the reinforcers and feedback that direct the person to the appropriate course of action. The cornerstone to any social skills program should be a component that addresses the generalization of skills and competencies.

The social skills instructor must also ensure that students possess sufficient background knowledge to respond effectively to the training tasks. Familiarity with the child's knowledge base is important to ensure that new information is organized and presented in such a way that it builds on already existing knowledge. In addition, familiarity with the child's knowledge base assists the teacher in presenting information in a manner that challenges, but does not exceed, the individual's abilities. While a strong knowledge base is necessary to social problem solving, it is by no means a sufficient condition for effective problem solving. Often the knowledge base remains inert. Inert knowledge is of limited value to the individual since it cannot be evaluated, restructured, or applied. It is the application and generativity of knowledge along with the ability to detect and correct the errors in it that is pivotal to problem solving and social cognition.

The complexity of training tasks is another important consideration in social strategy training. If the tasks are too simple and students are too familiar with them it may impede both creative problem solving and the ability to generate alternative solutions. After all, efficient problem solvers do not need to continually reinvent the wheel with each new problem encountered. Rather, they implement solutions that have been successful for them in the past. Feedback, practice, memory support, and the opportunity to determine which of a host of strategies to use help in facilitating effective process implementation (Gagne,

1985). The capable problem solver is one who is better at managing cognitive resources. In other words, good problem solvers constantly monitor and review the processes they use to solve problems, particularly when they become bogged down in a problem. Therefore, youngsters with poor social competencies must not only be provided with a sufficient background knowledge, but must also be taught how to change from being passive and inert thinkers to ones who are efficient managers, thinkers who oversee and direct their behavior in a critical way.

While it is generally agreed that one of the most important requirements for personal survival in settings such as work, school, and leisure is social competence, it is also agreed that many individuals, for a variety of reasons, do not possess such competence. They may not, for example, be fully aware of the need for social competence. They may lack the performance skills and strategies necessary to benefit from social interactions. The successful integration of a person into a social group often depends upon social abilities. According to some researchers (Phillips, 1978), social incompetence may be far more handicapping than academic problems. It becomes important, therefore, to help children acquire social skills in order to improve their social interactions. Many programs, however, that are designed to assist teachers in improving social competence fail to fully consider its complex nature. For example, failing to take developmental changes into consideration may result in teaching skills that are inappropriate for the age level in question. Research clearly shows the importance of developmental variability. Piaget and Inhelder (1958), Vygotsky (1981), and Kohlberg et al. (1975), for example, have all identified discrete stages of cognitive development that are greatly influenced by cultural and social interactions. They maintain that the child's exposure to higher-level task demands, creating disequilibrium in thinking, is a critical component in stimulating further cognitive development with resultant more complex schematas. Additionally, research consistently reveals that age and stage of cognitive development are closely related to the level of sophistication and mode of organization that a person uses in dealing with problems. In other words, social cognition structures are different throughout childhood, adolescence, and young adulthood. Further, as a result of maturation, children rely increasingly more on abstract constructs (Crockett, 1965; Gilbert, 1969; Livesley & Bromley, 1973; Supnik, 1967). By way of example, Peevers and Secord (1973), investigating the process of the formation of social impressions in five- to twenty-year-olds, found a significant relationship between age and the number, complexity, variety, and degree of differentiation of the construct in question. In addition, the older students demonstrated the use of dispositional terms that indicated a much greater sophistication in their awareness of personal characteristics. Similarly, Scarlett et al. (1971), utilizing a Wernerian analysis process with six-, eight-, and ten-year-olds, reported that older students utilized greater abstraction when describing their peers. This was seen as evidence of a greater differentiation of the construct in addition to increased hierarchical differentiation. The importance of using a developmental framework can be illustrated when considering the progression from a cognitive stage, where only a single point of view at a time can be considered, to a stage where others' views are considered as well. This is an important aspect to consider when attempting to teach the social skills of role taking and decentering.

There also exists a wide range of possible causes of social incompetence that the developers of intervention programs may not address. For example, failure may be directly related to other skills deficits. Bandura (1977) delineates several possible defects or deficits in learning and thinking that may be directly related to social incompetency. These are: (1) a learning deficit or performance deficit that represents either the nonpresence of a skill or the inability to use it at an acceptable level; (2) self-control performance deficits where one possesses the skills but for a variety of idiosyncratic emotional reasons is unable to use it; (3) self-control deficits where emotional lability hinders the learning of a skill; (4) environmental deficits or defects; (5) language and metalinguistic deficiencies that prohibit the person from "disambiguating" ambiguous information (the ability to comprehend, use, and monitor language is fundamental to learning and social interactions); and finally, (6) differences in exceptionality that necessitate differential programming. For example, psychotic disorders make children particularly difficult to teach. Some may have impaired attention or tend toward stimulus overselectivity (Lovaas et al., 1971). This can cause these children to focus their attention too narrowly, ignoring the overall problem and resulting in their inability to discriminate, a basic requirement of effective learning. An attentional deficit such as this, along with deficits in memory, have been shown to interfere with social skills learning, language learning, appropriate emotional responses, and the ability to learn via imitation (Rincover & Koegel, 1978). For example, in order to reproduce imitated skills the person must be capable of attending appropriately to the model and then encoding and symbolically storing its representation. Children with attentional and memory deficits that interfere with learning ability may respond better to behavioral shaping than more cognitively based methods.

The importance of attention is central to social cognition since social interactions are often nonexplicit and invisible. There are no step-by-step interpretive manuals. This may seem a superficial point. The lack of visibility inherent in social interactions, however, makes it important to attend to a great number of vicarious cues; otherwise critical information is lost. Children's attentional capacity may also be exceeded when they are required to think of too many things at the same time or when new information results in a mismatch with what they already know. Interference can occur when incompatible operations require focused attention (Broadbent, 1958; Deutsch & Deutsch, 1963; Treisman, 1964, 1969) or when the task demands are greater than the available cognitive resources (Kahneman, 1973; Norman, 1976). Lastly, attention to the model is influenced by the functional value of the model's behavior. The modeled behavior must have functional value to the individual in order to have reinforcing qualities.

The point to be made is that many social skills programs often do not differentiate between exceptionalities and developmental differences and simply emphasize a number of skills to be taught with guided practice. The remediation of skill deficits is seen to be purely a matter of assessing deficit areas and providing the opportunity for guided practice in the appropriate skills. Concern for, and assessment of, the range of possible cognitive deficits that may affect the efficacy of social skills training programs should be part of any approach. Viewing the enhancement of social competence via social skills programming in too simplistic a manner may result in inappropriate or inadequate programming and minimal learning.

Moving too fast may encourage behaviors that have been successful in the past to take priority over newer ones and consequently become more embedded. Students should be encouraged to slow down and analyze the problem qualitatively before attempting to respond quantitatively. It may also cause the neglect of the readiness phase of instruction that can provide students with the prerequisite knowledge and skills for effective problem solving. In an overzealous attempt to do everything the teacher may overextend and confuse the child. Seeing social competency as a panacea for all ills or teaching the same skills to all children irrespective of age or level of social competence may lead to minimal learning. Evaluation is not an afterthought. It should be continuous and formative. Failure to consider and understand the child's environment may hinder the generalization of skills. Instruction should take into consideration the nature and status of the learner's home environment and family support. Each child should understand the purpose of the program and participate in both its development and the evaluation process whenever possible.

The evaluation of the efficacy of social skills training programs is an important consideration. It should encompass not only the child's behavioral changes but also sociometric changes (e.g., the child's social standing). Social skills programs have been shown to produce changes in the child's overt behaviors but not their social status. In other words, while the child has changed, other people's attitudes and interactions remain unchanged. Therefore, an important part of any program should be an attempt to influence the attitudes of other people in the child's immediate environment—in the classroom, the school, and the family. Moreover, the traditional method of evaluating behavioral change based on frequency and rate of response often fails to account for some important social interaction variables. For example, the timing of the response or the appropriateness of a behavior within a given context is of equal or greater importance.

A possible solution to the above difficulties may lie in the use of descriptive self-reporting and interview techniques combined with analogue manipulation of the child's behavior. The former approach requires that children describe personal likes and dislikes in the behaviors, traits, and characteristics of themselves and their peers. These descriptions are then categorized and compared with the child's friends and nonfriends in order to develop a profile. This inferential process can facilitate awareness in the child of the reasons for making or losing friends and for peer acceptance or rejection. Furthermore, the process provides significant adults with the traits and behaviors that are relevant to the child. The technique supplies some degree of social validation of target behaviors in the program. Of course, the success of this approach rests on the child's language skills, the ability to provide labels for feelings and emotions, and the ability to understand the attributes subsumed by those labels.

Younger children often have difficulty in labeling behaviors that are important to them. This difficulty may be partly attributed to a lack of language proficiency but also to not understanding the attributes associated with the labels (e.g., nice, friendly, etc.). Children may need to be made aware of these attributes prior to entering social skills programs. Davitz's (1969) emotional dictionary has been used successfully, as has the compilation of emotionally descriptive lists.

The use of analogue manipulations of child behavior involves role playing with the use of confederates trained to depict specific social behaviors. It is important that the target audience be familiar with the confederate and that the target goals chosen simulate real-life circumstances. The use of videotape equipment helps control extraneous variables, such as prior interactions, which can mask social relations. Discussion, using a problem-solving approach, can create the analogue situation. In addition, emphasis should be placed on describing antecedent events, the associated interpersonal and intrapersonal responses, the range of emotions, and causal and sequential events of the analogue.

One model that incorporates the above approaches is the SPELT program (described in chapter 10 of this book). Generally, procedures for social problem solving in the SPELT approach follow the recommendations derived from empirical studies. The development of social cognition through SPELT places emphasis on the role of modeling as well as on the rehearsal and reinforcement of social problem-solving skills. The relationship between social problem solving and more academic problem solving is seen by the program developers as a rationale for incorporating social skills acquisition within the school curriculum. When social problem-solving skills are seen to be part of everyday instructional content, they can be taught without the need for other professionals to be involved.

The SPELT approach attempts to develop systematic thinking habits, to motivate students to achieve their own solutions to problems, to appreciate consequences, and to facilitate emotional and behavioral self-control. This approach to teaching the cognitive strategies that underlie social skills development is described in greater detail by Andrews et al. (1989).

An evaluation of the effectiveness of the SPELT approach to enhancing social cognition was carried out in a year-long longitudinal study (Mulcahy et al., 1989). The study involved a complete school system that had implemented their instructional program. The assessment indicated an increase in the students' perception of their problem-solving ability as well as their self-concept and suggests that the instructional approach does indeed influence the social competencies of students.

In summary, the authors applaud the effort put into instruction for the enhancement of social competence. The area still has many issues to address and improvements to make. This chapter has pointed to some of those issues and problems, including the need for programs that encourage the generalization of skills, that establish the appropriate training task difficulty levels, that consider cognitive and metacognitive prerequisites of the tasks, and that are consistent with the developmental levels and needs of the child. Sensitivity to these considerations will result in improved social competency training and a better understanding of social cognition in general.

REFERENCES

Anderson, S., & Messick, S. (1974). Social competency in young children. *Development Psychology,* 10(2), 282–293.

Andrews, J., Peat, D., Mulcahy, R. F., & Marfo, K. (1989). Developing social competence within regular classrooms through a cognitive strategies approach. In C. Violato & A. Marini (eds.), *Child development: Readings for teachers.* Calgary: Detselig.

Ausubel, D. P. (1952). *Ego development and the personality disorders.* New York: Grune & Stratton.

Bandura, A. (1977). Self-efficacy: Toward a unifying theory of behavior change. *Psychological Review,* 84, 191–215.

Barnett, D. W., & Zucker, K. B. (1980). The others-concept: Explorations into the quality of children's interpersonal relationships. In H. Foot, A. J. Chapman, J. R. Smith (eds.), *Friendships and social relations.* New York: Wiley.

Baumrind, D. (1975). The contributions of the family to the development of competence in children. *Schizophrenia Bulletin,* 14, 12–37.

Bellack, A. (1979). Behavioral assessment of social skills. In A. Bellack & M. Hersen (eds.), *Social skills training.* New York: Plenum.

Berman, A. (1981). Research associating learning disabilities with juvenile delinquency. In J. Gottlieb & S. Strickart (eds.), *Development theory of research in learning disabilities.* Baltimore: University Park Press.

Bierman, K., & Furman, W. (1984). The effects of social skills training and peer involvement on the social adjustment of adolescents. *Child Development,* 55, 151–162.

Bingham, G. (1980). Self-esteem among boys with and without specific learning disabilities. *Child Study Journal,* 10, 41–47.

Black, F. W. (1974). Self-concept as related to achievement and age in learning disabled children. *Child Development,* 45, 1137–1140.

Bransford, J., Sherwood, R., Vye, N., & Rieser, J. (1987). Teaching thinking and problem solving: Research foundations. *American Psychologist*, 41, 1078–1089.

Broadbent, D. E. (1958). *Perception and communication*. London: Pergamon.

Brown, A. L. (1980). Metacognitive development and reading. In R. Spiro, B. Bruce, & W. Brewer (eds.), *Theoretical issues in reading comprehension*. Hillsdale, N.J.: Erlbaum.

Brown, A. L., Campione, J. C., & Day, J. (1981). Learning to learn: On training students to learn from texts. *Educational Researcher*, 10, 14–21.

Bryan, J., & Bryan, T. S. (1982). The social life of the learning disabled youngster. Unpublished manuscript.

Bryan, T. S. (1974). Peer popularity of learning disabled children. *Journal of Learning Disabilities*, 7, 261–268.

———. (1976). Peer popularity of learning disabled children: A replication. *Journal of Learning Disabilities*, 9, 307–311.

Bryan, T. S., & Bryan, J. (1978). Social interactions of learning disabled children. *Learning Disability Quarterly*, 1, 33–38.

Bryan, T. S., & Pearl, R. (1979). Self-concepts as locus of control of learning disabled children. *Journal of Clinical Child Psychology*, 8, 223–226.

Bursuck, W. (1981). Sociometric status, behavior ratings and social knowledge of learning disabled and low achieving students. *Learning Disability Quarterly*, 4, 329–338.

Byrne, D. (1975). Role-taking in adolescence and adulthood. Unpublished Ph.D. diss., Harvard University.

Cartledge, G., & Milburn, J. F. (1978). The case for teaching social skills in the classroom: A review. *Review of Educational Research*, 48, 133–156.

Chandler, M. J. (1971). *Egocentrism and childhood psychopathology*. Paper presented at the meeting of the Society for Research in Child Development, Minneapolis, April.

———. (1977). Social cognition: A selective revision of current research. In W. F. Overton & J. M. Gallagher (eds.), *Knowledge and Development*. Vol. 1. New York: Plenum.

Covington, M., Crutchfield, R., Davies, L., & Olton, R. (1974). *The productive thinking program*. Columbus, Ohio: Charles E. Merrill.

Crawford, D. (1982). *ALCD-R & D Project: A study investigating the link between learning disabilities and juvenile delinquency*. Association for Children with Learning Disabilities, Research and Development Project, Phoenix.

Crockett, W. H. (1965). Cognitive complexity and impression formation. In B. A. Maher (eds.), *Progress in experimental personality research*. Vol. 2. New York: Academic.

Davitz, J. (1969). *The language of emotion*. New York: Academic.

deBono, E. (1975). *CoRT thinking lessons*. Elmsford, N.Y.: Pergamon.

Deshler, D. D., Schumaker, J. B., Warner, M. M., Alley, G. R., & Clark, F. L. (1980). *An epidemiological study of learning disabled adolescents in secondary schools: Social status, peer relationships, activities in and out of school, and times uses*. Research Report No. 19. Lawrence: University of Kansas Institute for Research in Learning Disabilities.

Deutsch, J. A., & Deutsch, D. (1963). Attention: Some theoretical considerations *Psychological Review*, 70, 80–90.

DeVries, R. (1970). The development of role-taking as reflected by behavior of bright, average, and retarded children in a social guessing game. *Child development*, 41, 759–770.

Elias, M. J., & Rothbaum, P. A. (1986). Social cognitive problem solving in children: Assessing the knowledge and application of skills. *Journal of Development Psychology*, 7, 77–94.

Feuerstein, R. (1980). *Instrumental enrichment: An intervention program for cognitive modifiability*. Baltimore: University Park Press.

Flavell, J. H. (1985). Social cognition. In J. H. Flavell (ed.), *Cognitive development*. 2d ed. Englewood Cliffs, N.J.: Prentice-Hall.

Flavell, J. H., Botkin, P. T., Fry, C. L., Wright, J. W., & Jarvis, P. E. (1968). *The development of role-taking and communication skills in children*. New York: Wiley.

Ford, M. E. (1982). Social cognition and social competence in adolescence. *Developmental Psychology*, 18, 323–340.

Forgas, J. P. (1981). *Social cognition: Perspectives on everyday understanding*. New York: Academic.

Gagne, E. (1985). *The cognitive psychology of school learning*. Boston: Little, Brown.

Gagne, R. M. (1977). *The conditions of learning*. 3d ed. New York: Holt, Rinehart & Winston.

Gerber, P. (1980). Social perceptual processing problems: Psychological and educational considerations. Unpublished manuscript.

Gilbert, D. (1969). The young child's awareness of affect. *Child Development*, 39, 619–636.

Goldstein, A., Sprafkin, R., Gershaw, N., & Klein, P. (1980). *Skill-streaming the adolescent*. Champaign, Ill.: Research.

Gottman, J., Gonso, J., & Rasmussan, B. (1975). Social interaction, social competence and friendship in children. *Child Development*, 46, 709–718.

Hogan, R. (1973). Moral conduct and moral character: A psychological perspective. *Psychological Bulletin*, 79, 217–232.

Jackson, N., Jackson, D., & Monroe, C. (1983). *Getting along with others: Teaching social effectiveness to children*. Champaign, Ill.: Research.

Kahneman, D. (1973). *Attention and effort*. Englewood Cliffs, N.J.: Prentice-Hall.

Kohlberg, L., Colby, A., Speicher-Dubin, J., & Lieberman, M. (1975). *Standard form scoring manual*. Cambridge, Mass.: Moral Education Research Foundation.

Kuhn, T. S. (1962). *The structure of scientific revolutions*. Chicago, Ill.: University of Chicago Press.

Lipman, M. (1982). Philosophy for children. *Journal of Philosophy for Children*, 3(3), 35–44.

Livesley, W. J., & Bromley, D. B. (1973). *Person perception in childhood and adolescence*. New York: Wiley.

Lovaas, O., Schreibman, L., Koegel, R., & Rehm, R. (1971). Selective responding by autistic children to multiple sensory input. *Journal of Abnormal Psychology*, 77, 211–222.

McGinnis, E., & Goldstein, A. (1984). *Skill-streaming the elementary school child*. Champaign, Ill.: Research.

Michelson, L., & Wood, R. (1980). Behavioral assessment and training of children's social skills. *Progress in Behavior Modification*, 9, 241–291.

Mulcahy, R. F., Andrews, J., Darko-Yeboah, J., & Marfo, K. (in press). In J. B. Biggs (ed.), *Teaching for learning: The view from cognitive psychology*. Victoria, Australia: ACER.

Mulcahy, R. F., Peat, D., Andrews, J., & Darko-Yeboah, J. (1989). *Evaluation of a cognitive strategies teachers' program*. Final report, Barrhead School Division, Barrhead, Alberta.

Neale, J. M. (1966). Egocentrism in institutionalized and noninstitutionalized children. *Child Development*, 37, 97–101.

Norman, D. A. (1976). *Memory and attention: An introduction to human information processing*. New York: Wiley.

Olson, D. R. (1976). Culture, technology, and intellect. In L. B. Resnick (ed.), *The nature of intelligence*. Hillsdale, N.J.: Erlbaum.

Peevers, B. H., & Secord, P. F. (1973). Developmental changes in attribution of descriptive concepts to persons. *Journal of Personality and Social Psychology*, 27, 120–128.

Perkins, D. (1987). Thinking frames: An integrative perspective on teaching cognitive skills. In J. Baron & R. Sternberg (eds.), *Teaching thinking skills: Theory and practice*. New York: Freeman.

Phillips, E. (1978). *The social skills basis of psychopathology*. New York: Grune & Stratton.

Piaget, J. (1970). Piaget's theory. In P. H. Mussen (ed.), *Carmichael's manual of child psychology*. Vol. 1. New York: Wiley.

Piaget, J., & Inhelder, B. (1958). *The growth of logical thinking from childhood to adolescence*. New York: Basic Books.

Rincover, A., & Koegel, R. (1978). Research on the education of autistic children: Recent advances and future directions. In B. Lahey and A. Kazdin (eds.), *Advances in clinical child psychology*. Vol. 1. New York: Plenum.

Rogers, C. R. (1952). *Client-centered therapy*. Boston: Houghton-Mifflin.

Scarlett, H. H., Press, A. N., & Crockett, W. H. (1971). Children's descriptions of peers: A Wernerian developmental analysis. *Child Development*, 42, 439–453.

Selman, R. L. (1971a). Taking another's perspective: Role-taking development in early childhood. *Child Development*, 42, 21–34.

———. (1971b). The relation of role-taking to the development of moral judgment in children. *Child Development*, 42, 79–91.

Shantz, C. (1983). Social cognition. In J. H. Flavell & E. M. Markman (eds.), *Handbook of child psychology*, vol. 3, *Cognitive development*. 4th ed. New York: Wiley.

Solomon, L. (1963). *Experimental studies of tacit coordination: A comparison of schizophrenic and normal samples*. Paper presented at the Brockton Veteran's Administration Hospital Colloquium Series.

Spivack, G., Platt, J. J., & Shure, M. (1976). *The problem solving approach to adjustment*. San Francisco: Jossey-Bass.

Stephens, T. (1978). *Social skills in the classroom*. Columbus, Ohio: Cedars.

Supnik, L. (1967). Source of information as a factor affecting the impression of others. Unpublished Ph.D. diss., Clark University.

Taft, R. (1955). The ability to judge people. *Psychological Bulletin*, 52, 1–23.

Triesman, A. M. (1964). Verbal cues, language and meaning in selective attention. *American Journal of Psychology*, 77, 206–219.

————. (1969). Strategies and models of selective attention. *Psychological Review, 76,* 282–299.

Trower, B., Argyle, M., & Bryant, B. (1978). *Social skills and mental health.* London: Tavistock.

Vygotsky, L. S. (1981). The genesis of higher mental functions. In J. V. Wertsch (ed.), *The concept of activity in Soviet psychology.* Armonk, N.Y.: Sharpe.

Walker, H. M. (1981). *The SBS social skills curriculum: Teaching interactive competence and classroom survival skills to handicapped children.* Eugene, Oreg.: Center on Human Development.

Walker, H., McConnell, S., Holmes, D., Todis, B., Walker, J., & Golden, N. (1983). *The Walker social skills curriculum: The ACCEPTS program.* Austin, Tex.: PRO-ED.

Weiner, B., Graham, T., Taylor, S. E., & Meyer, W. (1983). Social cognition in the classroom. *Educational Psychologist,* 18(2), 109–124.

Weissberg, R., & Gesten, E. (1982). Considerations for designing effective school-based social problem-solving training programs. *School Psychology Review,* 11, 56–63.

White, R. W. (1959). Motivation reconsidered: The conquest of competence. *Psychological Review,* 66, 297–333.

PART 3

ASSESSMENT AND EVALUATION

Advances in the field of cognitive psychology over the past two decades have led to a major change in educational assessment. Traditionally, assessment in education has focused on the product of cognitive activity—in essence, the amount and type of knowledge acquired. The current trend in educational assessment, however, has been one of attempting to evaluate the actual cognitive processes involved in learning, finding out how knowledge is acquired and used.

The complex relationship that exists among learning, thinking, and other cognitive processes makes it important to produce wide-ranging, and yet at the same time selective, assessment techniques. The new techniques for assessing the cognitive components of learning and thinking need to be increasingly sensitive to personal characteristics, such as cognitive structure, developmental level, and predispositions as well as to the context or situation in which learning takes place, and the possible interactions that occur among these variables. This concern for individual variability and process in learning and thinking means that assessment procedures are also required to be more complex, individualized, and cognitively sensitive.

In education, assessment and intervention should not be considered as discrete procedures but as interactive components that can mutually influence the direction of student learning and the type of educational decision making that is required. Discovering how students approach problem-solving tasks and the types of strategies that they use in their learning and thinking can provide teachers with the type of knowledge that they require to facilitate the design of further programming and instructional techniques.

Two questions appear to be central to the above concerns: How do individuals learn and think? How effective are programs of instruction for improving learning and thinking skills? In chapter 13, Joya Sen and J. P. Das assess the cognitive capabilities essential for competent functioning at the managerial level of business. They begin by reviewing some of the research in holistic and synthetic thinking in the field of business management. They believe that managerial success could be better predicted if initial screening assessment included more measures of cognitive processes, particularly those of planning, information coding, and attention. They see these, along with the possession of a strong knowledge base, as the major variables determining managerial competence. They also discuss procedures for developing good planning behavior and present an experiment that would help in the assessment of potential managers.

In chapter 14, Thomas O. Maguire reviews validity demands of classroom assessment and describes some of the assessment methods used to evaluate the type and quality of student learning. He concludes with an example of how these methods have been used to evaluate programs for gifted students.

In chapter 15, Carmel and Fred French discuss the nature of cognitive instructional programs, review some of the existing evaluations of thinking skills programs, and present their own model for evaluating cognitive instruction.

13

Planning Competence and Managerial Excellence: A Research Framework

Joya Sen and J. P. Das

Orientation to management has been split into the analytic and the humanistic approaches. Whereas the analytic (or so-called rational) stance has made the practice of management a science, often bringing in quantification and objectivity that were severely lacking in the old managers' hunches and gut feelings, rationality does not seem to be appropriate in complex situations that demand innovative or creative solutions. It is not even adequate when one is compelled to question policy or to determine the long-term goals of an organization. Therefore, there is growing disenchantment with logical-analytic thinking. There is a new interest in humanistic traditions as represented by Eastern mysticism (Leavitt, 1975). Zen or TM has been comfortably placed side by side with the functions discovered by split-brain research. Here, we are referring to the work of Sperry (1964) and others, which has influenced the thinkers in management (Mintzberg, 1976; Leavitt, 1975). This split-brain work was started some twenty years ago on epileptic patients, as well as on animal models. Yet the results of split-brain (hemisphericity) research have been taken out of context and extended to reflect a kind of social movement toward holistic and nonsequential thinking. W. Agor's *Intuitive Management* (1984) advocates the use of "right-brain" and "integrated-brain" thinking for managers. In contrast to such loose thinking, Luthans et al. (1984) compare the characteristics of top-level managers with those of middle- and first-level managers, and conclude that successful managers are especially adept at decision making and planning. One of the constructive approaches to ensuring the choice of good managers and the training of future managers in MBA programs is to determine what characterizes excellent managers, and which cognitive skills are associated with competent, outstanding managerial skills.

INTELLIGENCE MEASURES AS PREDICTORS
OF VOCATIONAL SUCCESS

Research on predicting vocational success in general is not new; intelligence and aptitude tests have been used for the last fifty years for selection and prediction (Thornton & Byham, 1982). The outcome has not been encouraging. For instance, Ghiselli (1966), summarizing this vast body of research, concludes that general intelligence tests do not correlate highly with proficiency in all types of jobs. Thornton and Byham (1982) conclude that the evidence in favor of predictability from intelligence tests is mixed, and hence no firm statements can be made in support of their predictability for occupational success. The use of intelligence tests are reluctantly recommended only for the selection of first-level supervisors. One of the harshest criticisms of the use of intelligence tests is contained in the widely noted article by McClelland (1973). The paper opens with provocative remarks such as we blindly promote "the use of tests as instruments of power over the lives of many Americans" (p. 1). McClelland states that education level or grades in school are unrelated to vocational success in a wide variety of jobs. Even for highly intellectual jobs such as academic research, college grades have little predictability. This latter statement has relevance to MBA education, where entry to the program is mainly determined by aptitude and intelligence tests. Such testing for aptitude/intelligence is considered by McClelland as a "sentencing procedure." Two of his recommendations as alternatives to aptitude/intelligence testing are the basis for the theme of this chapter. McClelland recommends that job sampling and description of roles that managers are expected to play in their various jobs should be carried out, and that generalized competencies should be delineated by focusing directly on the thought patterns required for the roles. We propose to consider both of these, and elaborate on the ideas developed by Klemp and McClelland (1986).

THE ROLES OF MANAGERS

People's perceptions vary in regard to the essential qualities of an outstanding manager and the merely good manager. In fact, they vary even in regard to what a manager's role should be. The overarching concerns in this area are contained in Janis and Mann (1977), Leavitt (1975) and Mintzberg (1973, 1976). All suggest alternative ways of thinking about manager's roles. Leavitt, for instance, advocates the use of nonrational thinking. Outstanding managers exercise what Leavitt calls imaginative problem finding, problem solving, and problem implementing. Some amount of "organized anarchy" ought to be encouraged in managerial goal-setting activity, and undue emphasis on rational rules should be abandoned.

What are the roles attributed to managers? A recent book by Horton (1986) focuses on the roles of chief executive officers by obtaining data based on long interviews with eighteen of them. Coding and analyzing the contents of interviews, Horton observes four clusters of competencies: goal and action management, directing others, human resource management, and leadership. Interviews are expensive ways of gathering data on managerial roles. A cost-effective way is to produce a checklist on which respondents can rate good and outstanding managers. There is not a dearth of such checklists. In Thornton and Byham's (1982) book several can be found.

It would seem, however, that managers perform adequately or in an outstanding manner only in some specific roles, and not in others. How do we describe succinctly the roles managers play? Mintzberg (1973) presents ten major roles that are clustered under three categories: interpersonal, informational, and decisional. The ten roles were derived by interviewing high-level managers and observing their daily activities. The list includes leader, entrepreneur, disseminator, resource allocator, negotiator, monitor, spokesperson, disturbance handler, figurehead, and liaison. Which roles are typically fulfilled by production managers, by administrative and staffing, and by sales managers ought to be delineated, simply because these are expected to differ. Paolillo (1987) has provided reliable information on this based on a fairly large number (352) of respondents. It was found that the following roles are filled by production managers: entrepreneur, disturbance handler, resource allocator, and negotiator.

The ten managerial roles in each of the categories may not have class membership only in those categories. The categories themselves overlap to a certain extent as perceived by managers and nonmanagerial employees. Using scaling theory to divide the roles into categories, Shapira and Dunbar (1980) found two categories: (1) roles concerned with the generation and processing of information, and (2) roles that involve decisions. The decisional roles had higher correlations with each other than the informational roles. Thus there is evidence that the ten roles may not be perceived to be distinct and uncorrelated by respondents.

Table 13.1 is a sample questionnaire that encapsulates the essence of each role in concrete behavior. Checklists of adjectives or key words are psychologically less appealing to the respondent, and may have less meaning when the respondents are asked to describe their perceptions of a manager's roles. Making up the checklist as Mintzberg did by observing the day-to-day activities of managers is of course a valid and necessary first step. Once such a list is generated, the words in the checklist are placed in meaningful sentences describing the behavior in concrete terms. Subsequently, in a study we propose, the list of roles that have been translated into behaviors is administered to samples of individuals (students, nonmanagement employees, etc.) to describe managers in the functional roles of production, administration-staffing, or sales.

Table 13.1
Managerial Role Scale

There are managers who work in PRODUCTION, others who do STAFFING and ADMIN-ISTRATION, and yet others who are in SALES. Look at the questions in this form. In this form, your opinion about the roles of the three different kind of managers is solicited. Consider each kind of manager separately; first start with PRODUCTION MANAGERS. Do you consider that "Conducts ceremonies such as staff retirement dinners" to be absolutely essential, expected, but not essential, not expected for the job?

You have three copies of this form. Use one copy for production managers. When you have finished answering the questions, use the next for staffing and administration managers, and the next for sales managers.

Production Managers

Conducts ceremonies such as staff retirement dinners
        absolutely essential   expected, but not essential   not expected

Gives advice, encouragement, and leadership
        absolutely essential   expected, but not essential   not expected

Keeps in touch and keeps the channels of communication open
        absolutely essential   expected, but not essential   not expected

Seeks information and understanding of the organization
        absolutely essential   expected, but not essential   not expected

Keeps everyone informed about goals and policies
        absolutely essential   expected, but not essential   not expected

Acts as a spokesperson
        absolutely essential   expected, but not essential   not expected

Initiates changes for improvement and juggles many projects
        absolutely essential   expected, but not essential   not expected

Resolves conflicts and handles crises
        absolutely essential   expected, but not essential   not expected

Knows where the company should go and makes resources available
        absolutely essential   expected, but not essential   not expected

Negotiates deals and has the authority for seeing them through
        absolutely essential   expected, but not essential   not expected

The list of role descriptors can be also administered to managers who are within and those who are outside the functional roles if our aim is to contrast their role perceptions. The role descriptors are shown in table 13.1; they need to be tried out in comparative studies.

The descriptors can be easily grouped under the three categories of interpersonal, informational, and decisional roles by the reader. But these role divisions are a priori, and may not correspond to the distinctions perceived by respondents. That is, which roles would cluster together, and would the three role clusters emerge? Cluster analysis is appropriate to use here, and its results will answer some additional questions, such as whether the clusters for managerial functions are identical or not, and whether there are differences in clusters obtained from data on different samples such as MBA students, nonmanagement employees, or managers in different functional positions.

The availability of time to reflect and plan and to engage in synthetic thinking is frequently scarce in managers' daily routine. The activities of most managers are brief, varied, and discontinuous. In fact, if 50 percent or more of manager's acts last less than nine minutes, Mintzberg is right in stating that managers have no time to plan, organize, or coordinate and have no control over their own schedules and appointments. Kurk and Aldrich (1983) replicated Mintzberg's (1973) observations ten years later. Managers again were found to have no time to engage in reflection. The fault obviously lies partly in the structure of the organization and the role expectations of peers, bosses, and employees of the managers. Appropriate training for effective management must be designed that promotes planning and decision making. Global and holistic thinking and planful behavior can be promoted in training programs for potential managers.

COMPETENCY

Intellectual competencies include planning and causal thinking, diagnostic information seeking, and synthetic thinking. Klemp and McClelland (1986) report the results of separate studies on the typical competencies in which outstanding managers distinguish themselves. In four out of five studies, they were clearly above average in conceptualizing the problem and in synthetic thinking, which entails understanding how different parts, needs, or functions of the company fit together, noticing patterns and consistencies that are interpreted, spotting the most important issues in a complex situation, and finally using unusual (novel?) analogies to understand and explain the essence of a situation. Planning and causal thinking were the next frequent discriminator, and diagnostic information thinking was slightly less frequent than planning as a significant characteristic of outstanding managers.

Competencies reflect intellectual or cognitive processes; thus they are themselves the end product of processes. Generic processes, then, should be the focus of study. A consideration of such processes leads ultimately to an understanding of intelligent behavior, of which managerial behavior is a subset. What could these generic processes be? The answer is not an easy one. Recent developments in the field of intellectual or cognitive processes tend to converge on two alternative models of cognitive processes. These are the computer models (Hunt, 1980; Sternberg, 1985), and the neuropsychological view of cognitive processes (Luria, 1966, 1973; Das, 1985). To give a simple example of cognitive processes from the computer-type models, consider Sternberg's generic processes, which are selective encoding, selective combination, and selective comparison. Their use is especially visible in nonentrenched or novel tasks (Sternberg, 1981). Thus, these processes are required in a variety of decision-making and planning situations, which characterize manager's responsibilities. We suggest that all three activities are involved in planful behavior as well as in decision making in managerial roles. We prefer a neuropsychological model to computer models (although the two are not in conflict), because the latter has a base in brain structure. Leavitt and Mintzberg have also used the functions of the brain to conceptualize managerial roles. The model (Luria, 1966; Das, 1973, 1984a; Das et al., 1975, 1979) suggests that there are three functional organizations of brain activity that are reflected in behavior: planning, coding of information, and attention and arousal.

Luria (1966, 1970) studied a variety of behavioral dysfunctions that resulted from lesions in the brain. His recorded observations span some forty years. He distinguishes among three main functional divisions, or blocks of the brain ("functional", because we would not be able to see these divisions if we did a postmortem on the most intelligent person on earth). The lower part, block 1, is involved in arousal. It consists of the brain stem and the lower brain structures, and is responsible primarily for levels of attention and arousal.

The second block of the brain, concerned with coding of information, engages in two broad kinds of processing activities: simultaneous synthesis and successive synthesis. Since we have already written a great deal on simultaneous and successive processing (Das et al., 1979), we will present here merely an overview of the two coding functions. In simultaneous processing, information is integrated into quasi-spatial arrays, such that all parts of the information that are simultaneously organized are surveyable. Simultaneous processing occurs in both the left and the right hemispheres, and includes both verbal and nonverbal information. Successive processing is concerned with integrating information in a temporal sequence. Successive processing of information related to both verbal and nonverbal material is similar to simultaneous processing.

The final division, block 3, regulates planful behavior. It is involved in "planning," which entails making decisions, evaluations, and judgments. It is also concerned with strategies for solving problems. But that is not all. It also entails the aptitude for asking new questions. We spend a lot of our time in making up problems as well as in solving problems, and indeed, this question seeking or problem finding (e.g., Arlin, 1977) may well be one of the highest orders of planful behavior. These planning functions are organized in the frontal lobe, especially in the prefrontal area.

Those who are uncomfortable in relating intellectual behavior to the brain and its ill-understood functions, may be more satisfied with a schematic diagram of the three blocks of the brain provided by Kirby (1980). In that picture, the relation among the functional blocks can be elaborated as follows. Input from the external environment reaches both block 1 and block 2. From that point on, there is a continuous interaction among the three blocks. The arousal functions of block 1 certainly influence both coding and planning. On the one hand, in block 2 the coding processes themselves provide a basis for planned action; on the other hand, plans and decisions and strategies influence the way we code information. These planning functions also modulate our arousal response.

The above discussion on the processes of coding information, attending and being aroused or alerted to the salient features of events or situations, and planning and decision making (see Figure 13.1) can be easily related to management. There is little disagreement in recognizing that managerial skills do involve all three processes.

Let us move deeper into a consideration of the nature of planning. Until now, we have advanced the hypothesis that planning is a uniquely human cognitive function. It has its structural base in the frontal lobes. The process of planning entails such activities as the generation, selection, and execution of plans or programs, judgment, evaluation of one's own behavior, and evaluation of others' behavior. Planning also refers to a tendency to act on the basis of such evaluations. Besides structure and process, planning has a knowledge base. Our plans operate on information that has been coded; in other words, information that has been properly analyzed. Without coded information, planning becomes empty, and in the absence of a plan, information coding is blind.

The relative independence of planning from coding has been suggested by philosophers and psychologists alike. Kant, for instance, thought that although people can acquire facts and utilize these facts in a scholarly manner, they may not have good judgment. In fact, Kant was somewhat skeptical of a necessary relationship between gathering of information on the one hand and competence in judgment on the other. We have all noticed that a wide range of competence in judgment and decision making may be found, given the same amount of intelligence as measured by standardized tests.

Standardized intelligence tests mostly measure the coding processes, and only tangentially measure the functions subsumed in planning. None of the IQ tests assess motivation, which may be conceived of as an interaction between block 1 and block 3 functions, nor do they measure arousal. Perhaps this is one of the major reasons for their reduced relevance for predicting success in the world outside the school. It must be granted that those individuals who have high IQs are often flexible and reflective, can choose wisely from among available strategies to achieve their goals, and tend to be highly motivated. But IQ tests mostly assess block 2 functions.

A reasonably high level of general intelligence may ensure adequate coding functions. As far as attention-arousal levels are concerned, BMAs and managers use this process adequately. Gross deficiency in attention-arousal functions is not expected among this population. So we focus on the performance

Figure 13.1
The Three Functional Blocks for Higher Mental Activities

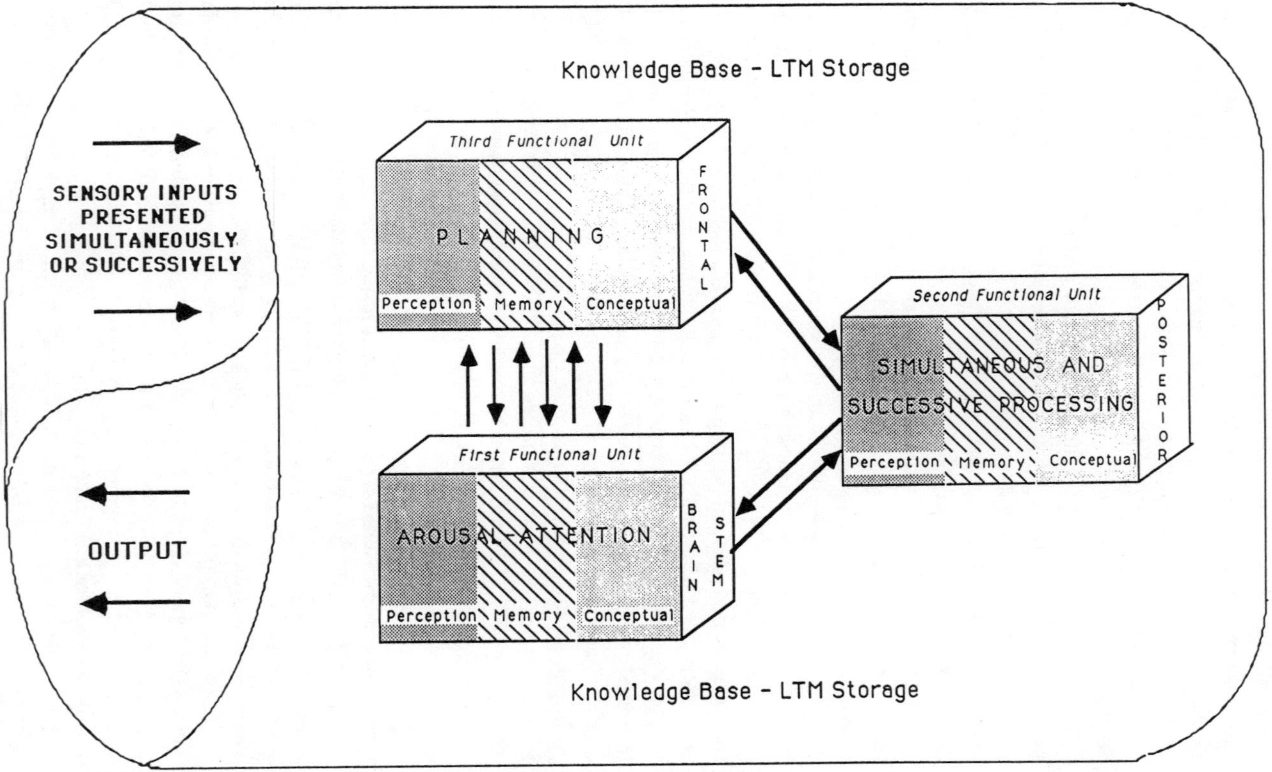

of our samples on planning tasks. These tasks involve planning behavior in perception, memory, and higher-order conceptual activities. Separate tests for each of these exist, the most relevant for managerial competence being the conceptual tasks.

TACIT KNOWLEDGE

How does one acquire knowledge that will be relevant to managerial planning? Is this knowledge explicitly acquired through deductive and inductive inferences that the individual makes or is this tacit knowledge? In answer to this, we believe with many other researchers that practical knowledge that leads to success in real-world pursuits is acquired without formal instruction (Wagner & Sternberg, 1986). Also, the acquisition of tacit knowledge will not be related to the narrow range of variations in intelligence in our samples. Thus, we relate these answers back to McClelland's advocacy against the usefulness of intelligence/aptitude tests in predicting real-life competence. First, we briefly consider Polanyi's (1976) definition of tacit knowledge, and then introduce Wagner and Sternberg's research on managers and academic leaders in regard to tacit knowledge.

Polanyi takes the position that all empirical knowledge is tacit knowledge, since no strict rules exist for empirical knowledge. The evidence exists for this knowledge, but the evidence is but a starting point; from this we go on to acquire tacit knowledge. Polanyi's example of reading a sentence expands on what he means by this. In reading a sentence the letters and the words are important, but the aim of reading is to understand the sentence. So we transcend the letters and words, which serve as subsidiaries, to get at the meaning. Tacit knowledge and inference are implicit. They differ from logical inference, which is explicit. This is relevant for planful behavior. The process of planning frequently uses implicit inferencing, and the planner is not aware of the logic. Nevertheless, tacit inference requires the manager to make a connection between the evidence and the focal target; otherwise the evidence has no meaning by itself. Further, the focal target is fully within the awareness of the planner or the manager, but the evidence can be at unconscious and subconscious levels. This is why the manager may not be aware of either the integration of evidence or the evidence itself while keeping the goal or the problem to be solved at the level of awareness at all times. How then do we facilitate the development of tacit knowledge?

A sample of a tacit knowledge test item from Wagner and Sternberg (1986) is given below. The situation portrayed in it calls for planning and decision making in the context of management.

You have just been promoted to head of an important department in the company. The previous head had been transferred to an equivalent position in a less important department. Your understanding of the reason for the move is that the performance of the department as a whole was mediocre. There were not any glaring deficiencies, just a perception of the department as so-so rather than as very good. Your charge is to shape up the department. Results are expected quickly. Rate the following pieces of advice colleagues have given you by their importance to succeeding in your new position:

—— a. always delegate to the most junior person who can be trusted with the task
—— b. give your superiors frequent progress reports
—— c. promote open communication

Wagner and Sternberg distinguish among three kinds of tacit knowledge: knowledge about managing self, managing tasks, and managing others. As the terms signify, the first one is concerned with self-motivation and self-organizational aspects of performance. The authors go on to propose local orientation and global orientation within the three types of "managing" knowledge. In the first kind of orientation, the manager is concerned with short-term payoffs from accomplishing a task, rather than caring for overall career goals, personal reputation, or the goals of the company. In contrast, a global orientation involves focusing on future career-related goals. To give a concrete example, if a subordinate is inconsiderate to the manager, the manager may have a justifiable reason to punish that employee by demotion. On the other hand, the company does not view demotions favorably. Thus, if the manager does not take the option to demote the employee, he would be showing global rather than a local orientation.

Wagner and Sternberg found reliable relationships between years of management experience and tacit knowledge with a local orientation and tacit knowledge about managing tasks. Tacit knowledge and level of company (included or excluded from the Fortune 500 list) or years of schooling beyond high school, however, did not relate to each other. They also found that acquisition of tacit knowledge does not appear to be closely related to verbal intelligence performance. On the whole, it appears that tacit knowledge relates to knowledge base in some specific areas, but not to intelligence. Those who are in management positions had better tacit knowledge than undergraduate students who had little experience of managing. At the same time, it is not clear how tacit knowledge is acquired during one's career as a manager, and whether its acquisition can be accelerated.

In relating tacit knowledge to the model of intelligence we have suggested, it appears that the acquisition of knowledge specific to a job or role may be separated from the flexibility with which that knowledge is used. In other words, generic competencies in planning should interact with tacit knowledge as well as with academic knowledge in solving problems that arise in managing career, self, or others. In some roles, the importance of generic competence in planning would be greater than specific knowledge about the company that correlates with seniority or years of service. It remains for future research to determine the relative contribution of generic planning and tacit knowledge to successful managerial performance in designated roles. The research will be by no means simple.

PROMOTING PLANFUL BEHAVIOR

The two components of managerial competency are knowledge and process. Knowledge can be acquired in formal instructional settings and through experience. The latter is characteristic of tacit knowledge. Although the interdependence of the two kinds of knowledge is not apparent, one is incomplete without the other. Book knowledge must be validated in experience, and experiential knowledge should be structured through formal instruction. Managers need this interfacing. They need to bring their formal knowledge down to field experience. They ought to give their practical knowledge, their insights, "hunches," and "sensing," a formal structure. Tacit knowledge must ascend and formal knowledge must descend for their full utilization in cognitive processing.

Can we promote better planning among potential managers, as well as managers in the field? Formal student knowledge must descend to the level of experience. Experience of managers in the field must ascend to be formally structured. Let us consider the following examples for promoting both and planning as well.

An irrigation project in a rural area in eastern India ran into serious difficulties. The villagers at the head of the irrigation canal blocked the flow of the water and diverted it to their own farm land. This action prevented those at the end of the canal from using the water. The irrigation engineer who was directing the project ordered the headers to remove the blocking; he was supported by the villagers at the end of the canal. Tension ran high. The director was threatened with physical attack by the "head" villagers; his supporters from the "end" villagers were going to stand behind him. A riot was inevitable.

How can the project director manage the conflict? What generic competencies are needed to resolve the conflict?

We have discussed Klemp and McClelland's three intellectual competencies (planning and causal thinking, diagnostic information seeking, and conceptualization and theory building); these will help the management of the conflict. All three can be understood within the neuropsychological model; but let us see how the project director may utilize these. The director should conceptualize and build a theoretical framework in order to understand the situation. This can be done by seeking diagnostic information, but more important by searching for causal links.

In concrete terms, the project director sets out initially with a hypothesis such as the following: The "headers" are simply insecure about their water supply, hence they wish to block. Diagnostic information seeking reveals some insecurity, but also exposes a great deal of mistrust in the past; promises of adequate supply of agricultural resources such as seeds and fertilizers have not been fulfilled. Although the irrigation problem is new, the mistrust has generalized to all dealings with the government. How to remove or significantly reduce the mistrust becomes an important concern. Another hypothesis is that the headers are known to be simply greedy and selfish. Not all of the villagers are this way, but some are and they have emerged as the bargainers. Diagnostic information seeking shows that indeed three persons are playing on the selfishness and greed of the villagers. Thus, another problem for the management is to persuade the three leaders to be less greedy. The above deliberations exemplify causal thinking, hypothesis testing, and relating recurring event to a framework. Such cognitive activities contain elements of cognitive processes of simultaneous-successive coding, attention, and particularly planning. Excellent managers excel in conceptualization of the problems (Klemp & McClelland, 1986) in constructing a general formulation that will guide the resolution of the conflict.

SCREENING FOR POTENTIAL MANAGERS

The first stage in screening for potential managers involves checking their efficiency in planning using simple visual search tasks and in the complex conceptual or logical search where feedback from four to five sources must determine the plan for solution of the problem. In the first stage, planning as applied to the solution of a real-world rather than a laboratory problem will be checked by using the tacit knowledge questionnaire.

A set of generic planning competency tasks and a test of the three categories of tacit knowledge are taken as independent variables in an experiment for the selection of potentially good managers. MBA students are the prime candidates for inclusion in this experiment; but the design can be extended to other groups such as nonmanagement employees.

As mentioned, a group of MBA students are chosen as subjects for the experiment. Their academic performance records in terms of grades over the last two exams are available. They are administered two generic tests of planning. These tests have not been found to relate significantly to IQ among normal (not retarded) individuals, and are less likely to relate among college students or educated adults of managerial potential because of the restriction of range in IQs.

Visual search is one of the planning subtests of the Cognitive Assessment System (CAS) (Naglieri & Das, 1987, 1988). It comprises twenty search tasks grouped under either the automatic search or controlled search component. The subject's task is to find a picture, number, or letter identical to one located in a box in the center (the field). The score is the time in seconds it takes the child to locate the target embedded in a field of similar items (picture among letters) whereas controlled search time refers to those where target and field items are the same. Automatic search is essentially a measure of attention as the target "pops up" from the field, whereas in controlled or planned search, people have to make a deliberate effort to locate the target.

Crack the Code is a planning subtest from the CAS. In this subtest the student's task is to determine the correct sequence of a number of colored chips given a limited amount of information. The subject is given two to five trials with feedback to determine the one correct order of chips for each of the seven items. The subtest is organized into seven items with two or three trials per item and a three-minute limit per item. An example of one of the problems is given below.

Five different color chips are used in this problem: white, black, orange, yellow, and blue. The colors are arranged in rows; against each row is the number of chips correctly placed. These are the feedbacks that the subject should use to get the correct answer.

White	Blue	Black	Orange	Yellow	3 correct
White	Black	Orange	Yellow	Blue	Zero
Black	Orange	Yellow	Blue	White	Zero
Blue	Orange	Black	White	Yellow	3 correct
Orange	Yellow	Blue	White	Black	Zero
?	?	?	?	?	

Answer not shown to subject:

Blue	White	Black	Orange	Yellow

The tacit knowledge questionnaire with at least one example each from the categories of managing self, career, and others is also administered. Then a test of generic planning with management content is administered as described below as a test of strategic planning. This is like planned composition, a task that has been identified as a reliable measure of planning (Das, 1984b). The first part of the task is a variant of Crack the Code; in place of colors, strategies are substituted. A test of strategic planning follows.

Suppose in a pharmaceutical company you are the chief executive officer. The company can have the following overall strategies in order to prosper: (1) be innovative; (2) achieve a good share of the market; (3) be known for its economical price—low cost of product; (4) produce high-quality goods.

Innovation requires an outlay of capital in research and development. But in the last five years, research and development money has increased fivefold, while the number of new products has remained the same. Achieving a market share requires aggressive advertisement, but the company's star product (i.e., Bayer Aspirin) is about to be replaced by a new breakthrough medication for fever. Recognition of affordability requires getting the components of the products, from manufacturing to packaging, from developing countries where labor is cheap. But this has a disastrous effect on domestic employment. The product of high quality may cost so much as to make it uneconomical.

In the fifty-year history of the company, the following weights had been given to the strategies with results indicated. Your job is to achieve 100 percent growth by rearranging the strategies; but you must take into account the information from the past.

A past manager gave first place to 3, second place to 4, third place to 1, and fourth place to 2. None of 3412 are in the correct position. The profit dropped to 0 percent because not even one of the strategies were in the correct place.

Another manager gave first place to 4, second place to 1, third place to 2, and fourth place to 3. Two of 4123 are in the correct position. The profit was 50 percent, because only two of the strategies were in the correct place. You do not know which two.

Another manager gave first place to 2, second place to 3, third place to 4, and fourth place to 1. Two are in correct position. The profit was also 50 percent because, again, only two of the strategies were in the correct place.

How will you assign the priorities so that the right strategy will have the right place to give a 100 percent outcome? Having found the solution (4321 or 2143), write a one-page essay justifying how the plan produced the best results when the solution is 4321, and another essay when it is 2143.

The essay is rated for organization and individuality (unique and original) on a seven-point scale, as well as on the following mechanics of writing: expression, wording, mechanics (syntax, spelling, punctuation). The rating is done by preferably three judges independently (see Ashman & Das [1980] for details). The whole group of students are divided into quarters (lowest 25% to highest 25%) on the basis of their MBA course performance. Then, their performance on the composition (mean for each group) is compared to check the relationship between tacit and formal knowledge.

Thus, in the first phase of selection we should be able to distinguish between two broad categories of individuals: those likely to be poor managers and those who are potentially good and excellent. On the basis of our tests of planning and performance on tacit knowledge questions, we can further select the MBA students. Those who consistently score above the eightieth percentile on both measures are likely to be excellent managers.

Subsequent situational tests like the irrigation problem could be devised for further confirmation. The situational tests have to be constructed in such a way that formal knowledge common to all MBA students is required for solution, and strategy planning using both formal and tacit knowledge can be elicited by providing feedback in the following manner.

We use the irrigation problem to discuss the two points made above. Suppose our MBA students have formal knowledge of irrigation. We divide them into groups of three to four and ask them to solve the problem as we introduce different feedback information such as the following: (1) the farm land area that will be inundated if the headers block the water 100, 75, and 50 percent. With blocking, headers get 50 percent of water. How can this information be used in managing the conflict situation? (2) The effect of salinization due to water logging. (3) The possibility of growing different crops by the farms at the end of the canal who get only 30 percent of the water. These crops may be exchanged for some of the headers' crops. Tacit knowledge feedbacks will include (4) the number of occasions in the past when promises by the government officers have not been kept and the fact that the irrigation officer has an untarnished record, (5) the presence or absence of a charismatic leader among the "headers" and end users, and (6) personality characteristics of the irrigation project director (e.g., authoritarian, indecisive, etc.).

The MBA student groups engage in problem solving as their examiner or instructor introduces one or more of these feedbacks at different times. At the end of a half-day exercise, the students are invited to articulate their learning experience.

This chapter began with a discussion of the current research in holistic and synthetic thinking in management. This was followed by a review of the use of intelligence measures for predicting managerial success as well as the role and psychological competencies of managers. The conclusion drawn from this review was that a good predictor of success would be an instrument that includes the assessment of cognitive processes, particularly planful behavior, information coding, and attention. These are considered to be the general competencies that in part determine managerial competence. A further determinant is a strong knowledge base, including both formal and tacit knowledge. The acquisition of such knowledge and its flexible application in managerial settings were distinguishable as separate components contributing to managerial excellence. It appears that the latter depends predominantly on the general competence of planning. Procedures for promoting planful behavior were delineated and an experiment for screening potential managers' planning processes was presented. We believe that such experiments will contribute toward developing the psychologically valid measures of the processes underlying managerial excellence.

REFERENCES

Agor, W. (1984). *Intuitive management.* New York: Prentice-Hall.

Arlin, P. K. (1977). Piagetian operations in problem finding. *Developmental Psychology,* 13, 297–298.

Ashman, A., & Das, J. P. (1980). Relation between planning and simultaneous-successive processing. *Perceptual and Motor Skills,* 51, 371–382.

Das, J. P. (1973). Cultural deprivation and cognitive competence. In N. R. Ellis (ed.), *International review of research in mental retardation.* Vol. 6. New York: Academic.

―――. (1984a). Intelligence and information integration. In J. Kirby (ed.), *Cognitive strategies and educational performance*. New York: Academic.

―――. (1984b). Aspects of planning. In J. Kirby (ed.), *Cognitive strategies and educational performance*. New York: Academic.

―――. (1985). Review of concept formation. *9th mental measurement year book*. Lincoln, Nebr.: Burros Institute.

Das, J. P., Kirby, J., & Jarman, R. F. (1975). Simultaneous and successive synthesis: An alternative model for cognitive abilities. *Psychological Bulletin*, 82(1), 87–103.

―――. (1979). *Simultaneous and successive cognitive processes*. New York: Academic.

Ghiselli, E. E. (1966). *The validity of occupational aptitude tests*. New York: Wiley.

Horton, T. R. (1986). *What works for me*. New York: Random House.

Hunt, E. (1980). Intelligence as an information processing concept. *British Journal of Psychology*, 71, 449–474.

Janis, I. L., & Mann, L. (1977). *Decision making: A psychological analysis of conflict, choice and commitment*. New York: Free.

Kirby, J. R. (1980). Individual differences and cognitive processes. In J. R. Kirby & J. Biggs (eds.), *Cognition, development and instruction*. New York: Academic.

Klemp, G. O., Jr., & McClelland, D. C. (1986). What characterizes intelligent functioning among senior managers. In R. J. Sternberg & R. K. Wagner (eds.), *Practical intelligence: Nature and origins of competence in the everyday world*. Cambridge, Mass.: Cambridge University Press.

Kurk, L., & Aldrich, H. E. (1983). Mintzberg was right: a replication and extension of the nature of managerial work. *Management Science*, 29(8), 975–984.

Leavitt, H. J. (1975). Beyond the analytic manager, pt. 2. *California Management Review*, 17(4).

Luria, A. R. (1966). *Human brain and psychological process*. New York: Harper.

―――. (1970). The functional organization of the brain. *Scientific American*, 222, 66–78.

―――. (1973). *The working brain*. Middlesex, England: Penguin.

Luthans, F., Rosenkrantz, S. A. & Hennessey, H. W. (1984). What do successful managers really do? *Journal of Applied Behavioral Science*, 21, 255–270.

McClelland, D. C. (1973). Testing for competence rather than for intelligence. *American Psychologist*, 28, 1–14.

Mintzberg, (1973). *The nature of managerial work*. New York: Harper & Row.

―――. (1976). Planning on the left side and managing on the right. *Harvard Business Review*, July–August, 49–58.

Naglieri, J., & Das, J. P. (1987). Construct and criterion-related validity of planning, simultaneous, and successive cognitive processing tasks. *Journal of Psychoeducational Assessment*, 4, 353–363.

―――. (1988). Planning-Arousal-Simultaneous-Successive (PASS): A model for assessment. *Journal of School Psychology*, 26, 35–48.

Paolillo, J. (1987). Role profiles for managers in different functional areas. *Group & Organization Studies*, 12(1), 109–18.

Polanyi, M. (1976). Tacit knowledge. In M. Marx and F. Goodson (eds.), *Theories in contemporary psychology*. New York: Macmillan.

Shapira, Z., & Dunbar, R. (1980). Testing Mintzberg's managerial roles classification using an in-basket simulation. *Journal of Applied Psychology,* 65(1), 87–95.

Sperry, R. W. (1964). The great cerebral commissure. *Scientific American,* 210(1), 42–52.

Sternberg, R. J. (1981). Intelligence and non-entrenchment. *Journal of Educational Psychology,* 73(1), 1–16.

———. (1985). *Beyond IQ: A triarchic theory of human intelligence.* New York: Cambridge University Press.

Thornton, S. C., III, & Byham, W. C. (1982). *Assessment centers and managerial performance.* New York: Academic.

Wagner, R. K., & Sternberg, R. J. (1986). Tacit knowledge and intelligence in the everyday world. In R. J. Sternberg and R. K. Wagner (eds.), *Practical intelligence: Nature and origins of competence in the everyday world.* Cambridge, Mass.: Cambridge University Press.

14

Assessing the Outcomes
of Learning

Thomas O. Maguire

Concurrent with a renewed emphasis on teaching generalizable learning and thinking skills today is the changing focus of educational measurement. Among the emerging research themes are the applications of cognitive psychology to assessment (Snow & Lohman, 1989; Embretson, 1985) and the new understanding of teachers' assessment practices (Stiggens & Bridgeford, 1985; Gullikson, 1984; Wilson, 1990). Taken together, these themes suggest that while there is renewed interest in issues of construct validity as they apply to classroom assessment, the breadth, complexity, and intensity of demands that are made on teachers from all sides make it difficult to change the current concentration of classroom testing practice on lower-level skills. The purpose of this chapter is to show how the Biggs and Collis (1982) SOLO taxonomy can be used to improve the validity of assessment of some higher-level objectives within the context of current classroom activities.

VALIDITY DEMANDS OF CLASSROOM TESTS

Snow (1989) presents a five-row by three-column network of constructs that is useful for research on assessment in learning from instruction. He divides achievement into five categories of constructs: conceptual structures of declarative knowledge, procedural skills, learning strategies, self-regulatory functions, and motivational orientations. On the other dimension, he places three constituents of instructional theory: aptitude constructs, learning-development or transition constructs, and outcome or achievement constructs. By placing achievement in a context of instruction, metacognition, and conative orientations, Snow reminds us of the complexity of the assessment situation and provides direction for carrying it out.

If we apply Snow's ideas to validity, we begin to see that our instruments must be capable of detecting development from "naive theories" to "deep understanding" and from "components of skill" to "efficient intuitive use." Our instruments must accommodate "multiple flexible strategies" for learning, and they must take into account growth and maturity in self-regulatory functions of attention and action control and motivational orientations toward selective intrinsic interest and eventual mastery. Simply put, the usual end-of-unit test with its emphasis on recall of facts is not going to be up to the task.

Snow points out that we will need a multiplicity of instruments and approaches because the range of tasks for assessment is so broad: from daily assessment for teacher planning to yearly assessment for system policy development, from specific assessment of proximal goals to more general assessments of long-range goals, and from assessment of cognitive outcomes to assessment of conative orientations. He calls for a program of construct validation and measurement development designed to produce better, more coherent approaches to assessment.

Cole (1990) maintains that how we conceive of achievement influences much that occurs in education, from how we teach and learn to how we set policy for our schools. She divides characterizations of achievement into two kinds: basic skills and facts and higher-order skills and advanced knowledge. Although the basic skills and facts conceptualization has had a good deal of prominence in the past few decades, the concern for the higher-order achievement such as critical thinking and problem solving has always been there and in the past few years cognitive psychologists have shown renewed interest in this sort of achievement. Although Cole does not attend to the political dimensions of her two characterizations of achievement, it should be kept in mind that for many reasons they have developed a sociopolitical life of their own. Accountability, back to basics, and whole education are not value-neutral in the minds of the public. Adoption of change is not entirely within the scope of the educational community. Nevertheless, there is a responsibility to analyze current practice, make suggestions, and argue for improvement.

For people reared in the psychometric tradition (that branch of psychology that deals with measurement), there may be a tendency to forget or even ignore the philosophical discussions of educational goals and what they imply for assessment. As one example, Cole briefly shows how Broudy's (1988) uses of schooling relate to her two concepts of achievement.

In outlining his argument for general education, Broudy (1988) lists four uses of schooling: replicative, applicative, associative, and interpretive. The replicative use of knowledge refers to the use of facts and principles in the exact form in which they were learned. Broudy points out, however, that much replicative knowledge is not retained beyond the classroom setting (although to some extent that depends on the individual). For example, the Russian vocabulary learned only to satisfy the language requirement for a Ph.D. may be soon lost, whereas addition facts used almost daily would remain.

The applicative use of schooling refers to the direct application of facts or principles to new situations. Much technical training and apprenticeships, and some professional education, is directed toward the applicative uses of schooling. The process of applicative schooling involves showing students how to structure, categorize, or recognize situations where the known facts and principles can be applied.

The other two uses, associative and interpretive, refer to how we use the associations and connotations that are built up around concepts and principles, and how we make translations and abstractions in order to conduct our lives. Broudy points out that the real value of education lies more in the latter uses of schooling than in the former. He justifies the former, however, by showing how they contribute to what he calls the "allusionary base," the conceptual storehouse of implicit knowledge that each of us possesses. As he notes (p. 21), "The associative resources provided by schooling and experience plus the interpretive repertoire of concepts and images constitute the allusionary base. The resources of the allusionary base are not used by simple replication of this or that school learning, and their adequacy cannot be judged by tests of replication or application. On the contrary, the success of general education is to be measured by the depth and quality of the allusionary base."

The point of describing Broudy's ideas is to show how consistent they are with Snow's. Where Brody argues for associative and implicative education building on an allusionary base, Snow from a psychologist's perspective talks about deep understanding, efficient intuitive use, multiple flexible strategies, adaptive control, and achievement motivation developing from a set of initial states. Cole's desire for an overarching framework linking the philosophical with the psychological is not a distant dream. The place of student assessment is significant. It must derive from the philosophical and psychological principles that are selected to guide education.

After reviewing over two hundred studies on the impact of classroom evaluation practices on students, Crooks (1988) concludes that classroom evaluation affects students by guiding their judgment on what to learn, how to learn it, and how much effort to put into the learning. If assessment is to work in concert with instruction and serve the broad goals of education then there must be greater focus on deeper learning.

From a cognitive perspective, it is important to direct students' attention to their own progress in order to improve their learning. According to Crooks, there has been too much emphasis on grading, especially comparative assessment. This appears to diminish intrinsic motivation to learn and accentuates the extrinsic rewards and punishments. Feedback that focuses on interpersonal comparisons tends to act against the development of self-efficacy for those students who are not among the top. This does not mean that teachers should allow even the brightest students to go unchallenged. Standards of performance should be set at a level that is both high and attainable. This may require different standards for different students. Evaluation tasks should be varied in format and nature to encourage transfer. Consistent with the idea that tests and assignments tell students what is important about a course, evaluation should be directed at the important features.

Crooks' review gives classroom level support to the more general recommendations of Snow and Cole. There is a need to change the way in which classroom assessment is viewed. It must be located within a philosophical framework (or at least make its basic educational assumptions explicit); it must have instructional utility; it must encourage students to take responsibility for their own learning; and, most important, it must possess construct validity.

There are many ways to improve classroom testing practice. Each approach has its strengths and weaknesses, and as Snow (1989, p. 14) points out, "In our efforts to use the new conceptions to improve educational measurement, there is no substitute for construct validation research patterned on the same logic that applies to conventional tests."

THE SOLO TAXONOMY AND
EDUCATIONAL ASSESSMENT

Much of the technology of achievement test construction has been directed at the writing and improvement of multiple choice items. Measurement texts for education students have a particular affinity for "objective measurement." Gronlund and Linn (1990) are not atypical when they devote fifteen pages of their text to essay examinations, and sixty-three pages to objective assessments (short answer, true-false, multiple choice, and multiple choice forms of "interpretive exercises"). They say, "Other things being equal, we always favor objective measurement over subjective measurement. There appears to be little justification for using essay questions to measure learning outcomes that can be satisfactorily measured by more objective means. Likewise, the problems of scoring and the inadequacy of sampling are ample justification for not using essay questions" (p. 217). Although there is some validity to this statement, the tone encourages a focus on Broudy's replicative and applicative uses of schooling. The associative and implicative uses must by their nature be evaluated using procedures that are structured but accommodating. If the latter uses are more important to students in the long term, then the emphases in assessment should be the reverse of those found in texts like Gronlund and Linn.

One approach that provides evaluative structure for a wide variety of tasks designed to assess higher-order objectives is the Biggs and Collis (1982) taxonomy for categorizing student responses, called the Structure of Learning Outcomes (SOLO). Under their system, assessments are made by placing student performances into one of five levels (prestructural, unistructural, multistructural, relational, and extended abstract) according to the degree of elaboration, organization, consistency, capacity, generalization, and abstraction expressed by the student. The levels can be thought of as stages of learning that an individual passes through in mastering new concepts.

Biggs and Collis (1982) describe the levels of the taxonomy used to evaluate the quality of learning in terms of the amount of memory capacity required to make the response, the kind of relating operations used to produce the response, and the degree of consistency and quality of closure displayed in the response. *Prestructural* responses require little memory. They may be a denial of the question or simply repeat the information contained in it. Often the responses reflect a lack of engagement between the student and the task. *Unistructural* responses concentrate on one relevant aspect of the task or concentrate exclusively on one part of the solution. Closure is premature. Conclusions are based on a single feature of the problem so that any generalizations that are made focus on a single issue. Students making *multistructural* responses treat two or more aspects of the task independently, and although the memory demands are higher than at lower levels, no attempt is made to integrate the dimensions of the problem. The result is a response that may contain inconsistencies or in which inconsistent information is ignored. As a consequence, a student could come to contradictory conclusions and generalizations from the same database. Students who provide *relational* responses attend to various aspects of the task in relation to each other. Integrating themes may be used to organize the result. Inconsistencies are addressed, but no attempt is made to go beyond the boundaries specified by the task. At the *extended abstract* level the task is treated in a context that goes beyond immediate information. Generalizations may be made to other situations of this type, but care is taken to describe the domain of generalizability. Conclusions may not be definite, but may be qualified to allow for logically possible alternatives. From this brief description, it is clear that motivation, regulation, and flexible internalization are all prerequisite to the production of an extended abstract response.

As will become clear, while the SOLO hierarchy is centered on declarative and procedural knowledge, the attainment of higher levels presupposes appropriate motivational orientations, self-regulatory functions, and learning strategies. In other words, students who approach desired states on all five of Snow's (1989) categories of achievement constructs will tend to produce responses to open-ended tasks that fall at the relational and extended abstract levels of the SOLO taxonomy. In terms of Broudy's (1988) uses of schooling, students will be able to use the facts, relationships, connotations, and structures that are contained in their allusionary base to make extended abstract responses, provided that the base is deep, extensive, and well connected.

Biggs and Collis (1982) provide sample applications of SOLO to the assessment of outcomes in various fields from arithmetic to foreign languages and at levels from elementary school to university. While tasks vary with grade level and subject field, in all cases they provide sufficient guidance and scope to enable the students to respond in a way that demonstrates the quality of their assimilation in terms of progressive structural complexity. For example, such tasks may ask students to organize their knowledge of a body of material, make sense out of evidence, reconcile conflicting accounts, make and justify arguments, present and support causal explanations, or solve novel problems. As the task is being set, the assessor should be mindful of the dimensions that are sought in the responses, and the integrating themes or features desired. While it is often not possible to anticipate all of the extended abstract responses that might be forthcoming, it will always be possible to show how they go beyond the confines of the task to place it within a demonstrably appropriate context. Indeed part of the extended abstract response is the demonstration or justification of extensions and abstractions.

In investigating the reliability and construct validity of the SOLO taxonomy as a basis for assessment, Biggs and Collis (1982) found that the interjudge agreement for two history questions was about 60 percent when the criteria for agreement was exactly the same categorical placement. But in fewer than 10 percent of the cases the difference between categories exceeded one category. Typical between judge correlations (treating taxonomic level as a continuous variable) using poetry, creative writing, and history, were above .75. Validity studies (Biggs & Collis, 1982; Biggs, 1979; Kirby & Biggs, 1981) suggest that higher levels of SOLO performance are related to higher ability levels, higher general school achievement, and higher levels of intrinsic motivation.

From this evidence, it is clear that the SOLO taxonomy could be a useful tool both for individual assessment and program evaluation. Indeed it has been used in a variety of situations: high school science (Collis & Davey, 1986); economics (Biggs et al., 1989); and even in the assessment of attitudes toward teenage pregnancy (Kryzanowski, 1988). Recently, Maguire (1989) applied the technique in an evaluation of programs for bright and gifted students in elementary and junior high school. Evaluation of such programs is often problematic. Program objectives are usually concentrated at Bloom's (1957) higher levels (analysis, synthesis, and evaluation) and students pursue these objectives in many ways: they may work independently on projects, they may work together in small groups, or they may participate in a mentorship program. This diversity in learning activity may lead to uneven levels of knowledge about a particular content domain, in spite of the fact that levels of attainment of higher-order objectives such as critical thinking may be uniformly high. In many situations the content provides a vehicle for instruction and may differ across students. It is not easy to find instruments that are relevant to program objectives, flexible enough to capture the creativity and divergence expected in performance from these kinds of students, yet at the same time possess utility and validity.

Utility and Validity of SOLO

In 1985, the Calgary Board of Education implemented a program to educate gifted students according to their needs. The plan called for a continuum of services, ranging from enrichment in the regular class through partial pullout at the neighborhood level to complete education in a special school for those gifted and talented students who required that level of attention. When the two ends of the continuum were in place in grades 3 to 9 about 250 students attended school in a congregated setting, and about 1,200 received enrichment within their regular schools. At that point, the board commissioned a study to explore various aspects of the implementation. The data presented here concern the part of the study that was directed at the performance of fifth and sixth grade students.

Three samples of students in grades 5 and 6 were identified. The *congregated* group was made up of the sixty-three students who attended a special school for gifted and talented students. Generally speaking, children were recommended to the congregated setting for one or more of three reasons: (1) they were so exceptionally bright that they needed the stimulation of other students at their own level; (2) they were bright but because of social, emotional, or behavioral problems stemming from this brightness, were not flourishing in the regular setting; and (3) they were bright, but their regular school did not have the capacity to provide the appropriate challenge. Not all students recommended for the congregated setting attended. Some parents preferred to send their children to the neighborhood school.

The *integrated* group was a sample of sixty-three students who were identified by the system as being gifted and attended regular classes in their own school. The *nominated* group was a sample of seventy-six students from the same classes as the integrated students. Teachers in schools with students in the integrated group were asked to name other students whose classroom performance indicated that the gifted designation might be appropriate. The students in the integrated and nominated groups came from sixteen schools. It is impossible to characterize their educational experiences in a single way. In some schools, gifted students were pulled out of classes for special instruction; in others efforts were made to extend the students within the regular instructional settings.

As an independent variable, "congregation versus integration" was not intended to contribute to theory. Rather it was viewed as a factor in policy development. The trustees were interested in global comparisons at the level of, "Do these organizational arrangements seem to make any difference?" From the perspective of the present chapter the answers to the organizational question are less important than the data that shed light on the validity and utility of the SOLO approach to assessment in the environment of bright and gifted elementary school students.

SOLO Tasks

To fit the requirements of evaluation, the tasks were designed so as to be relatively independent of particular course content while at the same time providing enough scope to allow structural consistencies and abstractions to emerge.

The open-ended tasks either had several "correct" solutions, or called for opinions. In this study, evaluation of responses focused less on the opinion expressed or the solution chosen than on the way in which it was justified or solved.

After some preliminary trials and revisions, two writing tasks and three arithmetic tasks were presented to the students. The general instructions for the tasks, the tasks themselves, and the response criteria for each of the five SOLO levels are shown in the appendix.

Data Collection

The three arithmetic tasks and two writing tasks were administered to the students in grades 5 and 6 at the end of the school year. It was clear from their responses that some individuals were more engaged with one task than another. In addition, many students did not allocate their time evenly among tasks. To overcome these problems it was decided to use a "best level" criterion to summarize performance. That is, the highest level from among the three arithmetic tasks and the higher level from between the writing tasks were taken as the indicators.

In addition to the SOLO tasks, a learning process questionnaire was administered to the students because reviews of previous research (e.g., Rogers, 1986) showed differences in cognitive strategies and styles between gifted and nongifted students. The instrument chosen was the Learning Process Questionnaire (LPQ) developed by Biggs (1985a). He breaks learning process preferences along two dimensions. The first divides approaches to learning into three groups (surface, deep, achieving), and the second distinguishes motives from strategies. The learning approach dimension categorizes aspects of quality and desirability, while the motive-strategy dimension captures features of Snow's (1989) learning strategies, self-regulatory functions, and motivational orientations.

The two-way classification gives rise to six cells. According to Biggs, students with high *surface motive* aim to meet requirements minimally. Their school life is a careful balance between failing and working more than is necessary. Students who use a *surface strategy* limit their efforts to the bare minimum and achieve their results through heavy reliance on rote memory. Students who possess *deep motive* have an intrinsic interest in what is being learned. They try to develop competence in particular academic subjects. To use a *deep strategy* is to discover meaning by reading widely and interrelating new ideas with previous knowledge. Having an *achieving motive* is to try to enhance ego and self-esteem through competition and to obtain the highest grades whether or not the material is interesting. Students who use an *achieving strategy* try to organize their time and working space to achieve specific goals. They follow up on all suggested readings, schedule their time carefully, and behave as model students regardless of the course.

The LPQ provides a subscale score for each of the six cells, indicating both the kinds of strategies that students use, and the kind of achievement motivation that orients their study. Motive and strategy scores can be combined to produce three "approaches to learning" scores: surface, deep, and achieving. Only the approach scores are used in this analysis.

As Snow (1989) points out, strategies, motives, knowledge, and skills are all tied together, both in the initial student states that precede instruction and in the final outcomes. LPQ results support the validity of the SOLO tasks if students who used deeper approaches to learning tend to produce higher-level responses.

The Canadian Cognitive Abilities Test (CCAT) (Wright, 1982) is routinely administered to students in the fourth grade in this jurisdiction. This test is a Canadian version of the Lorge–Thorndike Intelligence Test and provides scores on verbal and nonverbal abilities. For the purpose of the present study, raw scores were used throughout the analysis. The relationship between the CCAT scores and SOLO outcomes sheds some light on the validity of the latter. Verbal ability is a trait that underlies much student achievement. Most of the students in the present study fell within the top quartile of the population on verbal ability. Although the spread of their scores is restricted, there is still enough range to allow a high relationship with SOLO to emerge. Such a relationship would be evidence against the validity of the SOLO tasks because it suggests that the SOLO tasks tap generic abilities rather than school-related outcomes. On the other hand, no relationship would also stand against the validity because even in this group of bright students, verbal ability should play some part in performance.

Finally, evidence for SOLO validity should be manifested in differences among grades. Regardless of whether they had been in special programs, students in the sixth grade have one more year of experience and development, and according to Biggs and Collis this should influence their ability to create higher-order outcomes.

Analysis of Grade and Program Influences

As noted earlier, the question at the center of the board's agenda was, "Are there differences among levels for students in different programs?" The program designers hoped to find no great differences among groups because the program variations were intended to meet the needs of students. High-level performances in all groups would have satisfied developer goals.

The cross-tabulations of grade (5 or 6) by program (integrated, nominated, or congregated) by SOLO category (unistructural, multistructural, relational, or extended abstract) are shown in table 14.1 for writing and arithmetic. Using the "best level" criterion, no student was found at the prestructural level even though there were prestructural responses to some of the individual tasks. Also there were not many students who provided responses at the extended abstract

Table 14.1
SOLO Responses at Various Levels

Writing

Grade 5	Uni-structural	Multi-Structural	Relational	Extended Abstract	Total
Congregated	11	13	3	3	30
Integrated	12	13	4	0	29
Regular	12	19	5	1	37
Total	35	45	12	4	96
Grade Six					
Congregated	12	13	6	2	33
Integrated	17	7	6	4	34
Regular	7	17	14	1	39
Total	36	37	26	7	106

Arithmetic

Grade Five					
Congregated	7	15	8	0	30
Integrated	7	17	5	0	29
Regular	16	18	3	0	37
Total	30	50	16	0	96
Grade Six					
Congregated	2	14	14	3	33
Integrated	5	14	13	2	34
Regular	9	14	16	0	39
Total	16	42	43	5	106

level. In fact no student in grade 5 gave such a response to any of the arithmetic tasks.

For the first analysis it was decided to combine the relational and extended abstract categories so that there were only three levels of SOLO.

The log-linear approach to examining contingency tables (Fienberg, 1980) showed no significant difference among programs in relation to the SOLO responses for either arithmetic or writing. The influence of grade on category was significant, however, with the grade by SOLO results showing a larger proportion of sixth grade students giving relational and extended abstract responses than fifth grade students. The result could be accounted for on several grounds. The older students had been exposed to more schooling, they were more intellectually mature, and they had superior skills in written expression. All of these facts support the notion that the SOLO tasks were assessing a developmental phenomenon.

The lack of importance of the program by SOLO interaction was more difficult to understand. It had been anticipated that the regular students would do less well than the congregated and integrated students. This did not show up when the congregated and integrated groups were treated separately, but when they were combined and grade level disregarded, the chi squares calculated for the two by four contingency tables were significant for both writing (chi square = 9.2) and arithmetic (chi square = 9.6). For writing most students who gave extended abstract responses came from the combined groups, but at the unistructural end, there were also proportionately more students from the combined groups. In the case of arithmetic, the performance of the combined group was superior to the regular group. From the point of view of the developers and implementors, the results were disappointing. In spite of the curriculum documents and intentions of the teachers, it appeared as if the students had not accepted and incorporated a propensity to apply analytical and evaluative skills in a variety of circumstances. Nevertheless there were some very insightful performances and almost all of them came from the congregated and integrated groups.

SOLO, Intelligence, and Approaches to Learning

The relationship of learning approaches and intelligence to SOLO responses was explored by dividing the students according to their SOLO level in arithmetic and writing and carrying out one-way analyses of variance on five variables (verbal and nonverbal intelligence, and surface, deep, and achieving approaches to learning). The means, pooled standard deviations, and observed F values are shown in table 14.2

Writing Groups

Significant differences among SOLO writing groups occurred for deep and achieving learning styles and verbal intelligence. Post hoc tests for linear trend showed that higher SOLO groups tended to have higher scores on deep and achieving styles (p < .05) and a nearly significant trend (p < .10) on verbal intelligence. In the case of surface approach to learning, both the overall test and the test for trend were nearly significant (p < .10).

To get a better feel for the magnitude of the effect a comparison was made between the means for students at the unistructural level (the lowest group observed) and the relational level (since only eleven students gave responses at the extended abstract level). Unistructural respondents were about two-fifths of a standard deviation higher than relational respondents on surface approach, about two-fifths of a standard deviation lower on deep approach, but only one-

Table 14.2
Means for SOLO Groups on CCAT and LPQ

Writing

SOLO Grp.	CCAT Verb	CCAT N.Verbal	LPQ Surface	LPQ Deep	LPQ Achieving
Uni Str.	73.0	70.0	34.6	37.5	36.2
Multi Str	77.6	72.3	32.8	40.1	37.0
Relat.	79.0	72.7	31.9	40.5	37.2
Ext. Abst.	80.6	70.9	30.6	45.6	43.2
F obs.	3.85**	1.78	2.25*	4.20**	2.63**
S(pooled)	10.5	6.8	6.4	7.8	7.6

Arithmetic

SOLO Grp.	CCAT Verb	CCAT N.Verbal	LPQ Surface	LPQ Deep	LPQ Achieving
Uni Str.	74.6	70.6	33.4	40.3	36.8
Multi Str	74.2	70.6	33.4	39.4	37.1
Relat.	80.8	73.3	32.7	39.6	37.7
Ext. Abst.	83.8	75.0	32.4	37.0	34.2
F obs.	5.61**	2.40*	.19	.31	.36
S(pooled)	10.4	6.7	6.5	8.0	7.8

** significant p<.05   *significant p<.10

eighth of a standard deviation lower on achieving approach. On verbal intelligence, unistructural students were about three-fifths of a standard deviation below the relational students.

Students who gave higher-level responses to the SOLO writing tasks were also more deeply engaged in their learning while students who produced lower-level products seemed to have more superficial approaches. Of course these patterns do not apply to all students as a closer examination of score distributions would have shown. In particular, for the achieving approach, the observed trend is largely due to the performance of the eleven students in the extended abstract group. Generally speaking the results found here with bright elementary school children echo those of Biggs (1985b) and Kirby and Biggs (1981), who found that a deep approach to learning is tied to higher-level responding in samples of postsecondary and secondary students.

The trend on verbal intelligence appears to be at an appropriate level. Most of these students were in the top quartile relative to the national norms and so there was a range restriction. The tendency for the brightest of the bright to give higher responses seems consistent. (Interestingly, the correlation between verbal intelligence and deep approach to learning was only .13, so the cognitive and conative characteristics that related to the performance in this group of students are quite independent of each other.)

Arithmetic Groups

No approaches to learning differentiated among the groups defined on their SOLO arithmetic levels. The significant difference on verbal intelligence is likely a reflection of the strong verbal component that carries through the arithmetic tasks. The nonverbal scale of the CCAT is made up of spatial tasks and number series problems, but it does not have a strong base in numerical abilities. This may account for the smaller differences among groups ($p < .10$) found with the nonverbal scale.

The lack of relationship with learning approaches is more troublesome. Observations in classrooms, discussions with teachers, and examinations of the identification process all suggest that verbal abilities play a much more important role in identification and programming than numerical and other nonverbal abilities. In fact the first and third quartiles for nonverbal intelligence for this sample are almost the same as the values in the norming sample.

This being the case, the SOLO arithmetic tasks with their emphasis on open solutions may have been seen as being quite different from problems encountered in school. Using surface, deep, or achieving strategies should make a difference in how students approach the kinds of problems found in the curriculum as it is taught, but if the indicators that are created are too far removed from the arena of familiar experience, then raw creativity and intuition may be more important. In terms of Snow's (1989) model, adaptive learning styles directed toward novel problem solution may be relatively rare at this stage of mathematical development. This is partly borne out by the fact that only five students gave extended abstract responses and all of these were sixth graders.

The SOLO taxonomy has great potential for both individual assessment and program evaluation. It does not appear that instruments are tapping a generic trait. Rather the use of the approach with appropriately designed questions seems to tap a complex of deep understanding, motivation, and intuition as applied to a particular task. Since the attractiveness of the task characteristics differ from one student to another, level of performance also differs from time to time and from task to task. Among the present sample, about 40 percent of the students had the same response level in both arithmetic and writing. This is as it should be if the assessment is to reflect the variations in classroom learning and performance.

As Snow (1989) points out, "Deep understanding, higher order skill, strategic flexibility, adaptive control and achievement motivation are exhibited when students have to generate explanations, assemble skilled performances, and persist through learning to problem solving and problem finding" (p. 13). The SOLO taxonomy provides educators with one strategy for assessing these complex achievements. The specific structure upon which the taxonomy is built provides teachers and students with a developmental tool for both learning and instruction. It provides a vehicle for communication and feedback. It allows us to describe growth in understanding. It points to deficiencies and prompts connectedness and extension. It is one of the assessment tools that allows us to tap into Broudy's (1988) important and enduring goals of schooling, the associative and interpretive levels.

Finally, the evidence presented here and elsewhere indicates that properly constructed SOLO tasks provide valid assessments of learning within a framework suggested by Snow (1989) and consistent with many of the directions suggested in Embretson's (1985) anthology that links cognitive psychology to educational assessment. The SOLO approach to assessing higher-order objectives gives promise to assessment that has fidelity with the learning and instructional activities of the class and is reflective of the cognitive and conative processes of the students. In short, it gives promise to grounded authentic assessment.

APPENDIX

WRITING TASKS

Instructions

In the following pages there are two problems. They involve thinking and writing. In the first problem, you will be asked to make a decision and give reasons for it, and in the second you will be asked for an opinion. Please write as clearly as possible. If you need more space use the back of the page. When you have finished one question, you can go on to the next one.

Question 1

Pat is part of a community softball team and, like the rest of the team, has gone to three practices a week for the last month to get ready for league games. As the season begins, the team is doing very well. Pat, however, does not get to play as much as some of the better players. Half-way into the softball season, soccer season starts, and the better players go to soccer practices rather than softball practices. They come to play in the games, however, and so Pat still does not get to play. One day in the last inning of a game in which Pat's team was winning by a large score, the coach told Pat to go to bat. Pat was angry and said no. The coach kicked Pat off the team for being uncooperative.

Suppose that you are in charge of all of the community teams and the coach and Pat come to you to settle the dispute. What would your decision be? Why would you make that decision?

Question 2

Exceptional students are students who have a special talent or problem. Some examples are blind children, very bright children, deaf children, very athletic children, retarded children, and artistic children. Some people think that there should be special schools for exceptional children. Other people think that it is better if all schools have children of all kinds.

There are many reasons for holding one view or the other. Explain your position.

Scoring Key and Examples

Prestructural response. Gives an opinion without a reason, restates the problem. Example from Task 1: I would decide that Pat had a reason to be mad.

Unistructural response. Chooses one side or the other and supports it unequivocally with a single argument or using one relevant aspect of evidence. Example from Task 1: My decision would be for Pat because she was trying to play well during most of the season but the coach let the better players play the game instead of Pat. Even when the other players missed practices they got to play more so Pat deserved to be angry.

Multistructural response. Chooses one side or the other but discusses the validity of the claims of each or gives multiple arguments in favor of one. Inconsistencies or conflicts are ignored or discounted. Example from Task 2: I think that they should all be together because they can learn from each other. For example, an athletic child could help a blind child play soccer and the blind child could help him understand what it is like to be blind. Also if you always have handicapped people they may not learn how to relate to people without disabilities.

Relational response. Notes competing demands of the two sides and attempts to reconcile them. Conflicting data are placed in a system that accounts for the given context. Example from Task 2: I feel that there should be special schools for exceptional students. By having these schools, children will be able to work better in a situation that helps them to develop their talents or to cope with their handicaps. Many children cannot work well in a regular classroom as they require special attention. It is also not a good idea to make children work at a higher or lower level of learning than they are capable of. It is better for other students in a regular class if exceptional students are not there because they require the teacher's time. So to be entirely fair to the teacher, the classmates, and the students, special schools should be provided for these exceptional students.

Extended abstract response. Places the problem into a context and shows how it is an example of a more general case. Example from Task 1: I would ask Pat to apologize to the coach for being rude. After the superficial conflicts pertaining to this incident were resolved, however, attention would have to be drawn to the greater problem. The first thing that I would do would be to ensure that there was a higher league for better players. This way the difference in skill would not be that great. Next I would establish a minimum number of times to bat every player must receive and a maximum for every player. Obviously I would first have to do some research to find out what these limits should be. This way, weak players such as Pat would receive some times to bat and very good players would not always be at bat.

ARITHMETIC PROBLEMS

Instructions

In the following pages there are some arithmetic problems. They are a little different from the usual kind of arithmetic problem, because in these problems there are many ways to be correct. Sometimes you will be asked to give your opinion. When you give an opinion, try to be as clear as possible.

Question 1

Lori's lucky number is 3. Make up five arithmetic word problems in which the answer is three. Make the problems as different from each other as you can.

Scoring Key

Prestructural response. Gives an answer that is not related to the problem.

Unistructural response. All problems are of integer form using a single operator, e.g., _____ + _____ = _____

Multistructural response. At least two different operators are used to produce the word problem.

Relational response. Beyond the multistructural response, at least one of the word problems involves more than one related stage.

Extended abstract. Indication that a generating function can be used to produce an infinite number of solutions.

Question 2

Question 2 consists of three parts. Answer problems A and B and then answer problem C.

Problem A: Janice and her two friends buy a pizza. Unfortunately the pizza is not cut into pieces. The three girls have a special machine that will cut anything in half. How can they use the machine to share the pizza as fairly as possible? Use a diagram to illustrate your answer.

Problem B: Robert and his three friends buy a pizza. Unfortunately the pizza is not cut into pieces. The four boys have a special machine that will cut anything in half. How can they use the machine to share the pizza as fairly as possible? Use a diagram to illustrate your answer.

Problem C: How are problems A and B different?

Scoring Key

Prestructural response. Ignores problem C.

Unistructural response. Ignores the machine requirements, cuts pizzas into three and four parts, and then sees the difference as being in the number of pieces.

Multistructural response. Makes equal pieces for B and solves problem A by discarding or making unequal-sized pieces. Sees difference in problems as being one of the number of pieces.

Relational response. Produces equal results in problem A for all practical purposes. Sees one problem as harder than the other, with the difficulty related to the number of people. May speak of certainty of a fair solution in the two cases.

Extended abstract. Solves A by an approximation, and then discusses the differences in terms of how 2*n is never divisible by 3.

Question 3

The diagram shown below was used to illustrate a problem in an arithmetic book. Describe the kind of problem that it would be useful for solving. Be sure to explain your answer.

Scoring Key

Prestructural response. Response unrelated to problem.

Unistructural response. Refers to one arrow, may be a single example without explanation using specific values.

Multistructural response. Gives two or more examples with different values. Or the two arrows are treated separately. Does not integrate length and direction of the two arrows.

Relational response. Shows how directions and lengths relate to each other using an example.

Extended abstract. Shows how the diagram can be used to illustrate problems of a general form.

REFERENCES

Biggs, J. B. (1979). Individual differences in study process and the quality of learning outcomes. *Higher Education,* 8, 381–394.

———. (1985a). *LPO Manual.* Hawthorn: Australian Council for Educational Research.

———. (1985b). The role of metalearning in study process. *British Journal of Educational Psychology,* 55, 185–212.

Biggs, J. B., & Collis, K. F. (1982). *Evaluating the quality of learning: The SOLO Taxonomy.* New York: Academic.

Biggs, J. B., Holbrook, J. B., Ki, W. W., Lam, R. Y. H., Li, W. O., Pong, W. Y., and Stimpson, P. G. (1989). An objective format for evaluating the quality of learning in various secondary subjects. A symposium presented to the sixth annual Conference of the Hong Kong Educational Research Association, Hong Kong, City Polytechnic of Hong Kong, November 11–12.

Bloom, B. S. (ed.). (1957). *Taxonomy of educational objectives: The classification of educational goals,* handbook 1, *Cognitive domain.* New York: McKay.

Broudy, H. S. (1988) *The uses of schooling.* New York: Routledge.

Cole, N. (1990). Conceptions of educational achievement. *Educational Researcher,* 19(3), 2–7.

Collis, K. F., and Davey, H. A. (1986). A technique for evaluating skills in high school science. *Journal of Research in Science Teaching,* 23, 651–663.

Crooks, T. J. (1988). The impact of evaluation practices on students. *Review of Educational Research,* 58, 438–481.

Embretson, S. (ed.). (1985). *Test design: Developments in psychology and psychometrics.* New York: Academic.

Fienberg, S. E. (1980). *The analysis of cross-classified categorical data.* 2d ed. Cambridge, Mass.: MIT.

Gronlund, N. E., & Linn, R. L. (1990). *Measurement and evaluation in teaching.* New York: Macmillan.

Gullikson, A. R. (1984). Teacher perspectives of their instructional use of tests. *Journal of Educational Research,* 77, 244–248.

Kirby, J. R., and Biggs, J. B. (1981). Learning styles, information processing abilities and academic achievement. Final report, Australian Research Grants Committee, Balconnan ACT.

Kryzanowski, E. M. (1988). Attitudes towards adolescent pregnancy and parenthood. Unpublished Ph.D. diss., Department of Educational Psychology, University of Alberta.

Maguire, T. O. (1989). Gifted education in the Calgary Public Schools. Calgary: Calgary Board of Education.

Rogers, K. B. (1986). Do the gifted think and learn differently? A review of recent research and its implications for instruction. *Journal for the Education of the Gifted,* 10(1), 17–39.

Snow, R. E. (1989). Toward assessment of cognitive and conative structures in learning. *Educational Researcher,* 18(9), 8–14.

Snow, R. E., & Lohman, D. F. (1989). Implications of cognitive psychology for educational measurement. In R. L. Linn (ed.), *Educational measurement.* 3d ed. New York: Macmillan.

Stiggens, R. J., & Bridgeford, N. J. (1985). The ecology of classroom assessment. *Journal of Educational Measurement* 22, 271–286.

Wilson, R. J. (1990). Classroom processes in evaluating student achievement. *Alberta Journal of Educational Research,* 36, 4–17.

Wright, E. N. (ed.). (1982). *The Canadian Cognitive Abilities Test, multilevel edition.* Scarborough: Nelson.

15

Evaluating Programs That Claim to Teach Thinking Skills: Critical Issues and Options

Carmel French and Fred French

A multiplicity of programs claiming to teach problem solving, metacognitive strategies, critical thinking, reasoning, and cognitive instructional strategies abound as evidenced in this volume and in work by Chipman et al. (1985) and Chance (1986). Despite the multiplicity of programs to teach "thinking," no specific and comprehensive basis to understand the effectiveness and efficiency of such programs exists, with the possible exception of work by Baron (1987). Nevertheless, school jurisdictional administrators, to name but one group, would like to know more about the effectiveness and efficiency of these programs.

There is a real need to understand the nature and merits of these programs since, as stated by Sternberg (1983), thinking skills programs have the potential to be both a tremendously valuable component of learning and another bandwagon in education that may cause considerable harm. Differentiating among these options is critical for education and the learner.

THE NATURE OF COGNITIVE INSTRUCTIONAL
PROGRAMS: BASIS AND EVOLUTION

In order to evaluate the effectiveness of thinking skills programs, a clear understanding of such programs is needed. While this may appear to be a simplistic given in any evaluation, there are many approaches to the teaching of thinking. Baer (1988) states that educators and psychologists have yet to develop a body of knowledge about the nature of thinking, much less the teaching of thinking. Yet over two hundred programs that claim to train thinking skills exist. Herein lies the first issue facing evaluators of the effectiveness of programs claiming to teach thinking.

Waksman (1982) uses the term "cognitive education" to cover the teaching of thinking skills, intellectual skills training, and the production of strategies by children that help them to produce and monitor plans and/or actions aimed at improved cognitive processing. Use of such a generic term, however, may mask wide divergence in the purposes of a specific program that, while falling under the rubric of cognitive education, has a very different purpose and hence a different approach to the improvement of thinking. Nevertheless, some type of common terminology is necessary to facilitate discussion of the topic. For the purposes of this chapter, the term "cognitive education programs" will be used to address programs aimed at the teaching of thinking, critical thinking, problem solving, reasoning, reflective practice, decision making, and cognitively based instructional strategies. While each of the specific programs may have very specific objectives that need to be accounted for in any evaluation, the common element of reflective practice, of attempting to develop and/or reinforce a monitoring component in the learner so that the learner approaches tasks more methodically and more reflectively, exists in each of these programs in one form or another.

Brandt (1984, 1988), in an attempt to deal with the disparity of examples of thinking programs, conceptualizes the teaching of thinking in three ways: teaching *for* thinking, teaching *of* thinking, and teaching *about* thinking. According to Brandt (1988), teaching *for* thinking involves the development of language and conceptual abilities through various forms of teacher/student interaction, including questioning, group discussion, and cooperative learning. Teaching *about* thinking involves encouraging students to be aware of their own thinking and its regulation, particularly through self-regulation. Teaching *of* thinking teaches particular mental skills and processes, such as summarizing and decision making.

While Brandt's conceptualization is helpful, a review of existing programs that claim to teach thinking reveals a certain degree of overlap along these three dimensions. DeBono's (1976) CoRT program utilizes group discussion, questioning, and awareness of one's own thinking and its regulation. As such, it fits within the teaching *about* and *for* thinking conceptualizations. The latest revision to French's (1983) Learner Strategies program attempts to provide for all three of Brandt's conceptualizations. As such, any evaluation of cognitive education should address all three program components.

In general, many of the programs defy classification because of their dynamic and interactive nature with regard to knowledge acquisition, problem solving, and basic cognitive skills. For example, Philosophy for Children (Lipman, 1985) is designed to teach children to reason and to enjoy thinking. The program teaches over thirty specific thinking skills and the disposition and attitudes to develop a community of inquiry to use those skills.

In addition to explicit cognitive instructional programs, there is a need to consider other programs within the curriculum that may have either an explicit or implicit impact on the development of thinking. One example is the whole language movement (Newman, 1985). The principles of the whole language philosophy appear very similar to the principles found in cognitive instructional programs. Proponents of both, while not readily collaborating in the past, draw from the philosophy of learning rooted in the work of Socrates and Dewey. Cognitive educators also utilize the principles of Piaget (1972) and Vygotsky (1962). A more extensive review of this overlap is provided in French (in press).

It is interesting to note, however, that until recently, few attempts were made to integrate the teaching of thinking into the content area of the curriculum such that metacognitive, strategic, declarative, procedural, and self-knowledge were addressed. Current research on reading, writing, math, and science is contributing to the belief that in addition to domain-specific or declarative knowledge, teachers must possess a breadth and depth of understanding of the process of learning (Glaser, 1988). As well, several recent attempts to integrate thinking skills directly into the curriculum have been made (French, 1983, 1987a, in prep; Paul et al., 1987). Hence, knowledge of the implications of the broader curriculum is important for evaluating cognitive instructional programs.

Based on the descriptions provided by Campione and Brown (1987), Dillon (1986), Cross and Paris (1988), Sternberg (1985), Messick (1984), Flavell (1977), Vygotsky (1962), Feuerstein et al. (1980), and Glaser (1988), cognitive instructional programs are a collection of learning, reasoning, problem-solving, and instructional strategies aimed at helping learners acquire, maintain, and generalize the components of knowledge, such as declarative, procedural, metacognitive, and self-knowledge, necessary for effective functioning. Such practices work toward active learner involvement, the acquisition of thinking and problem-solving strategies, motivation, the use of real-world experiences, language development, the use of content and process knowledge, self-monitoring, and mediated learning experiences.

Cognitive instruction is based on the belief that intellectual/cognitive functioning is subject to improvement, modification, and enhancement given the appropriate instructional practices. The term "cognitive instructional practices" is a generic rubric covering the teaching of thinking, reasoning, instructional effectiveness, and problem solving. This is not meant to imply that only generic strategies are taught in cognitive instruction. On the contrary, both generic and specific strategies exist and are explored by various learners.

EVALUATIONS OF THINKING SKILLS PROGRAMS

A study by Narrol et al. (1982) appears typical of earlier research into the effectiveness of cognitive instructional programs. In this study designed to examine the effectiveness of instrumental enrichment (IE) in improving the cognitive performance of educationally handicapped adolescents in vocational secondary schools, five experimental and four control groups took part in an eight-month instructional program. Pre/post- analysis of data indicated significant effects of IE on the cognitive performance of those students in the IE group.

The instruments used in the study included the Lorge–Thorndike Intelligence Test Level 3, Form A, Non Verbal, the Primary Mental Abilities Test Letter Series Level 4–6, the Piers Harris Children's Self-Concept Scale, and the School Morale Scale. Without belaboring the issues of the appropriateness of the normative group, the validity, reliability, and recency of these measures, it may be sufficient to raise two other concerns with the use of these tests.

Specifically, the more critical issues concern whether these tests accurately reflect the skills and concepts addressed in the IE program; and, whether the training program teaches for the tests. With regard to the latter issue, it would appear that the Lorge–Thorndike and the Primary Mental Abilities tests cover content very closely related to the content of the IE program. Thus, gains differentiating between experimental and control groups would be expected to occur not only because of the effect of the instructional program, but also because of the tests selected to measure the effect. The affective measures would, with the exception of validity and reliability, appear appropriate.

Narrol et al. should not be faulted over the issue of test selection since it is one that continues to plague the evaluation of cognitive instructional programs. Instruments used to gauge the impact of thinking skills programs are many and varied (see Nickerson et al., 1985 for a more complete set of examples). Nevertheless, it appears that tests to facilitate the evaluation of process-oriented thinking skills programs do not exist. Nickerson et al. (1985) made a similar argument, which still appears to be the case.

It appears, as noted by Neisser (1979), that measures such as IQ tests do not address some aspects of what intelligence and thinking include. In the example of IE, aspects in thinking would appear to include the ability to actively confront the material, to control impulsivity, and to organize one's work. Use of IQ tests to tap these types of cognitive activities may fail to provide a complete picture of the merits and/or limitations of the program. As well, since items on the tests resemble items in the training package, there is reason to suspect that one is teaching for the test.

The issue of assessment of process components has been the most problematic in evaluating thinking skills programs. Meichenbaum et al. (1985) reviewed this issue and concluded that a multimethod assessment to provide converging evidence on these phenomena was necessary. Sternberg (1985), in his review of their work, concludes that there is much to be concerned about in assessing metacognitive knowledge and executive control. The use of participants' conscious access to cognitive processes is problematic in that much thinking is not available to conscious awareness.

Wiggins (1989) and Haney and Madus (1989) find that traditional tests do not reflect the objectives of the thinking skills programs. Indeed, Nickerson (1985) notes that current tests used to evaluate thinking skills programs often interfere with judging the programs' effectiveness. Rogers (1989) states that traditional quantifiable tests are inappropriate with an experienced curriculum and do not accurately measure the strengths of the curriculum or the processes of the students. Further, Garner and Alexander (1989) note that conventional tests with their right/wrong format, especially those that are timed, do not provide an accurate indication of what students have learned through a thinking skills program. Thinking skills programs encourage the student to stop, think, employ a strategy, and consider options. Timed tests, however, penalize students who carry out the processes they have learned. Yet many of the tests used in current evaluations of cognitive instructional programs focus on speed of performance or at least require speed of performance.

More recently, Neill and Medina (1989) state that standardized intelligence and achievement tests contribute to the reification and ranking of the construct intelligence. Standardized tests are constructed with the assumption that the skill being measured is one-dimensional and static and that all individuals perceive information and solve problems the same way (Campione & Brown, 1987; Neill & Medina, 1989; Menick, 1987). Neill and Medina (1989) also point out that standardized tests force teachers to focus on narrow quantifiable skills at the expense of more complex academic and nonacademic abilities that are not as quantifiable.

In addition, Walker (1987) and Campione and Brown (1987) note the need to assess cognitive ability level in familiar domains to provide more specific and accurate indications of capabilities. Using standardized achievement and intelligence tests that assess an individual's cognitive abilities in unfamiliar domains can underestimate the individual's potential as an information processor.

According to Wiggins (1989), authentic evaluation "is most accurate and equitable when it entails human judgement and dialogue, so that the person tested can ask for clarification of questions and explain his or her answers" (p. 704). Such a testing procedure allows for observation of learners while they tackle and solve problems, marshal evidence, arrange arguments, and take actions to address the problem (Wiggins, 1989). The process of assessment suggested by Wiggins better reflects the process of most cognitive instructional programs and provides greater insight into the impact of a particular program on a learner. Yet this process is rarely used in research on cognitive instructional programs.

Another issue of concern is the methodology used to design studies of cognitive instructional programs. Relatively few longitudinal studies of cognitive instructional programs exist. Notable exceptions in Canada include the Mulcahy et al. (1987) four-year comparison of IE, and work by French (1987a, 1988, 1989, 1990) comparing a variety of cognitive instructional models, including a learner strategies model designed by French (1983), a language experience approach, a problem-solving model, a critical thinking model, and a learning strategies model based on the work of Alley and Deshler (1979).

Nevertheless, the need for longitudinal research is critical to the evaluation of cognitive instructional programs, particularly since most programs argue that it will take at least two to three years for an effect to be significant. While varied opinion regarding the length of time necessary to attain an effect from a cognitive instructional program exists, Sternberg (1986) concludes that a program of less than a semester's duration does not appear to warrant serious consideration. At least one year's instruction appears necessary. Indeed, Feuerstein et al. (1980) state that approximately three years of training is necessary in order to see an impact that can be maintained and generalized. The opinion that more than a year's duration is necessary to see effects that are maintained and generalized is supported by findings by French (in press).

While longitudinal studies appear to cover a wider variety of measures with more participants, thereby providing a greater breadth of understanding of the effect and greater potential for noting the generalizability of the results, these longitudinal studies are also subject to methodological problems (for example, the use of intact groupings as opposed to random sampling, the use of varied instructors within and across techniques thereby leaving the teacher factor free to vary, and the use of the same limited instruments to determine the effect of the instructional approach).

French (in press) has attempted to control for the effect of varied instructors by using the same research assistants across different instructional conditions. This, however, raises the problem of the instructor utilizing aspects of each program under study in the teaching of one of the other programs, not to mention the cost involved. Brown and Palincsar (1984), in a short-term study of the role of dialogue in teaching, encountered the problem of individual differences in teachers resulting in a very different implementation of strategy dialogue across instructors. Coupled with an overemphasis on quantitative product-oriented measures, the impact of work in this study while significant has been reduced.

The increased number of cognitive skills programs available requires an evaluation of their theoretical, pragmatic, and research base on a range of issues. For example, Sax (1989) and Garner and Alexander (1989) addressed the issue of the duration of intervention. Interventions of short duration do not take into account the long-term effectiveness of the program. Garner and Alexander (1989) also discuss the issue of teacher fidelity when evaluating cognitive skills programs. It is difficult to control for the quality of teaching, motivation, and adherence to the suggested teaching techniques or philosophy during the research process. Indeed, the actual selection of teachers to participate in the evaluation of a program is another factor that has to be considered (Sax, 1989). Choosing only teachers who like and volunteer to participate in a specific program does not provide an accurate estimate of how effective this program will be among teaching professionals in general. Other issues that should be evaluated are the short- and long-term gains of the program, its cost effectiveness, and whether any secondary effects result (Garner & Alexander, 1989; Nickerson, 1985).

EVALUATING THINKING SKILLS PROGRAMS: A PROPOSED MODEL

Work by Baron (1987), Ennis and Weir (1985), and Nickerson et al. (1985) has helped in building the proposed evaluation model that follows. Generally evaluations can be either formative or summative. Nickerson et al. (1985) define formative evaluation as the type of evaluation that is conducted while a program is being developed. Summative evaluation is defined as evaluation that is more formal, often involving a statistical comparison of pre- and post-test results among the experimental and control groups, and designed to assess the program's effectiveness in attaining its goals. Nickerson et al. (1985) conclude that the focus should be on summative evaluation since educators need to know whether a program is likely to be effective in helping students to think.

Posavac and Carey (1985), in commenting on the general types of evaluation, note that four types exist and are dependent on the nature of the question asked. Two of the types that may be of interest to the cognitive researcher include the process and outcome types. Process evaluation is concerned with the effort that has to be put into the program in order to ensure its effectiveness. Outcome evaluation is concerned with what is accomplished as a result of the program being implemented. The outcome evaluation would appear to be similar to the summative evaluation.

Baron (1987) has made a similar point in her discussion of the types of evaluations available to the cognitive researcher. In addition, she draws a distinction between qualitative and quantitative evaluation. Specifically, qualitative designs are concerned with capturing the depth and detail of experiences of specific individuals in the program. Quantitative methods provide a standardized format for numerical rather than descriptive data. While some would argue against the merits of combining the qualitative and quantitative methodologies, there appears to be merit in taking an interactive approach rather than an either/or approach to the use of qualitative and quantitative methods. It is important to note not only what happens to groups of participants, but also what happens to individual participants. Wiersma (1986) has made a similar point in discussing the merits of ethnographic research.

The purpose for conducting the evaluation or research associated with cognitive education programs determines the type of evaluation that will be conducted. Nevertheless, given the developing nature of many cognitive instructional programs it seems reasonable to conclude that some type of interactive process involving formative, summative, and process-oriented evaluation that incorporates both qualitative and quantitative data would contribute much to the understanding and refinement of cognitive instructional programming.

Because many cognitive programs are implemented in schools rather than in tightly controlled clinical settings, a number of difficulties exist in the design of the evaluation. For example, controlling for the quality of teaching across groups, defining the control group, selecting randomized groups, and providing for some type of control group intervention that is appropriate from an experimental point of view and from the parents' point of view are all factors to be considered in such quasi-experimental designs.

Nevertheless, if generalization to other such classroom settings is desired, there is little option but to proceed and to attempt to address and control for the limitations inherent in such quasi-experimental designs. Baron (1987) and Nickerson et al. (1985) have made similar points. Therefore, the relative merit of the programs being evaluated seems more appropriate than does an attempt to categorically state that one program is better than another. Nickerson et al. (1985) identify a number of neglected issues in previous evaluations of thinking skills programs. Included is the need to assess negative effects of thinking skills programs. Earlier, Scriven (1972), in referring to goal-free evaluation, encouraged investigators to be open to unknown benefits and costs of programs. Further, Sternberg (1983) noted that while programs to train thinking skills have the potential to do considerable good they also have the potential to do considerable harm. French (1985), for example, found that of a group of thirty-six mentally handicapped adolescents receiving cognitive instructional training, four participants became so emotionally upset with the demands for verbalization that they had to be dropped from the study. This was despite the fact that no previous indications of emotionality were reported or found to exist.

How do evaluators set up an evaluation to account for potential negative effects that are unknown at the outset of the evaluation? Baron (1987) also comments on the problem of unknown benefits and costs, but provides no clear direction to evaluators to help address the problem of unknown effects.

Despite the seeming lack of a methodology to address the issue of unknown effects, suggestions from others may offer some promise. For example, Perkins (1985) refers to "taking the pulse" of the classroom on a regular basis. Costa (1983) advocates the development of "individual cognitive maps" to determine both what children know and how they behave when they do not know. Baron (1987) suggests using both a "wide-angle lens and a telephoto lens" to help determine and monitor the effects of thinking skills programs on children. In other words, it is important to move beyond simply gathering data at two points (entry and exit). Becoming a participant-observer as in ethnographic research (Wiersma, 1986) is one suggestion to cope with ongoing developments in evaluation. It is through this ongoing involvement of the researcher in the system under study that French (1985) discovered the emotional reaction of several participants and was able to intervene prior to the development of a more serious situation.

More recently French (in press) has moved to involve the teacher as a research confederate by asking the teacher to keep a log of events and perceptions throughout the process of the evaluation. Kantor et al. (1981), commenting on the collaborative relationship possible with teachers, conclude that experienced teachers have a knowledge of children and classroom settings that makes them potentially strong researchers. Baron (1987) also references the importance of daily journals for students to reflect on their progress and the progress of the group as a whole.

The use of a system of journal writing for student and teacher participants requires some form to objectively report the data. This necessitates a method to organize the data for meaningful interpretation. Dickson and Wiersma (1984), Schofield and Sagar (1977), and Schofield and Anderson (1984) have provided workable examples of such a content analysis with the caution by Schofield and Anderson that content analysis should not be applied to field notes since an after-the-fact content analysis may lead to erroneous conclusions.

Despite the possibility of alternative approaches to measuring the impact of cognitive instructional programs through the maintenance of journals and becoming a participant-observer, quantifiable student outcome data seem necessary to attest to the differences in student thinking and/or achievement as a result of the thinking skills program.

In order to respond to the problem of discerning how a child solves a problem, Baron (1987) describes the Connecticut approach of "nesting." The nesting approach requires the development of a series of questions, with one question designed to learn whether the child knows a concept and the second designed to determine whether the child can apply that knowledge. Use of the nesting technique is reported to be particularly relevant to the evaluation of thinking skills programs that are embedded in the content areas of the curriculum.

Another approach to determining what content children know and how they perform problem solving is under development by French and French (1989) and French (1990). Once again, the evaluation of thinking skills embedded in the curriculum through the use of math and reading comprehension tasks is being attempted in both oral and written assessments.

With regard to thinking skills programs that are independent of the curriculum, Ennis and Weir (1985) have developed a test of critical thinking that provides promise. Unfortunately, the test requires an essay format. Since many of the thinking skills programs and strategy training programs address oral communication, the Ennis–Weir test may not access fully the impact of a thinking skills program.

While addressing a different problem, Baron (1987) suggests that multiple approaches to evaluate the impact of thinking skills programs are necessary. Her suggestion to use oral discussions and writing to evaluate thinking offers a potential solution to the problem of evaluating programs that utilize predominantly oral dialogue in their training.

Many of the cognitive education programs are concerned with self-regulatory mechanisms utilized by participants during learning and problem solving. In order to assess participant use of such regulatory mechanisms various procedures have been employed. Included have been introspective and retrospective analysis of the verbal reports of the participants (a thorough review of the issues surrounding verbal reports as data can be found in Nesbitt & Wilson, 1977; Ericson & Simon, 1980; Afferbach & Johnson, 1984; and Meichenbaum et al. 1985) and the direct observation of task performance coupled with the drawing of inferences concerning the absence or presence of metacognitive acts (examples of the use of this technique can be found in work by Sternberg, 1983 with a review of the issue provided by Meichenbaum et al., 1985).

Lawson (1984), in an earlier review of the issue of being aware of thinking, particularly executive control, separated executive processing from metacognitive awareness for the very fact that not all thinking is available to conscious awareness due to the role of automaticity. Kirby (1984), in extending the work of Case (1980) on automaticity and integrating the work of Lawson (1984), suggests that automaticity plays a role only in strategies that are to be constructed as opposed to strategies that are well established. In other words, where an activity involves newer challenges building on an existing knowledge base, the issue of automaticity need not rule out participant access to thinking. With this in mind, French and French (1988, 1989) and French (1990) have constructed assessment activities that attempt to challenge children so as to minimize the impact of automaticity, thereby enabling children to access more information about their thinking. Borkowski (1985) presents a similar argument in reviewing metamemorial research. Nevertheless, it is important to remember that serious limitations exist in assuming that all thinking is available to conscious awareness.

An attempt to incorporate less obtrusive measures has been advocated by Baron (1987). Despite these attempts, however, it should be remembered that once nonfamiliar persons and/or nonfamiliar situations are introduced into any setting, a change in that setting and the individuals from their natural day-to-day functioning is possible. This is a particular problem for the person attempting to assess cognitive performance, since the very framing of even an open-ended question provides a previously untapped referent for the participant. In attempting to control for this, the participant-observer paradigm and use of suggestions from clinical practice (Gordon, 1980) should help the evaluator and/or researcher become a less obtrusive part of the environment.

Another useful procedure to reduce the obtrusiveness of assessment and the possible structuring of participant responses is to involve participants in instructing younger confederates of the researcher (Brown, 1980). French (1983) utilized this technique with considerable success providing access to the participant strategies told to a younger confederate of the experimenter whom the participants believed they were training.

Two remaining issues deserve attention in any model that pretends to provide a comprehensive overview of the merits of cognitive instructional programs. One issue pertains to the maintenance of thinking skills, while the other pertains to the generalizability of thinking skills.

With regard to the issue of maintenance, Feuerstein et al. (1980) argue that the real test of a cognitive instructional program would be in the maintenance of thinking skills following the conclusion of training. In fact, if the structure of the intellect were really changed following training, the thinking skills of the individual would continue to improve following the cessation of training. It appears that the only study that is looking at this hypothesis is the longitudinal research being conducted by Mulcahy (Mulcahy et al. 1989). Nevertheless, the need to review participants for periods up to at least a year following training is essential to determine the nature of the long-term effect of cognitive instructional programs. Without this data, the hypothesis that thinking skills programs influence how children learn to facilitate change in their ability to learn is nothing more than a hypothesis.

Borkowski (1985) has provided an extensive review of research on the transfer of skills in the area of memory. He argues, as did Butterfield and Belmont (1977), that most of the studies that have shown transfer have trained one or more of the components of the executive system that produce self-regulated problem solving. As with the discussion on maintenance, the issue of documenting transfer is essential to the determination of the effectiveness of cognitive instructional programs. Real change in participants should not only take place in the task on which the participant was trained, but also on related and nonrelated tasks. Work by Burger and Blackman (1979), Burger et al. (1979), Cavanaugh and Borkowski (1979), and Asarnow and Meichenbaum (1979) have helped provide a paradigm to assess near and far point transfer. More longitudinal follow-up on generalization will be necessary using the methods described by the above authors.

The integration of all these data points requires some type of methodology. In this regard, Denzin (1978) provides the concept of data triangulation—the combination of two or more different research strategies in the study of the same empirical units. Such combinations could be of data sources or data collection methods. In furthering this concept, an approach that seeks out as much information as possible in an exploratory yet refined manner using the rigor of quantitative and qualitative designs is needed. The evaluation of the merits and limitations of cognitive education are still in the exploratory stages. Failing to account for as many data points as possible in the exploration risks missing important information that may inhibit future development and/or advocate false hopes. The analogy of the octopus searching the ocean floor comes to mind in this regard; and, for the lack of any other term to capture the proposed methodology, this active searching and feeling out using a variety of means will be called the ''tentacle approach.''

The tentacle approach to evaluate the nature, merits, and limitations of cognitive education programs applied to a school setting relative to their efficiency, effectiveness, and accountability incorporate certain assumptions. For example, it is assumed that evaluation is an ongoing interactive process that incorporates formative and summative evaluation of not only the outcome, but also the process by which those outcomes were achieved. In this regard, both clinical and school-based research covering short- and long-term instructional periods utilizing both individual, small group, and intact classrooms is necessary to provide a comprehensive view of thinking skills programs. Within school-based research, the most likely design would be that of a pre-/post- control group quasi-experimental design incorporating quantitative and qualitative methodologies using an intensive case study approach with a random sample of participants to provide rigorous insights into the cognitive and affective functioning of selected individuals.

Given the developing nature of cognitive education programs, there is a need to answer three different types of questions while undertaking the evaluation. Specifically, it is necessary to know whether the program was implemented as designed; the effectiveness of the program with students, teachers, and others; and the reactions of students, teachers, and other significant persons relative to the program itself. In order to protect the integrity of the summative nature of the evaluation it will be necessary to hold program modifications until the conclusion of the post-testing or until some other appropriate time when changes can be implemented systematically and concurrently across programs.

A final assumption and requirement is that the researcher should function as a participant-observer such that the researcher blends into the school system and becomes one of the staff, thereby aiding the reduction of the obtrusiveness of the evaluation process.

Given the extreme difficulties with the assessment component of the evaluation of cognitive instructional programs, a brief overview of the assessment procedures necessary to account for the range of process and product variables to be assessed is presented as a part of the model.

Included as a part of the assessment process should be instruments and/or procedures that provide information on the following:

- the nature and extent of strategies (pre-/post- and at other appropriate times) in academic and nonacademic areas through the use of think-aloud, interview, and other types of procedures designed to challenge the participant by adjusting the difficulty level of the materials to be slightly above the instructional level of the participant.

- participant awareness of metacognitive and executive processes

- perceptions of the participants and significant others through the use of interviews, logs, and completion of checklists

- achievement and general ability

- critical thinking

- various affective measures, including self-esteem, acceptance of responsibility for academic outcomes, and attitudes toward the program, school, and school subject

- oral and written communication

- peer tutoring or teaching of younger confederates of the researcher

- information on the maintenance and generalization of thinking skills, utilizing near and far point transfer
- assessment data supplemented with information gained from school records, attendance, and discipline reports.

Control groups utilized in the evaluation also should be subject to careful analysis based on the same criteria as the experimental groups. This is necessary because many core and supplementary curricula encourage the teaching of thinking as a part of the subject matter. As well, analysis of teacher techniques are necessary since some teachers are more process-oriented.

The tentacle evaluation model incorporates three major areas that need to be addressed when making decisions on the effectiveness of any thinking skills program. These are represented in figure 15.1.

Figure 15.1
The Tentacle Evaluation Model

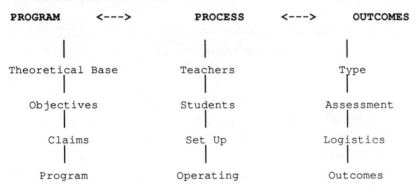

These three areas are interrelated, yet within each of these areas several specific aspects need to be examined to evaluate the effectiveness and efficiency of the program being employed. All three aspects need to be discussed and in place before a thinking skills program is introduced within the school setting. With regard to program, process, and outcome, it is important to consider the following:

Theoretical Base—foundation, if any, for the program
- the theoretical and research base of the program
- previous and current research and applications
- linkage of theoretical base and research to objectives and program procedures

Objectives—purposes of the program
- what objectives, if any, are stated
- whether the program objectives are explicit, implied, or convoluted

- whether the objectives are related to the theoretical base
- whether the objectives are implemented through the program

Claims—areas that the program is reported to affect and evidence to support such claims
- areas of knowledge that are influenced by the program—declarative, procedural, strategic, metacognitive, or all four
- the impact of the program on affective development
- the impact of the program on academic achievement
- whether acquisition, maintenance, and generalizability are addressed
- amount of time required for impact
- the need for and amount of teacher in-service required

Program—whether the program advocates general or specific knowledge strategies
- whether the program is a "stand alone" program or embedded in the curriculum
- whether the program is developed or developing, published or in the refinement process
- whether packaged materials are available and/or needed
- whether trained personnel are needed for in-service

Teachers
- the number of teachers piloting the program
- how the teachers are selected
- current philosophy, teaching style, and attitude
- student-teacher ratio
- qualifications and background experiences, particularly with process-oriented methods
- teachers' familiarity with the program

Students
- ability, attitude, and current grade level
- current affective and cognitive status, particularly with regard to level of declarative, procedural, and strategic knowledge as well as metacognitive, problem-solving, and decision-making knowledge and strategies
- exposure to different teaching styles
- selection procedures, whole group or random samples, actual teachers, volunteers, or research associates

Set Up—planning and preparation stage
- whether control groups and/or other thinking skills programs will be used for comparison
- how the thinking skills program was introduced—in-service (depth and duration)
- who provided the in-service, if any

- materials/manuals available
- teacher and student introduction to program and/or project

Implementing and Operating—carrying out the program
- whether the thinking skills program was carried out consistently and in line with stated objectives and procedures
- teacher and student motivation
- quality of implementation
- amount of time devoted to the program—daily, weekly, monthly, and yearly
- availability of resource person(s)—on-site, periodic follow-up
- monitoring of accuracy of program operations to determine consistency with assigned procedures

Type—method of evaluation
- have method in place before the program begins
- determine who is involved in the collection of outcome measures and the areas to be evaluated
- include both summative and formative techniques
- consider qualitative and quantitative techniques

Assessment—all measures used to collect data on the program
- decide which instruments to use to evaluate student progress/change—published normed/ criterion-referenced achievement or intelligence tests; tests by program's developer(s); school-based instruments; tests developed by participants; informal measures
- consider other methods of gaining information—direct observation of students and teachers; videotaping; interviews; questionnaires; journals; self-reports
- determine the appropriateness of the measurement instruments and/or techniques to the goals and procedures that pertain to cognitive instruction
- consider the person(s) who will collect the data
- choose or design methods/instruments to measure acquisition, maintenance, and transfer/generalizability
- devise ways to provide an ongoing review of how the program was set up and carried out
- examine the interaction among the various components of the program
- ensure that means are in place to look at all the claims of the program
- determine how the information will be gathered and presented
- ensure cognitive and affective processes and outcomes are addressed

Logistics/Efficiency—balance between input and output
- look at the financial accounts
- review the time commitments—in-service, lesson preparation

• decide whether the input of students and teachers is reflected in the outcomes

Outcomes—evaluating the information collected

• decide how the information gathered will be interpreted and used in the decision-making process
• set criteria to judge the effectiveness of the thinking skills program
• determine factors that influenced the program positively, negatively, or had little or no impact
• decide whether the claims by the program's author(s) were accurate
• make a decision to adopt the program as is, with modifications, or to reject
• set follow-up evaluation process in place, if necessary

Each of the steps within the tentacle model holds particular strengths and limitations. Taken together, they reduce the reliance on oral interviews, think-aloud procedures, and, written questionnaires as suggested by Sternberg (1985), Borkowski (1985), and Pressley et al. (1987). This is not meant to infer that combining a group of weak measures will result in a strong indication that a valid and reliable indication of the effectiveness or lack thereof of cognitive instructional procedures exists. What is implied and made explicit is the fact that by utilizing state-of-the-art measures, accounting for their limitations, and combining a wide variety of information windows of opportunity for further research into the evaluation of cognitive instructional programs are opened.

Problems implementing the tentacle model are to be anticipated. One problem concerns the cost. A second problem concerns consent of school systems for the collection of data, which may limit the effectiveness of instructional time. The third problem concerns the use of quasi-experimental research designs.

With regard to the problem of financial and time costs, one solution is to undertake intensive study of a random sample of the total student population involved in the cognitive education evaluation. This suggestion also reduces some of the concern with the use of nonrandomized sampling in quasi-experimental designs. A random sample of 30 percent of the population under study for participation in more intensive follow-up incorporating intensive experiences such as the oral interview, the think-aloud procedure, strategy assessment, and peer tutoring will help reduce costs and time. It is important to note, however, that many of the procedures itemized above do not require a great deal of cost or time away from instruction on the part of participants. Further, many of the data points referenced above are a natural part of the ongoing school routine.

Use of the experimental group as its own control is another possibility to help reduce the effects of nonrandomization. Cook and Campbell (1979) have discussed this procedure otherwise known as an interrupted time series design.

Perhaps the most critical aspect of implementing such a comprehensive model is timing and the cooperation of the school system, system personnel at all levels, parents, and students. Posavac and Carey (1985) state that the identification of relevant people, arranging appropriately timed preliminary meetings, and scheduling the evaluation at times convenient for school personnel and the other partners in the process are critical elements in organizing, implementing, and continuing a systematic and effective evaluation.

French (1990) has reported on the potential of a collaborative school-based research/evaluative model to address the needs, strengths, and limitations of the partners in the process. Rather than view the researcher as the academic who visits the school at key data collection points, the entire team—including teachers, administrators, faculty involved with the project, students, and parents—participates in the process. Each through a series of premeetings comes to understand the roles and responsibilities of the other, including the need for confidentiality and research rigor. While such a process may appear idealized, it has worked and is contributing to a large ongoing project in Nova Scotia known as the Annapolis Venture of the Reflective Learning Project at Mount Saint Vincent University. Approximately 50 teachers and 1,500 students are now involved in this four-year study of the relative impact of cognitive instructional procedures and programs from grade 1 through 11 (see French, 1990; French and French, in prep).

The evaluation of cognitive instructional programs in applied settings requires, as does any evaluation, intense procedures to ensure accuracy and completeness of the data. As noted by French (in press), the promise of cognitive instruction lies in the approach taken in refining and enhancing knowledge about cognition and how it affects the thinking process. Having a comprehensive system of evaluation contributes to the enhancement of that knowledge.

REFERENCES

Afferbach, P., & Johnston, P. (1984). Research methodology verbal reports in reading research. *Journal of Reading Behavior,* 16(4), 307–321.

Alley, G., & Deshler, D. (1979). *Teaching the learning disabled adolescent: Strategies and Methods.* Denver: Love.

Asarnow, J., & Meichenbaum, D. (1979). Verbal rehearsal and serial recall: The mediational training of kindergarten children. *Child Development,* 50, 1173–1177.

Baer, J. (1988). Let's not handicap able thinkers. *Educational Leadership,* 45 (7), 66–72.

Baron, J. B. (1987). Evaluating thinking skills in the classroom. In J. B. Baron & R. J. Sternberg (eds.), *Teaching thinking skills.* New York: Academic.

Borkowski, J. G. (1985). Signs of intelligence: Strategy generalization and metacognition. In S. R. Yussen (ed.), *The growth of reflection in children.* New York: Academic.

Borkowski, J. G., & Cavanaugh, J. C. (1979). Maintenance and generalization of skills and strategies by the retarded. In N. R. Ellis (ed.), *Handbook of mental deficiency: Psychological theory and research.* Hillside, N.J.: Erlbaum.

Brandt, R. (1984). Teaching of thinking, for thinking, about thinking. *Educational Leadership*, 42(3).

———. (1988) New possibilities. *Journal of the Association for Supervision and Curriculum Development*, 45(7), 3.

Brown, A. L. (1980). Metacognitive development and reading. In R. J. Spiro, B. C. Bruce, & W. F. Brewer (eds.), *Theoretical issues in reading comprehension: Perspectives from cognitive psychology, linguistics, artificial intelligence and education*. Hillsdale, N.J.: Erlbaum.

Brown, A. L., & Campione, J. C. (1977). Training strategic study time apportionment in educable retarded children. *Intelligence*, 1, 94–107.

Brown, A. L., & Palincsar, A. S. (1984). Reciprocal teaching of comprehension-fostering and monitoring activities. *Cognition and Instruction*, 1(2), 17–57.

Burger, A. L., & Blackman, L. S. (1979). Digit span estimation and the effects of explicit strategy training on recall of EM individuals. *American Journal of Mental Deficiency*, 83, 627.

Burger, A. L., Blackman, L. S., Holmes, M., & Setlin, A. (1979). Use of active sorting and retrieval strategies as a facilitator of recall, clustering, and sorting by EMR and nonretarded children. *American Journal of Mental Deficiency*, 83, 253–261.

Butterfield, E. C. & Belmont, J. A. (1977). Assessing and improving the cognitive functioning of mentally retarded people. In I. Bialer & M. Sternlicht (eds.), *The psychology of mental retardation: Issues and approaches*. New York: Psychological Dimensions.

Campione, J. C., & Brown, A. L. (1987). Dynamic assessment with school achievement. In C. S. Lidz (ed.), *Dynamic assessment: An interactional approach to evaluating learning potential*. New York: Guilford.

Carey, S. (1985) Are children fundamentally different kinds of thinkers and learners than adults? In S. F. Chipman, J. W. Segal, & R. Glaser (eds.), *Thinking and learning skills*. Vol. 2. Hillsdale, N.J.: Erlbaum.

Case, R. (1980). Implications of Neo-Piagetian theory for improving the design of instruction. In J. R. Kirby & J. B. Briggs (eds.), *Cognition, development, and instruction*. New York: Academic.

Cavanaugh, J. C., & Borkowski, J. G. (1979). The metamemory "connection" effects of strategy training and maintenance. *Journal of General Psychology*, 101, 161–174.

Chance, P.(1986). *Thinking in the classroom*. New York: Teachers College Press.

Chipman, S. F., & Segal, J. W. (1985). Higher cognitive goals for education: An introduction. In S. F. Chipman, J. W. Segal, & R. Glaser (eds.), *Thinking and learning skills*, vol. 2, *Research and open questions*. Hillsdale, N.J.: Erlbaum.

Cook, T. D., & Campbell, T. (eds.). (1979). *Quasi-experimentation: Design and analysis issues for field settings*. Chicago: Rand McNally.

Costa, A. L. (1983). Teaching for intelligent behavior. Unpublished paper, Sacramento, California State University.

Cross, D., & Paris, S. (1988). Developmental and instructional analysis of children's metacognition and reading comprehensions. *Journal of Educational Psychology*, 80(2), 131–142.

deBono, E. (1976). *Teaching thinking*. London: Maurice Temple Smith.

Denzin, N. K. (1978). *The research act: A theoretical introduction to sociological methods,* (2d ed.). Chicago: Aldine.

Dickson, G. E., & Wiersma, W. (1984). *Research and evaluation in teacher education: Empirical measurement of teacher performance.* Toledo, Ohio: University of Toledo.

Dillon, R. F. (1986). Issues in cognitive psychology and instruction. In R. F. Dillon & R. J. Sternberg (eds.), *Cognition and instruction.* Orlando, Fla.: Academic.

Ennis, R. (1987). A taxonomy of critical thinking dispositions and abilities. In J. B. Baron and R. J. Sternberg (eds.), *Teaching thinking skills: Theory and practice.* New York: Freeman.

Ennis, R., & Weir, L. (1985). Tests that could be called critical thinking tests. In A. L. Costa (ed.), *Developing minds: A resource book for teaching thinking.* Alexandria, Va.: Association for Curriculum Development.

Ericson, K. A., & Simon, H. A.(1980). *Protocol analysis: Verbal reports as data.* Cambridge, Mass.: MIT.

Feuerstein, R., Rand, Y., Hoffman, M. B., & Miller, M. J. (1980). *Instrumental enrichment.* Baltimore: University Park Press.

Flavell, J. H. (1977). *Cognitive development.* Englewood Cliffs, N.J.: Prentice-Hall.

French, F. (1983). *Learner strategies enabling thinking—A guidebook.* Edmonton: University of Alberta.

———. (1985). Cognitive strategy assessment and intervention with EMH adolescents. Unpublished Ph.D. diss., University of Alberta.

———. (1987a). *Learner strategies enabling thinking.* 2d ed. Halifax: Mount Saint Vincent University.

———. (1987b). *Student self generated strategies: An important dimension in learning.* Paper presented at the Canadian Psychological Conference.

———. (1990). *A longitudinal examination of strategic behaviour of junior high students: Assessment and intervention, year 1.* Paper presented at AERA, Boston, Mass.

French, F. (in press). Cognitive instructional practices in today's schools: Promise or fallacy. In R. H. Short, L. L. Stewin, & S. J. H. McCann (eds.), *Educational psychology: Canadian perspectives.* Toronto: Copp Clark Pitman.

———. (in prep). *Learner strategies enabling thinking.* 3d ed. Halifax: Mount Saint Vincent University.

French, F., & French, C. (1988). *Teaching thinking skills: Critical issues.* Paper presented at the Canadian Societies Conference, McMaster University.

———. (1989) *Evaluating thinking skills programs: One year later.* Paper presented at the Canadian Psychological Association Convention.

Garner, R., & Alexander, P. A. (1989). Metacognition: Answered and unanswered questions. *Educational Psychologist,* 24(2), 141–158.

Glaser, R. (1984). Education and thinking. *American Psychologist,* 39(2), 93–104.

———. (1988). Cognitive science and education. *Cognitive Science,* 40(1), 21–44.

Gordon, R. (1980). *Interviewing: Strategies, techniques and tactics.* 3d ed. Homewood, Ill.: Dorsey.

Haney, W., & Madus, G. (1989). Searching for alternatives to standardized tests: Whys, whats, and whithers. *Kappan,* 70(9), 683–687.

Hopkins, D., Bollington, R., & Hewett, D. (1989). Growing up with qualitative research and evaluation. *Evaluation and Research Education,* 3(2), 61–80.

Kantor, K. J., Kirby, D. R., & Goetz, J. P. (1981). Research in context: Ethnographic studies in English education. *Research in the Teaching of English,* 15(4), 293–309.

Kirby, J. R. (1984). Strategies and processes. In J. R. Kirby (ed.), *Cognitive strategies and educational performance.* Orlando, Fla.: Academic.

Lawson, M. J. (1984). Being executive about metacognition. In J. R. Kirby (ed.), *Cognitive strategies and educational performance.* Orlando, Fla.: Academic.

Lipman, M. (1985). Thinking skills fostered by philosophy for children. In J. W. Segal, S. F. Chipman, & R. Glaser (eds.), *Thinking and learning skills,* vol. 1, *Relating instruction to research.* Hillsdale, N.J.: Erlbaum.

Mann, L. (1979). *On the trail of process.* New York: Grune & Stratton.

Markman, E. M. (1977). Realizing that you don't understand: A preliminary investigation. *Child Development,* 48, 986–992.

Meichenbaum, D., Burland, S., Gruson, L., & Cameron, R. (1985). *Metacognitive assessment.* Paper presented at the Conference on the Growth of Insight, Madison, Wis.

Menick, N. (1987). Implications of Vygotsky's theories for dynamic assessment. In C. S. Litz (ed.), *Dynamic assessment: An interactional approach to evaluating learning potential.* New York: Guilford.

Messick, S. (1984). Abilities and knowledge in educational achievement testing: The assessment of dynamic cognitive structures. In B. S. Plake (ed.), *Social and technical issues in testing.* Hillsdale, N.J.: Erlbaum.

Mulcahy, R. F., Peat, D., Andrews, J., Clifford, L., Marfo, K., & Cho, S. (1989). *Cognitive education final report.* Alberta Education, Government of Alberta, Edmonton.

Narrol, H., Silverman, H., & Waksman, M. (1982). Developing cognitive potential in vocational high school students. *Journal of Educational Research,* 76(2), 107–112.

Neill, D. M., & Medina, N. J. (1989). Standardized testing: Harmful to educational health. *Phi Delta Kappan,* 70(9), 688–697.

Neisser, U. (1979). The concept of intelligence. In R. J. Sternberg & D. K. Detterman (eds.), *Human intelligence.* Norwood, N.J.: Ablex.

Nesbitt, R. E., & Wilson, T. D. (1977). Telling more than we can know: Verbal reports on mental processes. *Psychological Review,* 84, 231–259.

Newman, J. M. (ed.). (1985). *Whole language.* Portsmouth N.H.: Heinemann.

Nickerson, R. S. (1985). Understanding understanding. *American Journal of Education,* 24, 201–239.

Nickerson, R. S., Perkins, D. N., & Smith, E. E. (1985). *The teaching of thinking.* Hillsdale, N.J.: Erlbaum.

Paul, R., Binker, A. J. A., Jensen, K., & Kreklau, H. (1987). *Critical thinking handbook: 4th–6th grades.* Rohnart Park: Calif.: Centre for Critical Thinking and Moral Critique.

Perkins, D. N. (1985). General cognitive skills: Why not? In S. F. Chipman, J. W. Segal, R. Glaser (eds.), *Thinking and learning skills.* vol. 2. Hillsdale, N.J.: Erlbaum.

Piaget, J. (1972). *Psychology and epistemology: Towards a theory of knowledge.* Harmondsworth, England: Penguin.

Posavac, E. J., & Carey, R. G. (1985). *Program evaluation: Methods and case studies.* Englewood Cliffs, N.J.: Prentice-Hall.

Pressley, M., Goodchild, F., Fleet, J., Zajebowski, R., & Evans, E. (1987). *What is good strategy use and why is it hard to teach?* Paper presented at the University of Washington, Seattle.

Rogers, V. (1989). Assessing the curriculum experienced by children. *Phil Delta Kappan,* 70(9), 714–717.

Sax, G. (1989). *Principles of educational and psychological measurement and evaluation.* Belmont, Calif.: Wadsworth.

Schoenfeld, A. H. (1977). Measures of problem-solving performance and of problem solving instruction. *Journal for Research in Mathematics Education,* 10(3), 32–39.

Schofield, J. W., & Andersen, K. (1984). *Integrating quantitative components into qualitative studies: Problems and possibilities for research on intergroup relations in educational settings.* Paper presented at the annual meeting of the American Educational Research Association, New Orleans.

Schofield, J. W., & Sager, H. A. (1977). Peer interaction patterns in an integrated middle school. *Sociometry,* 40 (2), 130–138.

Scriven, M. (1972). Pros and cons about goal free evaluation. *Evaluation Comment,* 3, 1–7.

Sternberg, R. J. (1983). Criteria for intellectual skills training. *Educational Researcher,* 12(2), 4–6.

———. (1985). Instrumental and componential approaches to the nature and training of intelligence. In. S. F. Chipman, J. W. Segal, & R. Glaser (eds.), *Thinking and learning skills,* vol. 2, *Research and open questions.* Hillsdale, N.J.: Erlbaum.

———. (1986). Cognition and instruction: Why the marriage sometimes ends in divorce. In R. F. Dillon & R. J. Sternberg (eds.), *Cognition and instruction.* Orlando, Fla.: Academic.

Vygotsky, L. (1962). *Thought and language.* Cambridge, Mass.: MIT.

Waksman, M. (1982). Cognitive education—The emerging alternative in special education. Unpublished manuscript, University of Toronto.

Walker, C. (1987). Relative importance of domain knowledge and overall aptitude on acquisition of domain-related information. *Cognition and Instruction,* 4(1), 25–42.

Wiersma, W. (1986). *Research methods in education.* Toronto: Allyn & Bacon.

Wiggins, G. (1989). A true test: Toward more authentic and equitable assessment. *Phi Delta Kappan,* 70(9), 703–713.

16

Enhancing Learning and Thinking: Some Questions

Jac Andrews, Robert H. Short, and
Robert F. Mulcahy

Although some people suggest that education should return to teaching the three "r's," widespread support seems to favor a move toward other, even more fundamental aspects of education. These fundamentals involve teaching children how to become more active in their learning and thinking along with becoming more purposeful, independent, and creative in their problem solving and decision making. Thinking is not a fourth "r," but a variety of critical skills inherent in academic tasks such as reading, writing, and arithmetic that need to be more fully addressed by educators. For example, writing requires among other things, the ability to analyze, synthesize, and organize information, in addition to being able to monitor and evaluate one's own performance. Mathematical problem solving requires a variety of thinking skills beyond the ability to memorize rules and perform computations; and as noted by Leong (chapter 10 in this volume), and Mancini et al. (chapter 11), skilled reading performance is the result of integrated cognitive processing skills and a variety of knowledge-based subskills.

There is clearly a need for educators to focus their efforts on improving those higher-level cognitive skills that will enable children to become independent and productive learners and thinkers. Because of the rapidly changing technological environment in which we live, these skills are more important today than they have been at any other time. It is increasingly apparent that children need to know how to learn the new information and skills they will require in their lives and not just what to learn. Generally, research over the past decade indicates that many children are having difficulty learning, primarily because: (1) they tend to be passive rather than active learners; (2) they do not think that they have personal control over their learning and do not believe that their efforts will influence their achievement; (3) they tend to be dependent rather than independent learners; (4) they tend to be deficient in strategies, and/or inefficient in their use of strategies when doing school tasks; and (5) they do not monitor and evaluate their performance when doing school work. This type of evidence suggests that there is a need to develop learning and thinking skills in children that foster active, confident, independent, efficient, and self-controlled learning and thinking behaviors. Indeed, recent literature in the area has suggested that a more appropriate goal of education today is to produce learners who have the motivation and ability to learn on their own rather than to produce just learned individuals (Nickerson et al., 1985). The evidence is sufficiently clear that according to Pace (chapter 3), many Canadian provinces and American states have been actively developing official positions on the teaching of thinking skills and have now specifically included them in the formal curricula of their schools.

Nickerson (chapter 1) stresses that thinking is a multifaceted process that is only partially understood. He also points out that research has revealed systematic ways in which a person's thinking can go astray and that students do not necessarily emerge as capable thinkers as a consequence of completing courses in conventional subjects. Even though it is possible to process information and to think without being instructed, Nickerson (1988) suggests that when we say that we want to teach children to think "we really mean that we want to improve the quality of their thinking. We want to teach them to think more deeply, more productively, more effectively than they otherwise might. In a word, the challenge is not so much to teach thinking as to teach good thinking" (p. 2).

There are many reasons for enhancing thinking skills, not the least of which, argues Nickerson (chapter 1), is the potentially disastrous consequences for humanity of widespread inability to think well. In Nickerson's view, the ability to learn and think is quintessentially human. Accordingly, children who become good learners and thinkers are more fully expressing what it means to be human. To fail to develop that potential is a denial of a birthright of a fundamental sort. It is with this in mind that Nickerson maintains that the teaching of thinking should be a high-priority objective of education.

CAN THINKING BE TAUGHT?

Nickerson suggests that the teaching of thinking is not easy and cannot be accomplished with a "quick fix" approach. It requires preparation, commitment, perseverance, and a willingness on the part of the teacher, as well as a need to be inquisitive, fair-minded, understanding, empathic, flexible, metacognitive, insightful, creative, and curious. This is a tall order for any teacher and yet it still needs to be capped with a strong sense of self-efficacy as a thinking person.

Recent interest in the field of cognitive psychology has centered upon improving the learning and thinking skills of school-aged children. An increasing number of programs are being designed to develop children's thinking ability and they offer important guidance for school instruction. It is generally agreed that children need to be shown effective ways of approaching learning tasks to improve their performance and to increase their motivation to discover learning for themselves. They need to be encouraged to be more actively involved in the process so that they do not persist in the belief that learning and thinking are passive endeavors that are essentially someone else's responsibility. In order to help in this process, teachers need to constantly reinforce children's thinking as well as provide feedback about appropriate strategic approaches to tasks. They also need to constantly assist children in maintaining, evaluating, and improving upon their learning and thinking. Perhaps even more important, teachers need to be good models. Teaching thinking involves helping children to become aware of their own cognitive processes and to be effective managers of their own mental resources. They need to be given opportunities to discuss their viewpoints and to feel free to question, explore, and expose their own knowledge limitations or misconceptions without fear of ridicule. If these recommendations are appropriately applied within the context of classroom instruction, the evidence suggests that the quality of learning and thinking really can be improved. The teacher needs to be capable of fostering thinking, however, and the classroom and general school environment need to be nurturant and conducive to fulfilling the child's intellectual potential.

According to Costa (chapter 2), in the process of teaching thinking we should be more interested in observing how children produce knowledge than in their mere reproduction of knowledge. He suggests that intelligent behavior develops within a school environment where there is faith that children can indeed think, where thinking as a goal is nurtured, where there are ample opportunities for solving problems, and where the environment is highly responsive to thinking, allowing it to occur wherever possible. He further suggests that teachers are more likely to encourage thinking if they are in intellectually stimulating environments themselves, where the goals of the institution lie in the empowerment of others, in facilitating their creativeness, and in fostering a collective vision of excellence. Among other things, Costa suggests that thinking can be taught if teachers and administrators collaborate in the planning of cognitive skills acquisition and where, among numerous other attributes, there is an atmosphere that recognizes, values, and encourages thinking ability.

Thinking can be taught if teachers and the educational community value the systematic development of thinking. For this to happen, however, teachers need to treat children as thinkers and not merely as learners. They need to provide opportunities and set the stage for thinking, and motivate learners in the acquisition of knowledge and the development of talent. They are not just there to supply the answers. Children must be challenged to master the possibilities of the future and not just dwell on the literacy of the past.

HOW ARE LEARNING AND THINKING RELATED?

Thinking primarily involves the ability to formulate thoughts, to activate knowledge, and to utilize judgment. Thinking skills include processes such as attention, memory, and metacognition. They also include the cognitive strategies associated with the analysis of information and the evaluation of performance that a person uses to operate more effectively in a variety of learning situations. Most of these processes and strategies are used in conjunction with school content areas and various school learning tasks, such as writing assignments, finding main ideas, asking questions, and generating responses. It is because of the interaction between process and content that learning and thinking are viewed as being closely related to one another. As Nickerson (1988) indicates, "one cannot have more than superficial knowledge of any subject if one cannot use the concepts and relationships inherent to that subject in thoughtful ways" (p. 32).

The close relationship between learning and thinking has been discussed before. Jones et al. (1987) believes that learning and thinking share many related assumptions. There is clear support for the notion that the learner is an active, strategic, "planful," and constructive individual particularly in linking new information to prior knowledge. Skilled learners are seen as a people who understand assigned tasks and have the capacity to regulate their learning. Evidence suggests that proficient learners are able to improve the structure of poorly presented information and know how, when, and where to use appropriate strategies in addition to being able to understand and appreciate the quality of their performance. Learning takes place during the process of understanding something—the content. Thinking is related to understanding, which in turn is related to the very nature of knowledge.

Marfo et al. (chapter 6) note that the ability to learn and think has become synonymous with becoming educated and that preparing students to think has remained one of the central goals of education in nearly all societies. Since the early 1960s there has been a gradual bridging of the gap between the cognitive sciences, with their emphasis on critical, analytical, and productive thinking skills, and education, which has tended to emphasize the acquisition and application of knowledge. The bridging process has undergone considerable acceleration over the past decade. There is now a legitimate marriage between cognitive psychology and education and a cognitive education movement has been established. This movement is concerned with the improvement of the learner's basic cognitive functioning and with the application of cognitive functions and strategies to the improvement of academic achievement. The legitimacy of this movement can be witnessed in the proliferation of programs that are designed to enhance learning and thinking through direct instruction in cognitive strategies.

Much of the impetus for cognitive instructional programs has come from theories of information processing such as metacognitive theory (Borkowski,

1985; Brown, 1978; Flavell, 1976), Neo-Piagetian theory (Case, 1980), schema theory (Thorndyke & Hayes Roth, 1979), and problem-solving theory (Newell & Simon, 1972). There is also a trend toward defining human intelligence in information-processing terms, seeing it as being made up of cognitive components, many of which are amenable to change. In one particular component-based theory of intelligence, Sternberg (1986) describes three distinct types of cognitive process: knowledge and acquisition, performance, and metacognition. The last of these represents several higher-order processes that a person may use for executive decision making during the solving of a problem. Because cognitive processes are in large part learned, they are capable of being modified with systematic instruction. Instruction in the strategies that are used to improve a person's learning and thinking is based on the idea that cognition is amenable to being broken down into components and that cognitive performance can be improved by teaching children to employ thinking skills in their everyday learning.

WHAT SHOULD BE TAUGHT? CAN EVERYONE BE TAUGHT?

As has been mentioned, there are numerous programs that have been designed to improve children's learning and thinking, and there are a range of approaches available to meet the needs of specific problems. There are programs that focus on problem solving, intelligence, critical reasoning, creative reasoning, and thinking skills, but there is no single approach that is accepted by everyone. Strategy training approaches that are embedded in school and academic content, however, seem to be more favored by workers in the field. These approaches emphasize the close relationship between learning and thinking ability and focus on procedures for developing the appropriate skills for the content area in question. The decision of which particular skills to teach is made in the light of the child's developmental level, the amount of knowledge possessed, and the prerequisite skills already acquired.

Dansereau (1985) has suggested that learners scoring in the mid-range of standardized verbal ability measures can probably benefit more from strategy training than those at either extreme of the range. This does not mean, however, that all types of children cannot benefit from strategy instruction. Decisions regarding the type and sequencing of instruction can be guided by both theory and practice. Essentially, thinking skills such as comparing, classifying, hypothesis generating, and evaluating can be taught at any grade level, in any content area, with increasing complexity and sophistication. In other words, most thinking skills can be included in any school curriculum and taught throughout the child's school life. "Strategy" teachers "must balance a focus on content priorities with strategy instruction, not only as they plan sequences of instruction, but also during the act of teaching in the classroom. When strategy teachers identify content goals, they also consider the strategies that students need to use to learn the content well. These strategies then become secondary instructional goals to be incorporated as an integral part of the critical tasks" (Jones et al., 1987, p. 50).

In terms of instructional planning, it makes sense that the teaching of learning and thinking skills be undertaken as early as possible. Research shows that one difference between younger and older children is that the former fail to use spontaneous techniques to facilitate learning and problem solving. Although research also indicates that young children can be trained to be strategic in their learning and thinking, they require quite extensive instruction in the use of such strategies (Bray et al., 1977). In addition, the child's ability to select, maintain, and generalize strategies is relatively late in developing (Kendall et al., 1980; Butterfield & Belmont, 1977) and hence effective strategy use would appear to be related to the level of cognitive development attained (Peterson & Swing, 1983). Nevertheless, once young children have learned to use a strategy, they may benefit more from it than older children (Levin et al., 1979).

HOW SHOULD SKILLS BE TAUGHT?

Most programs designed to enhance learning and thinking ability are based on information-processing models in which "planful," organized, and independent activity is central. Programs already developed range from those enhancing intellectual competence (Feuerstein et al. 1980; Sternberg, 1985), operational reasoning (Nickerson & Adams, 1983; Lipman et al., 1980), problem-solving ability (deBono, 1980; Meichenbaum, 1980), and critical reasoning (Paul, 1984), to those providing procedural techniques and skills for mastering academic material (Dansereau, 1984; Deschler & Shumaker, 1986; Weinstein & Underwood, 1985). The programs tend to vary in scope, skill development, age/grade suitability, training requirements, curriculum integration, and cost and instructional methodology (Chance, 1986; Nickerson et al., 1985). The wide range of programs suggests that there is no one correct approach for teaching thinking. There appears to be growing support, however, for incorporating the teaching of thinking into the teaching of content (Bransford et al., 1986; Chance, 1986; Glaser, 1984; Mulcahy et al., 1986). According to Resnick (1987) content-embedded approaches appear to boost performance more comprehensively and have the following advantages: (1) they provide a knowledge base and the environment in which to develop thinking skills; (2) they provide the appropriate criteria of what constitutes good thinking, such as the use of inductive and deductive reasoning in the natural sciences and the use of critical reasoning in the social sciences; and (3) they ensure that important information and skills will be learned even if widespread transfer to other contexts does not always occur. Support for integrating the teaching of thinking skills with the teaching of academic disciplines is also voiced by Glaser (1984), who agrees that cognitive skills are best learned through the acquisition of domain-specific knowledge in the formal school curriculum. In addition, Joyce (1985) maintains that the teaching of thinking skills outside of the regular curriculum "creates a false dichotomy between basic subjects and intellectual activity. Worse, it says that it is all right to teach core subjects in a manner that does not stretch the intellect so long as we stimulate it elsewhere" (p. 5).

Even with this support for content-based teaching, it could still be possible that there is no single correct approach to teaching thinking. Some suggest that an "out of content" approach may be more appropriate for some individuals, such as preschoolers and culturally deprived adolescents, while "in content" approaches may be best suited to average achieving children and those who have mild to moderate learning difficulties. Alternatively, the best approach might be an integration of the two approaches. As Nickerson (1988) notes, "on the one hand it is important to treat the skills, strategies, attitudes and other targeted aspects of thinking in such a way that students come to understand their independence from specific domains and their applicability to many situations, on the other hand, it seems equally important to demonstrate their application in meaningful contexts so students witness their genuine usefulness" (p. 31).

Many psychologists and educators emphasize a strategy approach for the development of learning and thinking. This is due in part to evidence indicating that thinking is based largely on a repertoire of strategies that the individual can use in given tasks. Their view is that most learners should and indeed do assume much of the responsibility for their own learning. The reason why children with learning difficulties fail to achieve effectively is due to the fact that they are often rather passive in their learning and employ inappropriate or insufficient strategies in their approach to tasks. They also show poor organization and "planfulness" in their approach to problem solving.

The term "learning strategy" is used in a broad sense to include a number of competencies that are considered either necessary or helpful to effective learning. These competencies include information-processing strategies such as techniques for organizing, synthesizing, and elaborating information; active study strategies such as procedures for note taking, studying, and test preparation; and support strategies such as ways of coping with performance anxiety and focusing attention on the learning task. In addition, there are a wide range of metacognitive strategies that students can use to detect discrepancies in their learning as well as to monitor and direct their performance. Several investigators have shown that the emphasis on cognitive and metacognitive strategies results in improvements in thinking and problem solving (Mulcahy et al., in press). According to Bransford et al. (1986), a promising aspect of cognitive and metacognitive approaches to teaching is that they can be used to transform basic fact- and skill-oriented activities into lessons involving thinking.

One task force on learning and thinking strategies (Nickerson et al., 1985) recommends that the teaching of strategies be closely coupled to the teaching of conventional content material and that these skills be developed gradually over an extended period of time. According to Derry and Murphy (1986) improvement in academic aptitude "is not likely to result from anything less than a thoughtful systematic curriculum that complements direct training in learning strategies and thereby 'engineers' the gradual evolution of important executive control skills" (p. 1). Hence, cognitive theory, professional recommendations, and research provide ample support for the view that learning ability can be improved if children are taught learning strategies.

The current emphasis on the development and nurturance of cognitive strategies reinforces the time-worn philosophy that instruction should ensure that students become efficient, self-motivated learners. Because cognitive processes are acquired, they are modifiable through systematic instruction. The teacher plays a significant role as mediator between the learner and the external world. This mediational role helps facilitate the children's awareness of their own role in the learning and thinking process, encouraging them to practice the use of cognitive strategies in a variety of novel situations, and structuring the teaching and learning environment in a way that constantly challenges students to make decisions relating to the generation of new strategies or to the modification, extension, and application of existing ones.

Although it is rarely possible to fully individualize instruction when teaching large groups, it is possible to present and discuss strategic approaches to thinking about content material in such a way that all students can profit. Kendall and Zupman (1981) found that third, fourth, and fifth graders benefited from group-administered training in verbal self-instruction strategies and showed significantly greater improvements than students in a control group. Kestner and Borkowski (1979) found that instruction in interrogative strategies administered to first-grade students was effective in a group situation. Additionally, elementary and junior high school students have been shown to benefit from key word instruction (Levin et al., 1979; Pressley et al., 1982) as well as other memory and problem-solving strategies (Mulcahy et al., in press).

A number of investigators have shown the importance of metacognitive knowledge in the effective deployment of strategies (Baker & Brown, 1982). According to Shoenfeld (1979), "students need to be trained in a means for selecting the appropriate strategies for problem solving and for allocating their resources wisely" (p. 317). Students also need to be assisted in maintaining their attention and motivation while learning. This can be facilitated by providing them with sufficient time and the conditions for applying their strategies.

Important to the acquisition and employment of strategies is the quality of instruction. Children should be encouraged to use the strategies they have acquired with guidance and feedback (Borkowski et al., 1976). Teachers need to inform students how strategies can be beneficial to their academic and social lives and give them practice in a range of strategies (Anthony & Hudgins, 1978). Students need to be actively involved in the learning and thinking process, building a repertoire of strategies (Malin, 1979) and practicing the use of strategies in different contexts across a variety of problems (Schoenfeld, 1979). Generally, students respond more positively when the *Gestalt* of the strategy is taught first, followed by the details (Dansereau, 1985). Other considerations for instruction include: (1) providing a setting for social interaction and discussion in problem solution and decision making; (2) allowing for group problem solving so that children can both contribute to and learn from the group; (3) encouraging students to attempt novel and active approaches to learning and thinking and be open-minded; and (4) allowing students to express judgments and ask questions about the information they are acquiring.

Several authors in this book offer guidance in the teaching or learning and thinking skills. Biggs (chapter 4) presents a model that depicts learning outcomes as a result of the interaction of student characteristics, teaching context, and learning processes. One of the important aspects of his model lies in understanding how children approach learning. He presents three approaches in which students select learning strategies that are congruent with their motives. These are: (1) the *surface approach,* where the motive is to meet minimal institutional requirements and where the congruent strategy is to limit learning to essential details reproducible with rote learning; (2) the *deep approach,* characterized by an intrinsic interest in content, meaning, and competence with a congruent strategy involving reading widely and relating prior knowledge to present information; and (3) the *achieving approach,* where motivation lies in high grades and where the congruent strategies include managing time, work space, and content in the most efficient way. Biggs believes that improvements in learning require the full development of learning processes and suggests that good teaching minimizes superficial learning and maximizes deep and thorough learning. He further states that if exemplary teaching and learning are to take place, then the teacher and school system need to coordinate efforts and develop, support, and maintain consistent and effective learning strategies.

Patterson and Jamieson (chapter 8) believe that an important educational goal should be to change the emphasis from one of content mastery to one characterized by inquiry and investigation. They contend that teachers should provide opportunities to identify important content, reflect upon alternatives, assess the merits of opposing positions, pose questions, and substantiate and debate their positions. Bachor (chapter 9) stresses the importance of facilitating strategy acquisition and strategy competence and believes that it is important for students to appreciate the usefulness of strategic behavior. Marfo et al. (chapter 6) suggest that teachers should expose students to the idea that cognitive strategies exist and demonstrate to them that their usage increases the ability to acquire and apply knowledge in a variety of tasks and content areas. They also advocate that students should generate strategies for themselves. Their idea of an effective thinking teacher is one who can understand how students currently approach tasks and point out limitations; relate new approaches to old approaches; provide practice in strategy use; demonstrate the use of strategies across several areas; explain to students the purposes, values, and limitations of strategies; provide constructive feedback; and help modify and generalize strategies.

Price (chapter 5) stresses the need to encourage children to reflect on their own thinking and to be challenged to think during the question and answering process, while Evans and Dansereau (chapter 7) discuss the use of knowledge maps for helping in the understanding of text material and for general problem solving and decision making.

A consistent message of the above authors is that teachers need to engage their students in active learning and thinking skills. Teachers need to help students develop the ability to reason, to make decisions, and to solve problems through planful, systematic, and evaluative ways. Educators need to focus more on teaching how to learn rather than on just what to learn.

HOW IS A PROGRAM CHOSEN?

In determining which of a number of possible thinking enhancement programs to choose, school systems should consider the following:

1. Decide upon the best way to improve student ability over an extended time period. Review the relevant research literature on thinking skills enhancement and see what other school systems have used in the past.

2. Determine the special needs of the school system in question and delineate some of the obstacles that could impede the program.

3. Outline the specific steps necessary to reach the desired outcomes and suggest a timeline for achieving these goals.

4. Determine the ability and motivation required of the teachers who are to be involved.

5. List all personnel to be involved in the project (students, parents, teachers, vice principals, principals, superintendents, school board personnel, program coordinators, support staff, etc.) and determine each person's responsibilities.

6. Consider whether thinking skills should be taught to all grades throughout the whole school curriculum.

7. Plan for continuous in-service for the teachers involved.

8. Plan to continuously monitor teacher and student performance.

9. Design ways to assess the program's impact.

10. Present the program plans to a select committee for approval and refinement.

When a program is finally decided upon it must be realized that success is not guaranteed. According to Sternberg (1987) a program needs to be commensurate with the attributes of the teachers and students involved and the resources available. Teachers and students need to be aware that they are both involved in the learning and thinking process. Teachers need to promote the idea of thinking and support the view that the process of thinking is as important as its product. They need to facilitate and mediate thinking in classroom discussion and allow students to become active and independent thinkers who use thinking skills in every context. Sternberg suggests that teachers will need to modify certain programs to meet the needs of individual children and should encourage them to introduce their own modifications. He suggests that teachers should provide students with background information on the chosen program to help motivate and orientate them to some of the objectives of the program. The success of a program depends at least as much upon student understanding and attitudes as it does upon teacher understanding and attitudes.

HOW CAN THINKING BE EVALUATED?

Student performance is traditionally assessed with the use of standardized tests. Whenever standardized instruments are used, however, there is usually little opportunity for the teacher and student to interact. The answers required by the test tend to be unequivocal and quantitative, and feedback from the teacher tends to be corrective. Results from this type of assessment typically reflect the amount of acquired knowledge rather than how children arrive at a particular answer. The use of process-oriented assessment, however, places emphasis on the procedures that children use in a particular task and reveals valuable information for remedial intervention. The qualitative assessment of the processes that children use to arrive at a solution allows the teacher to supply feedback that is less pedantic and more formative. Faulty thinking and inappropriate strategies can be amended and redirected. The role of the teacher, as evaluator, becomes much more supportive in nature and assessment of thinking capability becomes a shared responsibility.

In assessing learning and thinking, then, evaluation of how children arrive at a particular answer or level of attainment is seen to be just as important as the answer or level itself. The challenge, however, lies in developing assessment instruments that can be readily utilized by the teacher. Maguire (chapter 14) shows how the use of Biggs and Collis' (1982) taxonomy can provide teachers with a way to assess some higher-level objectives in the classroom. The taxonomy provides a structure, which they call "structure of learning outcomes" (SOLO), for categorizing and evaluating student responses. Maguire explains that the assessment is made by placing a student's performance into one of five categories (prestructural, unistructural, multistructural, relational, and extended abstract) that are considered to be the levels or stages of learning through which an individual passes in the mastery of new concepts. The structural complexity of a student's responses produces a measure of the quality of knowledge assimilation. The responses are rated according to the degree of elaboration, organization, consistency, capacity, generalization, and abstraction. The essential aim is to specify how well students have learned the material rather than how much of the material has been acquired. Maguire contends that the SOLO assessment technique is an example of a measurement technique that has great potential for assessing degree of understanding and quality of higher-order thinking skills.

French and French (chapter 15) supply a model for evaluating thinking skills programs. They consider the purpose of evaluation to be threefold, addressing the program itself, the underlying process, and its outcomes. Even though cognitive instructional programs have been growing in popularity, many questions remain regarding their effectiveness. Some of these questions include defining the nature of thinking, selecting the most important criterion measures to use, determining whether programs are implemented as intended, and assessing the quality of the teaching. The authors suggest that in evaluating a program it is important to consider its theoretical foundations, its objectives, and its potential impact. In process evaluation, it is important to consider such things as the teacher's educational philosophy and familiarity with the program being used, the teaching methodology and style employed, and the continual monitoring of the program's operation. In outcome assessment it is recommended that a multimethod, interactive approach be used, emphasizing summative and process evaluation of qualitative and quantitative data, and focusing not only on student knowledge but also on the generalization and application of knowledge.

Due to the complex nature of the process of thinking, its assessment, along with the assessment of thinking skills programs in general, would seem to require a multifaceted approach. The research evidence suggests that there are several methods available that can help in understanding the complexity of thinking and that can determine how effective enhancement programming has been.

ARE LEARNING AND THINKING JUST A SCHOOL CONCERN?

Whenever the subject of the enhancement of learning and thinking is brought up, the discussion generally centers on how teachers can facilitate such processes and how learners can apply them to academic tasks in the classroom. If education is considered from a broader perspective, however, improving the quality of thinking can become the objective of any system that involves human beings. The issue of thinking, as in education itself, should be treated in a broader context in which technology, development, and culture are intertwined.

One area in which the enhancement of cognitive skills extends beyond the classroom is in social competence. The way people view themselves, the way they interpret social situations, and the way they process information from their social interactions have important implications for how successfully they relate with one another. A major assumption of social competence is that if people are able to predict and control what goes on around them, then they can identify lawful relationships and invariants that explain their own and other people's behavior across a variety of social situations (Weiner et al., 1983). According to Mancini et al. (chapter 12), reflecting, comprehending, conceptualizing, decision making, problem solving, and other learning and thinking skills are all important mediators of social competence. In addition, in order that people may act in a socially competent manner they must be able to: identify and understand the variety of social problems in which they engage; generate alternative solutions to problem situations; make decisions based on the projected consequences of their actions; and act upon their decisions (Goldfried & d'Zurrella, 1969).

These abilities can be thought of as "how to think" in social situations. Yet, a person must also know "what to think" in such settings. For example, the socially competent person should be aware of the personal characteristics that can affect a social task, in addition to the task requirements and the strategies that may help performance. Competency in these skills can directly influence the ability of people to initiate and maintain mutually satisfying interpersonal relationships. Enhancement of the skills can be facilitated by family, friends, and colleagues, as well as a variety of professionals.

Although Sen and Das (chapter 13) believe that effective business managers are good at a number of cognitive skills, including conceptualizing problems, noticing patterns and consistencies, spotting important issues in complex situations, and planning solutions, the really successful managers also require these same skills in their employees. As in education, business needs to provide opportunities for individuals to have more responsibility and authority as well as the freedom to be creative and independent thinkers. The enhancement of learning and thinking is central to all of society's personal and professional endeavors. It is "everybody's business."

Although knowledge of how people learn and think is becoming greater all the time there is still much to understand about these mutlifaceted and complex abilities of the human mind. This book presents some contemporary ideas about the enhancement of learning and thinking that will motivate readers to pursue their own interests and research in the area. In the end we are left with even more questions to answer and even more answers to question.

REFERENCES

Anthony, B., & Hudgins, B. B. (1978). Problem solving processes of fifth grade arithmetic pupils. *Journal of Educational Research, 72,* 63–67.

Baker, L., & Brown, A. L. (1982). Metacognitive skills in reading. In P. D. Pearson (ed.), *Handbook of reading research.* New York: Longman.

Biggs, J. B., & Collis, K. F. (1982). *Evaluating the quality of learning: The SOLO taxonomy.* New York: Academic.

Borkowski, J. G. (1985). Signs of intelligence: Strategy generalization and metacognition. In S. R. Yussen (ed.), *The growth of reflection in children.* New York: Academic.

Borkowski, J. G., Levers, S., & Gruenenfelder, T. M. (1976). Transfer of mediational strategies in children: The role of activity and awareness during strategy acquisition. *Child Development, 47,* 779–786.

Bransford, J., Sherwood, R., Vye, N., & Reiser, J. (1986). Teaching and thinking and problem solving. *American Psychologist, 41*(10), 1078–1089.

Bray, N. W., Justice, E. M., Ferguson, R. P., & Simon, D. L.(1977). Developmental changes in the effects of instructions on production deficient children. *Child Development,* 48, 1019–1026.

Brown, A. L. (1978). Knowing when, where and how to remember: A problem of metacognition. In R. Glaser (ed.), *Advances in instructional psychology.* vol. 1. Hillsdale, N.J.: Erlbaum.

Butterfield, E. C., & Belmont, J. M. (1977). Assessing and improvising the cognitive functions of mentally retarded people. In I. Bialer & M. Sternlicht (eds.), *The psychology of mental retardation: Issues and approaches.* New York: Psychological Dimensions.

Case, R. (1988). Implications of Neo-Piagetian theory for improving the design of instruction. In J. R. Kirby & J. B. Biggs (eds.), *Cognition, development & instruction.* New York: Academic.

Chance, P. (1986). *Thinking in the classroom: A survey of programs.* New York: Teachers College Press.

Dansereau, D. F. (1984). *Cooperative learning strategies.* Paper presented at the Conference on Study and Learning Strategies, Texas, S & M University.

————. (1985). Learning strategy research. In S. F. Chipman, J. W. Segal, & R. Glaser (eds.), *Learning and thinking skills,* vol. 1, *Relating instruction to research.* Hillsdale, N.J.: Erlbaum.

deBono, E. (1980). *Teaching thinking.* New York: Penguin.

Derry, S. J., & Murphy, D. A. (1986). Learning systems that train learning ability: From theory to practice. *Review of Educational Research,* 56(1), 1–39.

Deschler, D., & Shumaker, J. (1986). Learning strategies: An instructional alternative for low achieving adolescents. *Exceptional Children,* 52(6), 583–590.

Feuerstein, R., Rand, Y., Hoffman, M. B., & Miller, R. (1980). *Instrumental enrichment: An international program for cognitive modifiability.* Baltimore: University Park Press.

Flavell, J. H. (1976). Metacognitive aspects of problem solving. In L. B. Resnick (ed.), *The nature of intelligence.* Hillsdale, N.J.: Erlbaum.

Glaser, R. (1984). Education and thinking: The role of knowledge. *American Psychologist,* 39, 93–104.

Goldfried, M. R., & d'Zurrella, T. J. (1969). A behavioural analytic model for assessing competence. In C. D. Spielberger (ed.), *Current topics in clinical community psychology.* vol. 1. New York: Academic.

Jones, B. F., Palincsar, A., Ogle, L., & Carr, E. (1987). *Strategic teaching and learning: Cognitive instruction in the content areas.* Produced by the Association for Supervision and Curriculum Development, Alexandria.

Joyce, B. (1985). Models for teaching thinking. *Educational Leadership,* 42, 4–7.

Kendall, C. R., Borkowski, J. G., Cavanaugh, J. C. (1980). Metamemory and the transfer of an interrogative strategy by EMR children. *Intelligence,* 4, 255–270.

Kendall, P. C., & Zupman, B. A. (1981). Individual versus group application of cognitive behavioural self-control procedures with children. *Behavior Therapy,* 12, 344–359.

Kestner, J., & Borkowski, J. G. (1979). Children's maintenance and generalization of an interrogative learning strategy. *Child Development,* 50, 485–494.

Levin, J. R., Pressley, M., McCormick, C. B., Miller, G. E., & Shriberg, L. K.

(1979). Assessing the classroom potential of the keyword method. *Journal of Educational Psychology,* 71, 583–594.

Lipman, M., Sharp, R., & Oscanyan, F. (1980). *Philosophy in the classroom.* 2d ed. Philadelphia: Temple University Press.

Malin, J. T. (1979). Strategies in mathematical problem solving. *Journal of Educational Research,* 73, 101–108.

Meichenbaum, D. (1980). Cognitive behavior modification with exceptional children: A promise yet unfulfilled. *Exceptional Education Quarterly,* 1, 83–88.

Mulcahy, R. F., Andrews, J., & Peat, D. (in press). Cognitive education: A longitudinal examination. In C. K. Leong & B. S. Randhawa (eds.), *Literacy and cognition: Theory, research and instructional implications.* New York: Plenum.

Mulcahy, R. F., Marfo, K., Peat, D., Andrews, J., & Clifford, L. (1986). Applying cognitive psychology in the classroom: A learning/thinking strategies instructional program. *Alberta Psychology,* 13(3), 9–12.

Newell, A., & Simon, H. A. (1972). *Human problem solving.* Englewood Clifs, N.J.: Prentice-Hall.

Nickerson, R. S. (1988). On improving thinking through instruction (in preparation for *Review of Research in Education*). BBN Laboratories.

Nickerson, R. S., & Adams, M. J. (1983). *Introduction in Project Intelligence: The Development of procedures to enhance thinking skills: A teachers manual.* Cambridge, Mass.: Harvard University/Bolt Beranck & Newman.

Nickerson, R. S., Perkins, D. M., & Smith, E. E. (1985). *Teaching thinking.* Hillsdale, N.J.: Erlbaum.

Nickerson, R. S., Armbruster, B., Begab, M., Cox, B., Feuerstein, R., Gothold, S., Greenhalgh, C., Millard, W., Paris, S., Pearson, P., Rosotto, G., Smith, R. G., Ward, J., & Wittrock, M. (1985, winter). *Report from the excellence in schools task force in learning strategies and thinking skills outcome,* 4(2).

Paul, R. W. (1984). Critical thinking: Fundamental to education for a free society. *Educational Leadership,* 42, 4–14.

Peterson, P. L., & Swing, S. R. (1983). Problems in classroom implementation of cognitive strategy instruction. In M. Pressley & J. R. Levin (eds.), *Cognitive strategy research: Educational applications.* New York: Springer-Verlag.

Pressley, M. G., Levin, J. R., & Delaney, H. D. (1982). The mnemonic keyword. *Review of Educational Research,* 52, 61–91.

Resnick, L. B. (1987). *Education and learning to think.* Washington, D.C.: National Academy Press.

Schoenfeld, A. H. (1979). Can heuristics be taught? In J. Lockhead & J. Clement (eds.), *Cognitive process instruction: Research on teaching thinking skills.* Philadelphia: Franklin Institute Press.

Sternberg, R. J. (1985). Instrumental and componental approaches to the nature and training of intelligence. In S. F. Chipman, J. W. Segal, & R. Glaser (eds.), *Thinking and learning skills: Current research and open questions.* Vol. 2. Hillsdale, N.J.: Erlbaum.

———. (1986). *Intelligence applied.* Toronto: Harcourt Brace Jovanovich.

———. (1987). Teaching critical thinking: Eight easy ways to fail before you begin. *Phi Delta Kappan,* 456–459.

Thorndyke, P. W., & Hayes Roth, B. (1979). The use of schema in the acquisition and transfer of knowledge. *Cognitive Psychology,* 11, 82–106.

Weiner, B., Graham, T., Taylor, S. E., & Meyer, W. (1983). Social cognition in the classroom. *Educational Psychologist,* 18, 109–124.

Weinstein, C. E., & Underwood, V. L. (1985). Learning strategies: The how of thinking. In S. F. Chipman, J. W. Segal, & R. Glaser (eds.), *Thinking and learning skills,* vol. 1, *Relating instruction to research.* Hillsdale, N.J.: Erlbaum.

Index

About the Contributors

JAC ANDREWS is an assistant professor in the Department of Educational Psychology at the University of Calgary. His research interests are in cognitive instruction and the education of exceptional children.

DAN G. BACHOR is a professor in special education at the University of Victoria in British Columbia. His research is in learning disabilities and mathematics education.

JOHN B. BIGGS is a professor and Dean of the Faculty of Education at the University of Hong Kong. His research focuses on learning and instruction. His work on the Structure of Learning Outcomes (SOLO) has given him international recognition.

SEOKEE CHO is director of the Gifted Education Division of the Korean Educational Development Institute in Seoul, South Korea. She is currently involved in a major research project on giftedness funded by Unesco. She also acts as a consultant to numerous agencies in the area of giftedness.

ARTHUR L. COSTA is a professor of education at California State University in Sacramento and is internationally recognized for his work in the area of the enhancement and teaching of thinking.

DONALD F. DANSEREAU is a professor at Texas Christian University in Fort Worth. He is widely known for his teacher/learning techniques of "scripted cooperation" and "knowledge maps."

J. P. DAS is a professor in the Department of Educational Psychology and director of the Center for Developmental Disabilities at the University of Alberta in Edmonton. His research interests are in cognitive processes, mental retardation, and learning disabilities.

SELBY H. EVANS is currently a research scientist with Lynne Gilfillan Associates and Texas Christian University in Fort Worth. His research interests focus on research design and methodology, problem-solving, and computer applications.

CARMEL FRENCH is an assistant professor in special education at Mount Saint Vincent University in Halifax, Nova Scotia. Her research is in learning strategy assessment, particularly in mathematical problem solving.

FRED FRENCH is an associate professor and the coordinator of the graduate program in school psychology at Mount Saint Vincent University in Halifax, Nova Scotia. His research is in the assessment of cognitive processes in children, the academic performance of children born at risk, and the impact of special educational administrative policies on program development and the learner.

SHARON I. JAMIESON is Executive Assistant to the Dean of Education in the Faculty of Education at the University of Alberta in Edmonton. She is currently completing her Ph.D. studies in the teaching of history and the impact of information technology on the role of the teacher.

CHE KAN LEONG is a professor in special education in the Institute of Child Guidance and the Department for the Education of Exceptional Children at the University of Saskatchewan in Saskatoon. Dr. Leong's research interests focus on psychological and neuropsychological processes of reading and its difficulties.

THOMAS O. MAGUIRE is a professor in the Department of Educational Psychology at the University of Alberta in Edmonton. His research interests are in educational measurement and program evaluation.

GABRIEL J. MANCINI is a consultant in the area of behavior disorders and lectures in the Department of Educational Psychology at the University of Alberta in Edmonton.

KOFI MARFO is an associate professor of educational psychology in the Graduate School of Education at Kent State University in Ohio. His research is in early intervention with handicapped children, parent-child interactions, and cognitive strategies and classroom learning.

ROBERT F. MULCAHY is a professor of special education in the Department of Educational Psychology at the University of Alberta in Edmonton. His research interests are in the area of cognitive instruction and exceptionalities. He is the author of a strategies program for effective learning and thinking (SPELT).

RAYMOND S. NICKERSON works for B.N.N. Laboratories Inc. He is internationally recognized for his work in the area of teaching thinking.

SANDRA FALCONER PACE is currently Associate Superintendent (Curriculum) for the Regina Public School Board in Regina, Saskatchewan.

ROBERT S. PATTERSON is a professor of education and past dean of the Faculty of Education, University of Alberta in Edmonton. His research interests focus on teacher education and history of Canadian education.

DAVID PEAT is Coordinator of Special Education for the Ministry of Education, Government of British Columbia. His research is in the area of cognitive education as it relates to the learning disabled and in the area of curriculum design and assessment.

M. A. PRICE is coordinator of the Learning Centre Community Early Childhood Services Program for children with special needs and Adjunct Assistant Professor of Educational Psychology at the University of Calgary. Her research interests lie in the area of cognitive education and dynamic approaches to assessment.

JOYA SEN is an associate professor in management at Concordia University in Montreal. Her research interests are in organizational behavior, industrial arbitration, and women's issues.

ROBERT H. SHORT is a professor in the Department of Educational Psychology at the University of Alberta. His research interests are in the area of cognitive processes, learning and instruction, and neuropsychology.